Mary Webb   NEGLECTED GENIUS

2/28/2011

Mary & Dale

With my compliments,

Mary Crawford

"MARY WEBB"

Mary Webb
Neglected Genius

MARY E. CRAWFORD
&
BRUCE J. CRAWFORD

*With contributions by
Gladys Mary Coles
& Thomas A. Goldwasser
and original illustrations
by William Bishop*

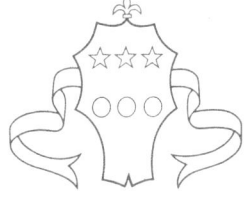

THE GROLIER CLUB
New York 2009

To Gladys Mary Coles,
  author, poet and friend, whose intellectual,
  intuitive, and imaginative ties
  to Mary Webb
  have enriched us all.

FRONTISPIECE: "Mary Webb" original illustration by William Bishop.

ISBN: 978-1-60583-024-7 (2-vol. set)
  VOL. I: Essays and catalogue.
  VOL. II: *Clematisa & Percival.* The first printing (by letterpress) from the manuscript, with original illustrations by William Bishop.

Frontispiece illustration and illustration on page 144
© 2009 William Bishop. All rights reserved.

"A Modern Writer" © 2009 Dr. Gladys Mary Coles. All rights reserved.

"A Bookseller's Retrospective on Collecting Mary Webb"
© 2009 Thomas A. Goldwasser. All rights reserved.

All other content © 2009 Mary E. Crawford and Bruce Jay Crawford.
All rights reserved.

Contents

Foreword *Dr. Gladys Mary Coles*	7
Acknowledgements *Mary E. Crawford*	9

MARY WEBB: NEGLECTED GENIUS

A Biographical Sketch *Mary E. Crawford*	13
A Critical Assessment *Bruce J. Crawford*	23
A Modern Writer *Dr. Gladys Mary Coles*	33
How I Came to Discover, Collect, and Appreciate Mary Webb *Mary E. Crawford*	47
A Bookseller's Retrospective on Collecting Mary Webb *Thomas A. Goldwasser*	52
Mary Webb & her Work: Some Views of the Critics	57
Catalogue *Mary E. and Bruce J. Crawford*	63
Synopses of the Six Novels, and a Selection of Poems *Mary E. Crawford*	145
Selected Bibliography of Writings by and about Mary Webb *Mary E. Crawford*	173
Index	201

Published to accompany exhibitions at

THE GROLIER CLUB
New York, New York
January 27 through March 13, 2010

and

STANFORD UNIVERSITY
Cecil H. Green Library
Stanford, California
May 17 through August 29, 2010

Foreword   Dr. Gladys Mary Coles

It is with great pleasure that I write the foreword to the Crawfords' Mary Webb catalogue. The exhibition represents an important point in the ongoing revival of interest in this lesser-known English novelist and poet, and undoubtedly will bring the wider attention that her work deserves. For me it is immensely significant, a landmark in my own journey with Mary Webb over three decades. With postgraduate studies behind me, my first reading of her novels, poems, and nature essays held the excitement of a rare discovery. I found the same highly individual voice and vision informing all her writing; language rich, lucid, arresting, with an irreducible spiritual quality; ideas and themes ahead of her time. And I was astonished that so fine a writer was neglected in literary studies. I determined to redeem her from obscurity, researching and writing the first major study of her life and work, *The Flower of Light*. In this critical biography, I combine the bittersweet story of a life as intense, innerly rich, and tragic as the Brontës' with a revaluation of her literary achievement. Other publications followed—my editions of her poetry and nature essays, introductions to her novels, a second biographical and critical study, articles in various journals, including the new *Oxford Dictionary of National Biography*—as well as extensive lecturing and broadcasts. It is extraordinary now to see my own publications among the secondary material in the Crawford archive, together with many of the primary and secondary sources I drew upon when researching *The Flower of Light*. I pay tribute to the dedication of the collector Mary Crawford, who shares my belief that Mary Webb is undervalued, and whose deep commitment to enhancing her literary reputation is evident in this remarkable archive.

Of the primary materials in the collection, the most important are the only extant manuscript of a Mary Webb novel, *Armour Wherein He Trusted*, left unfinished at her death in 1927 and published later by Cape in the *Collected Works* (1929); a letter of appreciation from Prime Minister Stanley Baldwin to Mary Webb, praising her novel *Precious Bane* ("a really first class piece of work"); a group of early letters from Mary (then Meredith) to her future mother-in-law; and the manuscript of *Clematisa & Percival*, an unpublished story written by her as a teenager and reproduced here in an accompanying volume.

In recent years I have had the privilege of meeting Mary Crawford and her husband Bruce on their visits to England, memorable meetings during which I was their guide to locations in Shropshire of significance in Mary Webb's life and work. Their wholehearted devotion to the quest, scholarly approach, and understanding impressed me immensely. The assembling in this exhibition of so many rare sources, disparate in their provenance, is a triumph of literary collecting.

Acknowledgements MARY E. CRAWFORD

I thank Dr. Gladys Mary Coles—to whom this book is dedicated—for her scholarship, guidance, and support in the preparation of this book and exhibition. Gladys Mary Coles's *The Flower of Light* (London: Duckworth 1978; reprinted Wirral: Headland 1998) is the authoritative biography and critical study of Mary Webb's life and work. I regularly consulted both this seminal work and her updated biography, *Mary Webb* (Bridgend: Seren Books, 1990, reprinted 1996), each of which proved an invaluable resource in enhancing my understanding of this unique author and in the preparation of this catalogue. Dr. Coles has so significantly expanded the understanding of Webb's genius that—without her definitive biographies—far less of substance would be known about Mary Webb's life and work. She was kind enough to carefully review our manuscript in its final stages and to suggest numerous important corrections and improvements. Over the past four years, Dr. Coles has graciously guided Bruce and me to many Shropshire locations important in the life of Mary Webb, and I credit these wonderful outings with giving us a deeper appreciation of Mary Webb and her work. I would also like to thank Dr. Coles for her contribution of the foreword and for her essay in this catalogue.

I am grateful to past and present members of the Mary Webb Society (www.marywebbsociety.co.uk), organized in 1972 and headquartered in Shropshire (the environment that was so elemental to Webb's creative spirit) who are devoted to the literature of Mary Webb.

I would like to express my gratitude to Mary Young of the Grolier Club of New York, whose warm encouragement led me to propose this exhibition. Thanks must also be extended to Ward Smith, George Ong, Szilvia Szmuk-Tanenbaum, Eric Holzenberg, Fernando Peña, and Megan Smith—all with the Grolier Club, and to Roberto Trujillo, Assunta Pisani, Andrew Herkovic, Becky Fischbach, John Mustain, David Jordan, and Annette Keogh—all associated with the Stanford University Libraries. I am grateful for the help of Stuart Snydman, Michael Olson, and Mattie Taormina (also from the Stanford Libraries) for their work in digitizing the Webb manuscripts and making images available to illustrate this book.

Many thanks to Thomas Goldwasser for arranging the acquisition of much of the important Mary Webb manuscript and first edition material in our collection, and for contributing an essay to this catalogue.

This catalogue is much better than the drafts I submitted thanks to the special expertise of numerous talented individuals who made editorial suggestions without changing the authors' personal voices. I especially thank Frank Sypher (our editor extraordinaire), George Ong, and Becky Fischbach. Our book designer, Jerry Kelly, brilliantly combined an authoritative catalogue and a first edition (the fine press printing of Webb's juvenile story), all the while balancing aesthetics and budget.

My late father-in-law, Ralph Crawford, was the first to introduce me to the work of Mary Webb. (Little did any of us realize that his innocent recommendation of *Precious Bane* as a weekend read would set us on a decades-long path of exploration.) Diane and Evan Crawford, our daughter and son, have been immersed in Mary Webb from childhood and have been helpful, supportive, and encouraging throughout, as we worked to create the best catalogue and exhibition that we could produce. My dear friend Sharon Thayer and I have for decades enjoyed sharing our interest in Mary Webb. Sharon joined Bruce and me in June 2008 in Chester, England where we met Gladys Mary Coles to discuss the Mary Webb exhibition and publication. Special thanks are also due to Spencer Tressler for his contributions to the Mary Webb dialogue, even with competition from his law studies.

Miriam Margoyles, talented actress and warm personality, whom we serendipitously met at a Dickens Fellowship meeting in 2007, made us aware over a memorable breakfast in Philadelphia of Carol Snape-Barker's dramatization of Mary Webb's life, *My Wife Did a Bit of Scribbling*. This two-person dramatization was initially created to celebrate the 1981 centennial of Webb's birth. It subsequently became a radio production, and was performed at the Ludlow Festival in the early 1980s. I would like to thank Carol Snape-Barker for her permission to re-enact her dramatization in March 2010 as part of the activities surrounding the Mary Webb exhibition at the Grolier Club, and the talented writer, director and actor, Jack Milner, and his actress wife, Rebecca Rainsford, for traveling from England to perform the parts of Henry and Mary Webb for the dramatic reading of *My Wife Did a Bit of Scribbling*.

Bill Bishop, artist extraordinaire, contributed his original graphic interpretations to accompany the first publication of *Clematisa & Percival*, as well as his original illustrations tipped into this catalogue.

I fervently hope, as a result of this catalogue and the exhibitions in 2010 at the Grolier Club and at the Stanford University Libraries, that many new readers will be introduced to the unique voice of Mary Webb—her intuitive brilliance, her passion, and her literary legacy.

My greatest thanks go to my husband and best friend, Bruce Crawford, for his endless support and encouragement. He was always there—offering ideas, assistance and/or a kick in the pants when necessary. His contributions are so great that it is only fair to credit him with co-authorship of this book. It truly would never have been written without his passionate intellectual and spiritual support. For this, my most grateful love and thanks.

Mary Webb

CAT. 1, PAGE 63

A Biographical Sketch   MARY E. CRAWFORD

Mary Gladys Meredith (known as a child as "Glad" or "Gladys," but after marriage and throughout this text as "Mary") was born in 1881 in the Welsh borderlands, the eldest by six years, of the six children of George Edward Meredith (1841–1909) and his wife, Sarah Alice (née Scott 1852–1924, and known as "Alice"). George Meredith, an Oxford M.A. and country gentleman of Welsh descent, ran a boarding school for boys and kept a home farm. Known as a cultured man who wrote poetry and painted, he was by reputation generous, humorous and a lover of nature.

In the seven years spanning 1887 to 1894, five additional children were born to George and Alice Meredith. Mary's siblings, close in age, gravitated toward each other's company. Mary's six-year seniority made her a solitary child and, according to Webb's biographer, Gladys Mary Coles, young Mary saw little of her mother, who was busy with the latest baby and a nursery filled with toddlers.

George Meredith, although busily engaged with his students and oversight of the farm, schooled Mary at home alongside his pupils. From her earliest days, precocious Mary was her father's special child. Coles states in *The Flower of Light* (1978) that George nicknamed his eldest child his "precious bane," from Milton's *Paradise Lost* (I. 692). She was given free run of her father's library. Young Mary acquired from her father a deep love of the Welsh borderlands and knowledge of local history, legends and folklore as he took her on long walks and drives. An amateur poet himself, Mary's father encouraged her to express her perceptions of nature in poetry and prose. Allowed to wander the Shropshire fields, woods, and lanes, Mary developed an acute perception of the smallest elements in nature (e.g., the sparkle of dew on grass, the sound of leaves falling from their branches, the ripple of water in changing winds).

When Mary was ten, Miss Edith Lory, known as "Minoni" to the Meredith children, joined the family as governess; she eventually taught all six of the Meredith children. Biographies state that Minoni did a great deal to widen young Mary's literary horizons at an impressionable age. Mary's studies included her favorite writers: Shakespeare, Milton, the Romantic poets, the Brontës, Richard Jefferies, and Thomas Hardy. Miss Lory later told Hilda Addison: "Gladys would sit by the hour while

I read Shakespeare to her, and she grew to love the plays more than anything in literature." Mary could quote at length from the major poets and was thorough and knowledgeable when discussing literature and history. At the age of fourteen, Mary was sent to Mrs. Walmsley's Finishing School in Southport for two years. Upon completion of this education, Mary helped her father and Minoni to raise her younger siblings after her mother, having suffered a riding accident during a hunt, had taken to her bed as a semi-invalid.

The next few years, while her mother kept to her bedroom, were among the happiest of Mary's life. Mary dedicated herself to her family with a maternal and protective attitude. She enjoyed being needed and shared with her father his "unfailing delight" in the children. As an adolescent, Mary was said to have created stories, poems, and plays to amuse her younger brothers and sisters. In keeping with her nature—firmly believing that her father and the children should have whatever they wanted—Mary was unstinting in her generosity. Coles in *The Flower of Light* (1978) states: "She [Minoni] had vivid recollections of Mary's creative zeal—arranging charades and plays to amuse her brothers and sisters, boldly ransacking her mother's wardrobes and chests for silk clothing in which to dress them as fairy characters or flowers—poppy, primrose, forget-me-not, daffodil." The family returned Mary's affection. As long as she lived, their eldest sister was particularly beloved by her siblings.

In the spring of 1900 Mary's mother unexpectedly reappeared, after many years spent in her bedroom as a semi-invalid, and rejoined the family without comment. Biographers speculate that Alice, a proper Victorian matron, arose from her bed when she believed that the lack of economic sense showed by her husband George and daughter Mary was leading the family to financial ruin. Nineteen-year-old Mary was henceforward relieved of family responsibilities. She was expected to obey her mother's wishes respectfully and to follow her iron discipline.

Alice Meredith's sudden reappearance was an emotional shock for Mary. Relieved of her family duties, she took her bicycle on long expeditions through the countryside. In 1901, after a particularly long bike ride, twenty-year-old Mary collapsed and became ill, causing her family grave concern. Her first symptoms were exhaustion, moodiness, weight loss, nervous irritability, goiter and protrusion of the eyeballs. Diagnosed with Graves' disease (a then-incurable glandular disorder in which the thyroid becomes overactive), Mary was tenderly nursed by her father for the next six months. During this time, she withdrew into an introspective isolation. Using the next two years' convalescence to read and write, Mary was encouraged by her father and Minoni to express her thoughts, perceptions, and observations in prose and poetry. Her early essays, written during these years, were published fifteen years later under the title *The Spring of Joy* (1917).

Sensitive and painfully conscious of her altered appearance, Mary found solace in writing over the following decade. She sought to capture her ever-changing thoughts and moods in verse and prose. With a keen sensory awareness, Mary was able to detect and describe with poetic feeling the subtlest qualities and minutest of details. Walter de la Mare in his introduction to *Poems and The Spring of Joy* (1928) said: "The mere statement of facts that she was interested in is poetical in effect. 'The pollen grain of chicory—an outer and inner hexagon united by rays—is a rose window in a shrine of lapis lazuli. It needs no light behind it, for it illumines itself.' Few observers have taken the pains to describe an object so minute in terms so precise, yet the words are poetical in effect; they are charged with life and significance, and only a loving rapture in the thing itself could have found them for this purpose." Mary's physical limitations helped crystallize her thoughts—her writing became a creative, imaginative, and philosophical outlet. She worked assiduously on her verse, submitting poems and prose for publication, and was more than occasionally gratified to see her work printed in local periodicals.

The Gates of Gold and Green

Nature has opened her gates again!
Her gates of gold and green;
Has opened them wide to welcome me
Back to her glorious liberty,
To her wholesome grass and sun and rain,
Through her gates of gold and green.

The infinite sky bends close to me
With a great protecting calm,
And wave upon wave of its peace profound
Steals on my spirit and circles me round
With the stillness of eternity
And a great protecting calm.

Mary Webb: *Collected Prose and Poems* (1977)

In January 1909, when Mary was twenty-eight, George Meredith died. Mary's intense, long-lasting grief for her beloved father undermined her already fragile health. Over the next three years, she again suffered long spells of recurring Graves' disease, with its accompanying symptoms of exhaustion, high fever, nervousness, severe headache, and gastric distress. The physical manifestations of her illness became more pronounced. Mary again sought solace in poetry and writing.

As Mary's health improved, she attended Cambridge University Extension lectures in Shrewsbury. In 1910, at a local literary discussion group, Mary met her future husband, Henry Bertram Law Webb (known to his family as "Bertie," but referred to throughout this text as "Henry"). A Shropshire native, Henry was a recent graduate of St. Catherine's College, Cambridge, whose parents had recently moved to the village of Meole Brace where the Meredith family was then living.

Mary loved Henry instantly and rapturously. They shared a deep appreciation for nature and literature and she considered him a brilliant scholar. In 1911, the Bodley Head published *The Silences of the Moon*, Henry's philosophical treatise about man's place in nature. He spoke encouragingly to Mary of her poems. Gladys Mary Coles says in *Mary Webb* (1990): "Henry gave Mary companionship and understanding such as she had known only with her father. He filled the emotional vacuum in her life." Henry proposed to Mary and was joyfully accepted. When they married on June 12, 1912, Mary was thirty-one and Henry was twenty-six.

After their wedding, in order to be near his newly-widowed mother, Henry and Mary moved to Weston-super-Mare on the Somerset coast, where Henry had secured a two-year position at a local boys' school. While at Weston, Mary persevered in her efforts to write poems and short stories. Although homesick for her native Shropshire, she was delighted that some of her writings were accepted for publication, and she gained in confidence. Mary began to formulate the plot of a novel to be set in the Shropshire landscape that she knew so well. Henry, for his part, found teaching both tedious and a distraction from his own writing.

Henry gave up his teaching post in 1914 in order to return to Shropshire, hoping for more leisure to write. The Webbs rented a small house at Pontesbury (near Shrewsbury) and planned to live on Mary's £100 annual allowance, given to Mary by her mother, supplemented by sales of their writing. Mary concentrated on poems and imaginative short stories, while Henry composed poetry and worked on translations of scholarly works from other languages. After long mental incubation, Mary rapidly penned her first novel over a period of only three weeks. *The Golden Arrow* was published in 1916, when Mary was thirty-five. Critics reviewed the novel favorably. It did not sell well, largely because the reading public was distracted by anxiety over the Great War.

In order to help the war effort, Mary chose to sell their surplus garden produce at Shrewsbury market. For two years, Mary and Henry sold their extra fruit, vegetables, flowers, and honey from their garden. The work was physically strenuous. On Saturdays, Mary would walk the nine miles each way to Shrewsbury where she would listen, watch, and absorb the odd words and impressions in market dealings. As the cost of living increased with the war years, Henry and Mary became impoverished—especially because Mary was not temperamentally equipped to economize. She suffered great anxiety for her three brothers—Kenneth, Douglas, and Mervyn—who were then serving on the Western Front.

After 1916, marketing efforts ceased. According to Coles, Henry Webb escaped military service during World War I, partly on the grounds of ill health (due to his bad back and acute short-sightedness) and partly because he was one of the few men left to teach young boys (first at the King's School in Chester and then at the Priory School in Shrewsbury).

Mary completed her second novel, *Gone to Earth*, during the year of the Battle of the Somme. Published in 1917, the novel (although set in Shropshire and never directly mentioning the war) is a passionate cry against man's inhumanity to man. Rebecca West, in her review of *Gone to Earth* in the *Times Literary Supplement*, stated unequivocally "Mary Webb is a genius." In a later symposium on novels for a leading London newspaper, West proclaimed *Gone to Earth* as "Novel of the Year" for 1917. Even though the novel was well received by critics, few people during wartime had the leisure or inclination to read fiction, and the booming guns of the Western Front drowned the voice of the poet. Mary was again disappointed by the lack of public attention for her books. She keenly felt her unique gifts, and was unhappy that her writing did not bring her the public recognition that she craved.

Because of the critical appreciation for her earlier two novels, Mary secured large advances from British and American publishers for her third book, *The House in Dormer Forest* (1920). She and Henry were able to purchase land on Lyth Hill south of Shrewsbury (with advance money, a loan from her mother, and a mortgage from the local bank) and build a small home that they named "Spring Cottage." When reviews of *The House in Dormer Forest* were generally disappointing, Mary realized that critics had entirely missed her underlying premise—the need for man to break away from the "herd mentality" in order to realize his own individuality. Coles states in *The Flower of Light* (1978): ". . . there were no indications of awareness of the novel's vital theme, no response to those insights and perspectives around which she had structured all and which she considered to be so important for the individual and for society." Mary slipped into depression. Her doctor recommended a change of physical environment to rouse her from her melancholic lassitude, and Henry urged Mary to move to London, both for his sake and for the sake of her growing literary reputation.

In January 1921, the Webbs moved to London, planning to return to Spring Cottage for holidays and long weekends. As hoped, Mary's health improved somewhat, and she began to meet people of standing in London's literary and journalistic circles. Henry took up a teaching post at the King Alfred School in London where, according to Coles, he was immediately "slotted in." Mary secured work writing literary reviews, essays, short stories, and poems for such London literary journals as the *Spectator*, the *Nation*, *T. P. and Cassell's Weekly*, and the *Bookman*.

Mary Webb had dual motives for taking on review work; she sought to promote her literary reputation as well as to earn money. Despite being well paid for her novels, reviews, and published poems, the Webbs lived with mounting debt: they were maintaining Spring Cottage in Shropshire while also renting in London, and Mary gave unstintingly of whatever they had.

Mary was keenly sensitive to the needs and suffering of others. Her sympathy over time had steadily grown into a veritable passion for giving. Yet, Mary's generosity did more credit to her heart than to her head as she gave extravagantly, often with little regard to her own or to Henry's basic needs. Hilda Addison, in *Mary Webb: A Short Study of Her Life and Work* (1931), quotes one of Webb's friends as saying, "She might have twenty pounds in the morning and hardly ten shillings at night" (p. 41).

Mary's fourth book, *Seven for a Secret* (1921), once again set in the Welsh border country, was dedicated to Thomas Hardy, with his permission. Mary wrote this novel during inspired weekends in Shropshire at Spring

Cottage. She yearned for her Shropshire countryside when in London but, when in Shropshire, longed for Henry, who often stayed in London (initially because of his teaching schedule and, later, by preference).

In *Precious Bane* (1924), her most famous book and last completed novel, Mary Webb again demonstrates her knowledge of and love for her native county, its legends, and its customs. The story is told in the first person, and makes use of the vernacular of the Welsh border, learned by Mary when she was visiting country cottages in her youth and in the stalls of Shrewsbury market. *Precious Bane* was awarded the coveted Prix Femina Vie Heureuse Anglais early in 1925, an award presented by the French magazines *Femina* and *Vie Heureuse*, for the best English-language work of imagination published during the year by a male or female author whose work (in the opinion of a committee of eminent French women writers) had not received sufficient recognition.

Webb was building an admiring circle of literary critics, but public acclaim remained elusive. One of the few notable figures who did recognize *Precious Bane* as a work of genius was Stanley Baldwin, then British prime minister and a cousin to Rudyard Kipling, who had grown up near Shropshire. Baldwin recognized the insight, accuracy, and great beauty of the story and, in January 1927, wrote a letter to Mary saying how much he had enjoyed reading the novel over the preceding holiday. She replied with a letter of effusive thanks, accompanied by a gift of violets for his desk.

Webb's diseased thyroid had been slowly poisoning her body. Pernicious anemia (then incurable) set in, diminishing Mary's resistance, and leading to a rapid decline in her health. More than ever, as Mary's body weakened, she needed her husband's love and support. Mary was distressed by Henry's infatuation with one of his young students and by his decision to spend extra hours after school privately tutoring the young girl at her family's home. For his part, Henry answered his wife's suspicions with an ever-increasing emotional distance.

Mary began *Armour Wherein He Trusted* at this time, set in the Welsh border country during the time of the First Crusade. Unlike her five already-published novels, whose story lines were developed over time but written quickly and with little revision, *Armour Wherein He Trusted* proved much more difficult for Webb. She suffered from vertigo, blinding migraine headaches and extreme fatigue, and changed plot course several times. In fact, Webb never completed this novel. It is a strange fragment, completely different in style from her other books. *Armour Wherein He Trusted* has an artificially contrived austerity—unlike the clarity, color, and warmth of her previous five novels. When compared to the vibrant portrayals of Shropshire life found in those other narratives, this story has the restrained feel of a watercolor. Webb describes the garden of Sir Gilbert Polrebec and his wife Nesta with great delicacy:

> It clung like a nest, this my garden, to the grey wall of our castle, and it was grey itself with the quiet greyness of doves. The lavender was all spiked over like a castle guarded by halberd-men, and the maiden pink held up fresh buds, the grey-leaved rose bloomed white beneath the heavy dews. There were no citizens of the litel grey garden save Nesta and I, the grey-brown bees and the portly grey pigeons walking in the sun, like abbots.
>
> *Armour Wherein He Trusted* (p. 99)

One day, Henry heard Mary speaking in great distress on the telephone to Arthur St. John Adcock, editor of the *Bookman,* saying that she could not finish the novel and, in despair, had torn it and thrown it on the fire. Henry retrieved the manuscript fragment of *Armour Wherein He Trusted* from the fireplace grate (cat. 148).

Mary spent her last summer alone at Spring Cottage on Lyth Hill in Shropshire. Henry, no longer in love with her, was estranged and remained in London. Webb died of pernicious anemia and Graves' disease at the age of forty-six on October 8, 1927. Her death went largely unreported in the London press.

* * *

Yet Mary Webb left behind the rich posthumous gift of her writings.

In early 1928, Prime Minister Stanley Baldwin mentioned to Sir J. M. Barrie and to John Buchan (Lord Tweedsmuir) how much he had enjoyed reading *Precious Bane*. Both authors, having known Mary Webb personally, told him that she was "one of the best living writers, but no one buys her books."

Shortly after this conversation, Baldwin learned of Webb's decease several months earlier. Surprised at the lack of press coverage upon her death, he paid tribute to Mary Webb's "neglected genius" in a speech given at a Royal Literary Fund dinner in April 1928 where he castigated the press for the undeserved oblivion into which her work had fallen.

Hearing in advance of Baldwin's plan to praise Webb in his talk, Jonathan Cape informed her three other publishers (Constable, J. M. Dent and Hutchison) of his intention to publish a collected edition of Webb's complete writings.

As Cape had calculated, Baldwin's praise generated an immediate demand for Webb's books. The wide reading public had finally "discovered" Mary Webb's genius. The *Evening Standard* published a biographical review of Webb on June 8, 1928. The following day, the paper began to serialize her first novel, *The Golden Arrow,* which ran until August 1928.

To meet the demand for books by Mary Webb, Jonathan Cape rushed out a seven-volume collected edition of her work, which included Webb's five previously published novels, the text of the novel fragment left unfinished at her death, a reprinting of her nature essays, a selection of her poetry, and some of Webb's short stories. Famous men of the day who had personally known Mary Webb—Martin Armstrong, John Buchan, H. R. L. Sheppard, Robert Lynd, G. K. Chesterton, Walter de la Mare, and Stanley Baldwin—wrote the introductions to the collected edition, each volume of which became a bestseller in its own right. By December 1929, Henry Webb was sufficiently well off from royalties earned on the copyrights of Mary Webb's books to retire permanently from teaching and devote himself to his own literary efforts. Henry later wrote four historical novels under the pseudonym of John Clayton.

In September 1929, Henry Webb, aged forty-three, married his then twenty-year-old former student, Kathleen Wilson. As Coles relates in detail in both *The Flower of Light* (1978) and *Mary Webb* (1990), the relationship between Henry and Kathleen had strained the Webbs' marriage and caused Mary grief in her last years. Henry and Mary Webb were childless; Henry and Kathleen Webb had two children.

The reading public was eager for anything related to Mary Webb. With encouragement from his new wife, Henry sold the manuscripts and typescripts of Mary Webb's poems and literary reviews. He also sold the manuscript fragment of her last novel, along with unpublished juvenilia and short stories. Such was the demand that Henry even sold his personal and dedication copies of Mary's novels, as well as Mary's "library"—the few dozen heavily-used, tattered books that Mary had acquired in childhood or had purchased to research the lore, history, flora and fauna of Shropshire.

According to Gladys Mary Coles, Henry and Kathleen Webb owned a home in Golders Green; a cottage in New Forest; a Bentley; and a yacht. The newly-wealthy Webbs also enjoyed traveling to Portofino, Italy to practice their Italian. In 1939, soon after editing *A Mary Webb Anthology*, Henry Webb died at the age of fifty-three in a fall from the pinnacle of Scafell in the Lake District. Coles suggests in the final chapter of her later biography (*Mary Webb*, 1990, p. 153), and in her published poem "To Henry Webb" (*The Echoing Green*, 1994, p. 67), that Henry's fall may have been suicide. While the Coroner recorded a verdict of accidental death, Coles points out that this was Henry's second "fall" in months. Mary Webb's estate in 1928 was valued at £936, Henry's estate (twelve years later) was appraised at £35,800. The almost forty-fold increase in value of Henry Webb's estate, despite a very comfortable lifestyle, was due in significant part to royalties he received from Mary Webb's writings.

Coles tells us that, in a twist of irony that would not have been lost on Mary Webb, Kathleen Webb (then a thirty-year-old widow with two children) inherited Mary Webb's literary estate. In 1943, Kathleen married Mary Webb's publisher, Jonathan Cape, later selling her Mary Webb copyrights to her new husband.

By a strange coincidence, Kathleen, like Mary Webb, died of an incurable disease at the age of forty-six.

Mary Webb is buried in Shrewsbury cemetery.

A Lover of Roses

Here lies a lover of roses. All her years
She fashioned shrouds in a cellar underground.
At last she owns a rose-tree; all around
Where she reposes fragrant petals fall,
Clear pink and shelly and ethereal,
Raining upon the daisied grass like tears –
Only she does not know and cannot see:
Darker than any cellar lieth she.

Fifty One Poems (1946)

A Critical Assessment   Bruce J. Crawford

Mary Webb's prose and poetry has been read and commented on by well-known writers, politicians, editors, ministers, family, and friends, who all weighed in with their opinions. Early critics naturally differed on details, but most agreed on several characteristics that sharply differentiate Webb's writing from that of other early twentieth-century British authors.

    Virtually all reviewers and critics agreed that Webb had extraordinary powers as an observer of the English countryside. She simply *saw, smelled,* and *heard* Shropshire with a sharpness and clarity to an extent that others did not. Further, Webb was able to record her observations in ways that made her readers *feel* that they were living in her landscape. It was easy for critics to agree that Webb brought her readers closer to the experience of living in intimate sympathy with nature, to a degree unequalled by any other contemporary English writer.

    Second, reviewers characterized Webb's best writing as poetic, in a very specific and traditional sense of the term. Her prose, in addition to creating (in the minds of sensitive and imaginative readers) vivid impressions of the outdoor experience, has a musical, lyrical quality that makes it sound both pleasant and richly expressive, whether read silently or aloud. Of all her works, *Precious Bane* rises, in its command of language, to the level of a truly great novel.

    Third, in portraying English rustics as working poor, Webb, unlike many other contemporary novelists, went out of her way to draw characters as complicated individuals, and not as brutes without imagination, sympathy, or depth. Webb's characters feel deep sympathy, love, and joy, and they can take genuine pleasure (as Webb herself did) from the experience of living in the country. Of course, not all of Webb's characters show such robust and high-minded feelings. It would be hard to imagine a more unappealing group of relatives than those shared by Amber Darke in *The House in Dormer Forest.* But Amber's heartless companions were put there by Webb for a reason: they permitted her to study and contrast character, amid the good and bad that can coexist in the tense relations of a family group.

    Webb went even further. She wrote about rural England as an environment where people, nature, folklore, language, and morality were inseparable. Her contemporary critics realized (some more acutely than others) that her work stood apart because there was a genuine artistic principle in her view of the interdependence of man and his environment. Her more astute critics also correctly perceived her position as essentially autobiographical.

Last, and perhaps most difficult to interpret, is the tendency of some early critics to describe Webb as a mystic, and her work as mystical. A good deal of this difficulty comes from how the definitions of "mystic" and "mystical" have evolved: from relatively clear and concise definitions, to very broad and subjective meanings, open to a wide variety of interpretations.

Samuel Johnson in *A Dictionary of the English Language* (1755) defines "mystical" and "mystick" as: 1. Sacredly obscure; 2. Involving some secret meaning; emblematical; and 3. Obscure; secret. He describes the noun "mysticalness" as involving "some secret meaning."

In 1902 William James, a professor of psychology and philosophy at Harvard, published his influential *Varieties of Religious Experience: A Study in Human Nature,* a series of lectures that he had given at the University of Edinburgh. Lectures XVI and XVII in James's book deal with the topic of mysticism. Early in the first lecture, James says: "The words 'mysticism' and 'mystical' are often used as terms of mere reproach, to throw at any opinion which we regard as vague and vast and sentimental, and without a base in either facts or logic." This usage is a far cry from the simple Johnsonian one of nearly 150 years before. Of the "mystical range of consciousness," James says: "It is on the whole pantheistic and optimistic, or at least the opposite of pessimistic. It is anti-naturalistic, and harmonizes best with twice-bornness and so-called other-worldly states of mind." At the end of the two lectures, James says of mystical states: "They tell of the supremacy of the ideal, of vastness, of union, of safety, and of rest . . . The supernaturalism and optimism to which they would persuade may, interpreted in one way or another, be after all the truest of insights into the meaning of this life."

James's book was an early twentieth-century standard in the field of the psychology of religion and influenced contemporary literary critics. But James's definitions of mysticism were far-ranging, difficult to interpret, and did much to obscure the true nature of Webb as an insightful novelist and poet.

So, what were early critics really trying to get at when they described

Webb as a "mystic"? Certainly that Mary Webb was contemplative and intuitive, and that she displayed an extraordinary sensitivity towards her natural environment. Critics were right to say she was pantheistic, in the sense that her spirituality and religious feeling resulted from her closeness to nature.

Webb was also acutely aware that people were capable of great good and great evil. She knew that some were capable of profound love and kindness, and others of extreme cruelty. To her, human nature was conflicted, locked in a tense battle between good feeling and behavior, and bad. Webb saw people engaged in moral battle. She used her native Shropshire, its folklore, legends, local superstitions, and rustics, as vehicles to explore this endless struggle of the human spirit. She wrote with delicacy and perceptiveness, drawing readers into an emotional intimacy with her scenes and characters. It is precisely this sense of spiritual intimacy, which Webb shares with her readers, that sets her apart.

Webb's early critics were greatly impressed by her close observation of nature and her ability to write about it. In *Precious Bane*, Webb writes:

> When a breeze came, the leaves lapped up the silence like the tongues of little creatures drinking. Up in heaven there were clouds like the bit of lace on Mother's wedding-gown, and a setting moon as green as a young beech leaf. And down under the polished water was another moon, not quite so bright, and other clouds, not quite so lacy, and the shadow of the spire, very faint and ghostly, pointing across the water at us.

No wonder her critics focused so intently on this aspect of her work; but this attention had its downside. The battle of the human spirit, which occupies so much of Webb's narrative, became lost in the critical assessments. Today, we need a fresh focus on these underlying but important themes.

In her first novel, *The Golden Arrow* (1916), Webb confronts the cruelty of the human spirit. At the beginning, John Arden warns of his mean-spirited neighbor: "Eli's got no honey in his heart." His assessment is confirmed in the most terrible way, when (in chapter 5) Eli ridicules his daughter Lily's dress, hair, and the "smudge on her nose." He tears Lily's clothes, demanding that she use the fragments to help make cheese. Webb casts the rustic farmer Eli in a cruel light:

> Eli's crafty face, with its downward seams from the mouth and nose and the two long, yellow teeth over the lower lip, was dark red with passion. His plain living, his long prayers, his loud confessions of sin, his harsh

treatment of himself and his unquestioning meekness to the God he believed in (a vengeful, taloned replica of himself)—all these things had to be paid for by some one. . . . A few times in the year, when things had gone wrong, the lust of torture came upon Eli, and the contemplation of a deferred and somewhat problematic torment of the wicked (i.e. the non-Eli) in hellfire could not slake it. At these times he exhibited the subtlety of a woman in finding weak points wherein to stick pins—a subtlety inherited by Lily. The ironic remarks of everyday life—the commonplaces of rudeness—gave place to a caustic finesse which burned like red-hot needles.

When Eli and his daughter return to their farmhouse, Eli further punishes Lily by cutting off her hair with sheep-shears. Later in the book (chapter 25) Eli curses Deborah Arden, calling her a whore. Deborah's boyfriend, Stephen, mocks Eli. In a vengeful passion on the ride home, Eli flogs his own horse to death.

In her middle novels, Webb continues with her focus on cruelty. In *The House in Dormer Forest* (1920) the servant Marigold is berated by the Darke family. She is threatened with losing her servant's place after being (wrongly) accused of sleeping with Peter Darke. Judging her tears as evidence of guilt rather than of confusion, terror and the pride of a country girl whose good name means all to her, Grandmother Velindre calls for Marigold to be beaten across the shoulders with a stick. Mrs. Darke says to Marigold: "Your dress is tight already! You know what that means!" Mary Webb ends the scene with Marigold and the Darke family: "Marigold, as she went downstairs, came slowly and by gradual steps to the conclusion that being good did not pay. And a faint, fluttering regret was born in the depths of her heart—regret that she had suffered the penalty without having tasted one crumb of the joy."

In *Precious Bane* (1924) Mary Webb reaches the apex of her literary career. The novel is a profound study in human character. The humble modesty of Prue Sarn and Kester Woodseaves is cast up against the selfishness, greed, and moral corruption of Prue's brother Gideon. In chapter 2 ("Telling the Bees") Gideon and his father have an argument. Threatened, Gideon knocks his father down, and the older man dies from the fall. Mary Webb says:

> All the while, Gideon stood like stone, remembering the horsewhip Father meant to beat him with, so he said after. And though he'd never seen anyone die afore, when Father went quiet, and the place dumb, he said in an everyday voice, only with a bit of a tremble – "He's dead, Mother. I'll go and tell the bees, or we met lose 'em."

After Gideon locks up the farmhouse for the evening, he says:

> "Best go to bed now, Mother . . . All's safe, and the beasts in their housen. I told every skep of bees, and I can see they're content, and willing for me to be maister."

According to Charlotte Sophia Burne's *Shropshire Folk-lore: A Sheaf of Gleanings* (1883), hiring a poor person to become a Sin Eater for the deceased at funerals was an early Shropshire custom. By eating bread and drinking ale passed over the corpse, accepting payment, and then making a ritual speech, a Sin Eater was believed to take on the deceased's sins, thus freeing the dead person from wandering the earth as a ghost. Mother Sarn is desperate that a Sin Eater be found to take on her late husband's sins, as he has unluckily died in his wrath and with his boots on. Tightfisted Gideon, unwilling to spend the money to hire a Sin Eater, preys on his mother's superstitions and blackmails her into giving him the farm:

> "Oot turn over the farm and all to me if I be the Sin Eater, Mother?" he said.
> "No, no! Sin Eaters be accurst!"
> "What harm, to drink a sup of your own wine and chumble a crust of your own bread? But if you dunna care, let be. He can go with the sin on him."
> "No, no! Leave un go free, Gideon! Let un rest, poor soul! You be in life and young, but he'm cold and helpless, in the power of Satan. He went with all his sins upon him, in his boots, poor soul! If there's none else to help, let his own lad take pity."
> "And you'll give me the farm, Mother?"
> "Yes, yes, my dear! What be the farm to me? You can take all, and welcome."

Much later in the novel, after the tragic burning of the harvest, Prue tries to persuade Gideon that he should marry his fiancée, Jancis—Gideon had slept with her before the ricks were burned and their marriage called off. Gideon flatly rejects the idea, and when Prue says "And suppose there was to be a baby, what then?" Gideon replies:

> "A baby? What? My child and hers? I tell ye, if any such thing came to pass, I'd strangle it. Hark ye, their blood's black. Foul, foxy, vermin. That's what they be. They're not fit to live."

Mary Webb had plenty to say about the meaner side of human character. Some of her portraits (like the ones of Eli, Gideon, and the Darkes) are downright chilling. To say that she was a "gloomy" writer is inaccurate, but to focus on her description of nature as the principal merit of her work is equally unfair.

In *The Golden Arrow*, Webb introduces a second theme that would be repeated in much of her mature work: the importance and challenge of independent action and thought, and the need to resist societal pressure to conform to prevailing customs. Stephen Southernwood persuades his girlfriend Deborah Arden to live with him outside of marriage; this arrangement is condemned by friends and relatives, and especially by their mean-spirited neighbor Eli Huntbatch. John Arden (Deborah's father, whom Mary Webb modeled after her own father George Meredith) has a different point of view. Webb sets up a brief visit between John and the two lovers:

> If other lives could have been hindered from impinging on those of Deborah and Stephen, they might have worked out their destinies in the swift way of great lovers. But Mrs. Arden with her definite morality, Joe with his obstinate and straitened view of sex, Eli with his ranting dogmatism, Lily with her petty spite, and the world in general with its terror of nonconformity—all these came round them as stealthily as the tide round a promontory, and (some of them with the best intentions) brought about tragedy. The only person to utter no word was John, for he had no moral code. Those that dwell in the lands of the sun do not need fires. "Thou shalt not" was mere foolishness to John, who was always so occupied in loving—the great affirmative—that he had no time for such negation.

Much to Deborah's joy and relief, John befriends Stephen. At the end of his visit, John asks Stephen to join him in the selfless act of caring for Eli's sheep. John says: "Well, since the owd mare died, he's [Eli's] good for naught, poor chap. He sits in the house like an owl in a tree, and when I go in, he says, 'The Lord's dealing with me. Take your silly face outside, 'oot!' And, of course, the animals and that must be seen after, so I thought to myself, if Joe'd borrow a horse and you'd ride Whitefoot, we'd soon round up the sheep." Stephen agrees, and Mary Webb concludes her chapter by saying of John: "To do a kindness and make several people happy as well, was his idea of bliss."

Later in *The Golden Arrow* (chapter 34), Webb again comments on the importance (and elusiveness) of independent thought and behavior. She says:

> Lesser men dwell in impregnable castles of content in the most lonely, the most populous place. Greater men set forth on quests against all the agony and mystery of life, and win their peace or go into a madhouse. But Stephen was too clear-sighted for the first, too much bondsman of

joy for the second. Therefore he lived at present in vivid sunshine—like a butterfly between two night-frosts, a poet between two portents.

Mary Webb, in *The House in Dormer Forest* (1920), again does battle against the corrupting influences of mindless habits and traditions. The house itself is used by Webb as a metaphor: it imprisons the Darke family, forcing its members into unhealthy conventions and a herd mentality. Webb, in chapter 6 ("The Advent of Ernest"), is harshly critical:

> A crowd of people shut up in one house, one creed, one strait view of life, must eventually wear each other out. Good nature is ground down by constant friction. Hatred leaps out like sparks from flint and stone. Society thinks that mistakes are made and crimes committed through the human soul being too much itself, going its own way. But crimes really happen through the soul being too little itself, striving to conform, or being crushed into conformity.

Mrs. Darke is Mary Webb's ultimate target. In chapter 11 ("Marigold's Warning"), Webb attacks with directness and intensity that is probably unsurpassed in any of her other work:

> She [Mrs. Darke] went in and out like a stranger, leaving no impress on anything in the house, for the desire for artistic self-expression comes from a healthy individualism and not from the disease of egotism, which is stunted development. Mrs. Darke was quite unindividual. She was a part of her class and creed, just as a bit of meteorological stone is part of a sun or a star. But it will never be a world unless it has movement. Nor would Mrs. Darke ever be an individual, because she had no living impulses. Her longing to be bowed down to, her greed of power, were also the results of this lack of growth. It was as if, very far away in the mists of the subconscious self, she heard a voice cry that she did not exist, never had existed, and in the fear of being nothing had resolved to seem to be everything. The outer form was all in all to her. She was one of those for whom ceremonial is made. She had always done her duty by her husband and children. She had seen to it that Solomon's winter coat was put away with pepper in the summer, and that his frayed cuffs were mended by Marigold or her predecessors. Her offspring had all suffered vaccination, baptism, dentistry, and confirmation at the correct times. She ruled Solomon's house in the orthodox manner. She had a gift for autocratic rule, and was a staunch believer in matriarchy. She disliked her own mother, who bore her, but she would never confess it even to herself. She had a certain dour loyalty to the dour laws she obeyed. That she did not love Mrs. Velindre was not astonishing, for in nothing but physical fact was that lady her mother. For the real mother is, first, a passionate lover of her children, recklessly spending herself in the manner of

all lovers. The idea of either Mrs. Velindre or her daughter in the guise of a reckless lover had in it more of mirth than conviction. They had somehow missed the gift, for it does not go inalienably with the production of offspring, and it is sometimes found in strange places—in the eyes of spinsters or invalids, in the smile of some whom the world despises.

This passage does far more than define Mary Webb's passion for individualism and her hatred of conformity. It shows Webb as fully competent to illuminate human character. It also shows that her exceptional powers of observation were in no way limited to the world of nature.

In her writing, Mary Webb takes on one more deeply-embedded conflict inside human nature. She knew (as many good writers of lasting fiction have known) that a genuine love for others (and the self-sacrifice that often comes with it) is at odds with lust and selfishness.

Precious Bane is, to a great degree, about this conflict. Prue Sarn deeply and sincerely loves the weaver Kester Woodseaves, and she sacrifices much in her daily life to her brother Gideon's dreams of financial riches. Gideon is a model of sexual lust and self-centered behavior. But this conflict arises much earlier in Webb's work, notably in one of her least-read and least-understood novels, *Seven for a Secret* (1922).

This novel has been criticized by many as having an abrupt and awkward ending. In the last chapter, Mary Webb (having ended her story) speaks directly to her readers. She challenges them to unravel the mystery of the novel's title (based upon an English children's counting rhyme), to accept the novel's ending, and to reflect upon Robert's return to life, Rwth's fate, and Gillian's redemption. The "secret that's never to be told" (as the nursery rhyme says) is left by Webb for her readers to unravel. Webb's unconventional finish did not sit well with critics.

Nonetheless, *Seven for a Secret* directly confronts issues surrounding love versus lust, and self-sacrifice versus selfishness. Robert Rideout and the servant Rwth (who cannot speak) both love deeply and selflessly. In chapter 21 ("Briar Roses"), Webb describes Rwth's feelings for Robert:

> . . . to sit and look at him [Robert] was heaven. To hear his voice was health and joy. To suffer for him—that was, all unknown to herself, the ultimate purpose of her life. Once he had come to the inn with a long red briar-scratch on his cheek, and had chanced to say that the old dog-roses by the rickyard wanted lopping, only he'd have to wait till he got some new hedging gloves.
>
> Next morning, mysteriously, uncannily, the dog-rose briars were neatly cut and the cut branches burnt in a little bonfire outside the gate. And had anyone at the "Mermaid" observed anything about Rwth they would have

seen that her hands were a mass of wounds, and they would have seen, as she plunged them into the bucket of soda and water to scrub the floor, the smile on her sad face, uplifted, ecstatic as that of a martyred saint.

Ralph Elmer, his manservant Fringal, and (in the beginning) Gillian Lovekin are of opposite minds. Fringal is simply mean and selfish. When others become confused or unhappy, he laughs convulsively to himself. He deliberately tortures others for his own amusement. Elmer and Gillian are sexually attracted to one another. They marry, in large part because Gillian's father Isaiah threatens to ruin Elmer if doesn't marry his daughter once he's deflowered her. Robert (who has always loved Gillian, despite her many faults) selflessly gives Gillian a piano as a wedding present (which he cannot really afford). Gillian undergoes a sea-change in attitude, culminating at the end of the novel. Mary Webb writes: "'Oh, Robert!' whispered Gillian, 'Robert! The powers of darkness have loosed their hold, and I'm not a child of sin any more.'"

Despite what critics have said about the ending to *Seven for a Secret*, Mary Webb made her point. Lust, and the selfish behavior that can accompany it, need not be overruling passions.

In 1891 Thomas Hardy, at a high point in his career as a novelist—and greatly admired by Mary Webb, who would dedicate *Seven for a Secret* to him—contributed his comments on "The Science of Fiction" to the *New Review*. Hardy says:

> A sight for the finer qualities of existence, an ear for the "still sad music of humanity," are not to be acquired by the outer senses alone, close as their powers in photography may be. What cannot be discerned by eye and ear, what may be apprehended only by the mental tactility that comes from a sympathetic appreciativeness of life in all its manifestations, this is the gift which renders its possessor a more accurate delineator of human nature than many another with twice his powers and means of external observation, but without that sympathy. . . .
>
> Once in a crowd a listener heard a needy and illiterate woman saying of another poor and haggard woman who had lost her little son some years before: "You can see the ghost of that child in her face even now."
>
> That speaker was one who, though she could probably neither read nor write, had the true means towards the "Science" of Fiction innate within her; a power of observation informed by a living heart.

Powers of observation, sympathetic appreciativeness of life, and accurate delineation of human nature, wonderfully described by Thomas Hardy, are together what define the extraordinary literary talent of Mary Webb.

Maesbooth
Meole.
July 23rd

Dearest Mrs Webb
 Thank you very much for the Bookman. Funnily enough, I had thought of writing a review for that Competition, — on "Silences" but I did not do so, not quite liking the idea of writing about a book of the kind for the sake of trying for a prize.
Are you feeling better? I hope the change, and also — what is much more — your

A Modern Writer   Dr. Gladys Mary Coles

Mary Webb (1881–1927), is usually classed as a regional and rural writer, her six novels set in her native county, Shropshire, a landscape of hills, valleys, woods and meres bordering on Wales. Yet while her work belongs in this tradition of English regional, country life writing, it also transcends these categories and is more in tune with our own times than with the period in which she wrote.

Her novels, functioning at several levels of meaning, are allegorical and symbolical, shot through with poetry and insight. She writes out of a twentieth-century consciousness and is a modern writer in her central concerns: the individual's search for self; the influence of the unconscious mind; inimical pressures of society on the individual; sexuality; the spiritual nature of love; and—of increasing contemporary relevance—the significance of the natural world and man's relationship with it.

Mary Webb's own intimate and intense relationship with nature—her "book of revelation"—was essential to her being, a life-force and one of the mainsprings of her writing, whether in prose or poetry, from first to last. An outstanding feature of her style is her evocative use of imagery drawn from the natural world (specifically of Shropshire), with exactness of descriptive detail deriving from her naturalist's knowledge. This, for example, from the opening paragraphs of her second novel, *Gone to Earth* (1917):

> It was cold in the Callow—a spinney of silver birches and larches that topped a round hill. A purple mist hinted of buds in the tree-tops, and a fainter purple haunted the vistas between the silver and brown boles.
>
> Only the crudeness of youth was here as yet, and not its triumph—only the sharp calyx-point, the pricking tip of the bud, like spears, and not the paten of the leaf, the chalice of the flower.
>
> For as yet spring had no flight, no song, but went like a half-fledged bird, hopping tentatively through the undergrowth. The bright springing mercury that carpeted the open spaces had only just hung out its pale flowers, and honeysuckle leaves were still tongues of green fire. Between the larch boles and under the thickets of honeysuckle and blackberry came a tawny, silent form . . . Clear-eyed, lithe, it stood for a moment in the full sunlight—a year-old fox, round-headed and velvet footed. Then it slid into the shadows.

As John Buchan said, in his Introduction to the *Collected Edition* of the novel (1928), "no one of our day has a greater power of evoking natural magic." Yet at the same time her novels are warmly human, rich in wit and irony, characterized by a unique blending of the mystical and the precise. The truths she expresses in her writing are particularly valuable today.

While my discussion of the themes and views which make Mary Webb a truly modern writer cannot be in depth in this short essay, I hope nonetheless to elucidate them, drawing on the extended assessments in my two biographical-critical studies, *The Flower of Light* and *Mary Webb*.

The spiritual nature of love, a major theme in her fiction, is explored extensively in her first novel *The Golden Arrow* (1916), written in the early years of her marriage to Henry B. L. Webb. This story of two contrasting sets of young couples in the Shropshire uplands dramatizes Mary Webb's belief that love is a fusion of the spiritual and the physical; and that a union of lovers at once psychic, sexual, and spiritual is a true marriage, with or without a legal wedding. But it is on the spiritual grasp of love that lasting happiness depends. As the central female character Deborah Arden explains (in Shropshire dialect) to her shallow, uncomprehending friend Lily Huntbatch:

> "If your man inna the lover of your soul . . . you've missed the honey and only got the empty comb. . . . for it's only when a man's the lover of your soul and wants you so as he's nigh beside hisself, as you're his 'ooman, right and true. I'm thinking it's only then as you've a right to be called his wife and sleep along of him."

Mary Webb's views on love were unconventional in the early decades of the twentieth century and offended some sections of Shropshire society to the extent that there was a ritual burning of her book.

Writing from keen personal experience, she emphasizes that suffering is intrinsic to love, illustrating in *The Golden Arrow* (structured on a complex pattern of opposites) the paradoxical quality of a love which both wounds and heals, breaks and makes whole—and the dual experience of extreme happiness and intense pain which this involves (as, in a wider sense, human existence comprises such a mixture). This union of opposites is symbolized in the title of the novel "the golden arrow," and echoed in imagery such as hawthorn and blossom ("the thorn's white over") or honeysuckle ("pain is the honeysuckle around the door").

In the pivotal figure of *The Golden Arrow*, John Arden, a visionary shepherd, the father of Deborah (and a portrait of her own father, George Meredith), Mary Webb projected her vision of love as "the great affirmative." She created in John Arden a "moral" centre, establishing the pattern of the novel as the other characters either rise or fall short of his standard. John Arden functions as a touchstone for the two couples, whose interwoven stories carry the narrative forward. Mary Webb's mode is naturalistic allegory, and in her symbolical world the outer and inner, the actual and the visionary, fuse indefinably, occur as one. To this purpose, she carefully selected her settings, features of the Shropshire landscape which would provide a vividly realistic world and at the same time lend themselves to the symbolical expression of her themes (as in her first novel, the contrasting parallel hill ranges, the pastoral Long Mynd and the craggy Stiperstones, allegorically re-named Wilderhope and Diafol Mountain with its ominous outcrop the Devil's Chair). She creates an essentially poetic world, uniquely her own, close-knit and self-contained, in which all interrelates and interacts—as Hawthorne put it, in the preface to *The Marble Faun* (1860), describing his own work—"a sort of poetic or fairy precinct."

Her concept of love, its spiritual nature, the struggle between the sacred and the profane, love and lust, self-giving and self-interest, is a recurring, cohesive theme in Mary Webb's novels. In *Gone to Earth* (1917), it is again intrinsic to character and plot—and the tragic fate of the central figure, Hazel Woodus. But in *Gone to Earth*, this theme is part of Mary Webb's more dominant and pressing concern: to show and question the barbarity of civilized society, man's pitiless inhumanity, the sacrifice of innocent, vulnerable young life. It is a novel most intimately related to the sad period in which it was written, the First World War, specifically 1916 and the Battle of the Somme, when the tragedy and carnage were intensifying—and is Mary Webb's compassionate response to the physical, emotional and psychological suffering. She was writing this novel when her three brothers were serving at the Western Front and she was living in Chester, a centre for the British and Belgian Red Cross and a military headquarters. Using symbol, myth and image, Mary Webb expresses obliquely in *Gone to Earth* the tragic spirit of those war years when multitudes, slaughtered, were indeed "gone to earth." Hazel Woodus is representative of that lost generation. But there is no direct mention of the war in its pages. Foremost a literary artist, Mary Webb, in translating pity and fear into image, wrote about what she knew and understood best—rural Shropshire, its people, customs, and rituals such as foxhunting, its folklore and legends. In *Gone to Earth* the dominant legend and motif is that of the Black Huntsman and his death-pack, a sinister myth which has a powerful hold over the mind and imagination of Hazel, who is ruled by superstition:

> Hunter's Spinney, a conical hill nearly as high as God's Little Mountain, lay between that range and Undern. It was deeply wooded; only its top was bare and caught the light redly. It was a silent and deserted place, cowled in ancient legends. Here the Black Huntsman stalled his steed, and the death-pack, coming to its precincts, ceased into the hill. Here, in November twilights, when the dumb birds cowered in the dark pines, you might hear from the summit a horn blown very clearly, with tuneful devilry, and a scattered sound of deep barking like the noise of sawing timber, and then the bloodcurdling tumult of the pack at feeding time.

Set in a remote area of the border hills, *Gone to Earth* is the tragedy of a country girl, eighteen-year-old, half-gipsy "child of nature" Hazel Woodus, desired and pursued by two men—the local squire, Jack Reddin, who awakens her sexually, and a young minister, Edward Marston, who marries her but reverentially does not consummate their union. Hazel becomes a divided being, torn by her polarity of desires and needs. In an ironic causal chain of events, both men, each of whom is a pillar of the social establishment, ultimately are instrumental in propelling Hazel to her death as, fleeing from the hunt, she tries to save her pet fox from the jaws of the hounds:

> The death that Foxy must die, unless she could save her, drowned all other sights and sounds. . . . she doubled for the quarry. . . .
> For one instant the hunt and the righteous men, Reddin the destroyer, and Edward the saviour, saw her sway, small and dark, before the staring sky. Then, as the pack, with a ferocity of triumph, was flinging itself upon her, she was gone.
> She was gone with Foxy into everlasting silence.

Both realistic and symbolic, *Gone to Earth* is imbued with a lyrical urgency that never falters, a sense of inevitability as the narrative moves to its compelling climax. Folklore, myth, and local legend are very finely assimilated into the fabric of the novel, especially the death-myths, such as the legend of the Black Huntsman and his pack, which embody Mary Webb's major theme and reflect the catastrophic period in which she was writing. Hazel Woodus (and her fox-cub) are representative of " all things hunted and snared and destroyed," and the hunt and the death-pack symbolic of universal cruelty, the barbarism in society that victimizes the defenceless, crucifying others whether physically or spiritually. The death-pack, which "hunts at all hours, light and dark" is made of "our fellows . . . all that have strength without pity. Sometimes our kith and kin, our nearest intimates, are in the first flight; give a view-halloo as we slip hopefully under a covert; are in at the death."

The death-myths are fulfilled at the close of the novel when the hunting cry "Gone to earth!" rouses "the shivering echoes"—a cry of universal pity and fear which encompasses all, hunters as much as hunted. In expressing obliquely the anguish of the contemporary world caught in a senseless war, *Gone to Earth* sounds a poignant chord which continues to echo.

The epigraph to her third novel, *The House in Dormer Forest* (1920), "Let the sleeping soul awake," is a key to its major theme: how society, with its codes and creeds, class system and herd-instinct, can stifle and destroy the individual trying to find himself and develop, "sing his own song." Like *Gone to Earth*, this important novel is an implicit response by Mary Webb to the devastation and carnage of the First World War—a criticism of the civilized world still applicable today. But while *Gone to Earth* is an impassioned plea and protest against human cruelty and hypocrisy, offering no clear answers, *The House in Dormer Forest* probes a solution, which for Mary Webb lies in the development of individual consciousness and awareness (and the freedom necessary for this development).

She was working on this novel when, after the armistice, widespread disillusion had set in across Britain, a mood of reaction and questioning of the established order which had led the country into a disastrous war. Mary Webb belongs with those writers, thinkers, and artists who were radically scrutinizing the inherited values and codes of behavior that had prevailed in 1914. *The House in Dormer Forest* reflects this climate of opinion in a postwar world casting its old skin and seeking for a new one.

Mary Webb looks closely and incisively at society in microcosm—represented by the Darke family, gentry with a long lineage who live in their gloomy ancestral mansion, Dormer Old House, reminiscent of Poe's House of Usher in its gothic qualities—"a place of ticking clocks and death-watch beetle." "Dormer" is situated "low by the water" in a "cuplike valley" surrounded on all sides by steep forest (the many variations on circular symbolism in the narrative underscore the theme of man's search for inner wholeness).

Richly entertaining, ironic, sharp and humorous, the most populated of her works, *The House in Dormer Forest* is less a rural novel than a social satire, with its emphasis on human relationships, the action centered on the ways in which the younger generation of Darkes are repressed, their inner development stifled by the archaic older generation who demand conformity—and how each of the younger Darkes rebel and arrive at an inner crisis, only three of the four ultimately achieving freedom from Dormer with its "spider's web of rules, legends and conventions."

Through her major character, Amber Darke (a portrait of herself when younger, and as she was before marriage), Mary Webb projects her own views and attitudes, her love for and need of "the green world," her mystical intuition and preoccupation with the unconscious mind. Amber loves "maternally, protectively, perceptively." She is in touch with her own deepest self, and has an awareness of the "subconscious." To her sister Ruby she explains: "It's something deep down . . . far down, like a pool in a mountain hollow." Repeatedly in her articles and reviews Mary Webb returns to the "well of the subconscious," which she defines (in her review "Birds, Beasts and Trees" for the *Spectator,* December 2, 1922) as that "which includes individual memory, race memory, deductions drawn from them, and something else as yet unnamed." There are many Jungian parallels in Webb's imaginative world. Her settings function symbolically—for example, in *The House in Dormer Forest,* the deep circular valley and, behind the house, the Beast Walk, a steep avenue of "strange beasts and birds cut out of gigantic yew trees," added to by each "regnant Darke." It was as if "each ancestor had breathed such ferocities as were in his soul into his especial creation." Here young Jasper Darke's spiritual crisis reaches its dramatic climax. A powerful image, the Beast Walk symbolizes man's dark unconscious mind, his propensity to revert to "the beast" within himself. And more explicitly, Mary Webb states: "when man is herded he remembers the savage." She was projecting her view of the dark side of civilized life—when the rise of Fascism and Nazism and yet another war with its barbaric Holocaust were not far off.

While at one level *The House in Dormer Forest* is a satirical, at times comic, novel of social behavior, at another it explores the modern theme of human loneliness and alienation, and is concerned with problems of "being" or "non-being," what is reality, what unreality. Like D. H. Lawrence, Mary Webb speaks for the freedom and growth of individual consciousness, demonstrating that our humanity must not be subservient to codes, systems, creeds, or "isms." On publication however, critics and reviewers failed to see the levels of meaning in this novel or comprehend its message.

In her fifth and most famous novel, *Precious Bane* (1924), winner of the coveted Prix Femina Vie Heureuse Anglais, Mary Webb takes forward the major themes of her previous fictional works, now embodied in a narrative set back in an earlier age, the second decade of the nineteenth century. Her setting is the remote meres, woods, and farms of Shropshire in a period when the influence of the Bible, local lore, and superstition deeply penetrated rural life—and the psyches of her characters. In creating this novel, like Thoreau at Walden, contemplating and observing, Mary Webb saturated herself in the atmosphere of the lonely meres, tree-ringed and shrouded in legend. In two interwoven stories of love and tragedy, the destinies of the main protagonists, sister and brother Prudence and Gideon Sarn, are worked out against a richly evoked landscape. The narrative, told by Prudence Sarn in intense and haunting language, is a tapestry of dark and light threads. Mary Webb achieves here a unique blend of romantic allegory, poetic parable, and personal testament.

More than any other of her novels, *Precious Bane* is projected from the center of her own bittersweet experience. In expressing individual truth and dramatizing her theme of the outsider, a person not the norm, rejected and persecuted by society but ultimately triumphing in spirit, Mary Webb is a modernist writer.

Precious Bane is Mary Webb's most technically perfect novel. The first person narrative form suited her well, and she employed it with unerring sureness of touch. Her comments and views are now presented as those of the narrator, so eliminating authorial interpolations and obtrusive didacticism (sometimes a weakness in her earlier fiction). This was to be the method of narration in her next, and unfinished, novel *Armour Wherein He Trusted* (1929) written in a male consciousness. In *Precious Bane,* all is seen through the eyes, mind and sensibility of Prudence Sarn looking back on her life; in this way, Mary Webb's own personality and vision—mirrored in Prudence—permeate the novel. The filtering of everything through this single, ardent consciousness gives the novel a curious, sustained intensity.

The title (from Milton's *Paradise Lost*) holds multiple meanings and significance. Mary Webb was afflicted with her own bane, Graves' disease, at the age of twenty, the then-incurable thyroid disorder causing protrusion of her eyes and a small goiter at the base of her throat: yet through her intense suffering she attained a richer inner life, developing both as a writer and a creative mystic. Often she endured "the critical, sly stare" of people suspicious of her appearance; and as a woman writer too, she was an outsider, her way of life not understood by local people in Shropshire farms and cottages. She sublimates her own experience in that of Prudence Sarn, whose bane is a "hare-shotten lip." Prue is painfully aware of the hostility of her superstitious neighbors in "the lonely farms," who spread rumors that she is cursed, changes into a hare at midnight and is a witch. But although shunned and an outsider because of her bane, she finds a "blessedness" within "which she might otherwise never have found," the mystical intuition she experiences in the apple-filled attic:

> ... there came to me, I cannot tell whence, a most powerful sweetness ... It was not religious, like the goodness of a text heard at a preaching. It was beyond that. It was as if some creature made all of light had come on a sudden from a great way off, and nestled in my bosom. On all things there came a fair, lovely look, as if a different air stood over them. ... I cared not to ask what it was. For when the nut-hatch comes into her own tree, she dunna ask who planted it, nor what name it bears to men. For the tree is all to the nut-hatch, and this was all to me.

This, Prue explains, is "a core of sweetness in much bitter." Her inner radiance, her beauty of mind and spirit, is discerned by the perceptive weaver, Kester Woodseaves, whose love for her is "the one maister-thread of pure gold" and who at the end of the novel saves her from the angry crowd who are attempting to drown her on the ducking stool.

Equally, the title is appropriate to the dark story of Gideon, whose bane is gold, which he sets out to acquire by means of the "innocent gold" of corn. Ruthlessly ambitious for wealth and power, at seventeen he foredooms himself, becoming his dead father's Sin Eater (an old Border custom), taking on his father's sins in return for his mother's promise to give him the farm and all that went with it. The tragedy which inexorably overtakes him, while it arises out of his own character, is also influenced by ironic chance and superstition.

Mary Webb achieves in *Precious Bane* a perfect synthesis of symbolism and realism: Sarn Mere is the essence of Gideon's character as well as the stage for his tragedy; it is the symbol of the dark unconscious mind in which he drowns, unable to cope with the sins he has committed. In the many fine descriptions of the mere, the detail is always meaningful. Here, for instance, the eerie atmosphere is evoked:

> It may be the water lapping, year in and year out—everywhere you look and listen, water; or the big trees waiting and considering on your right hand and on your left; or the unbreathing quiet of the place, as if it was created but an hour gone, and not created for us.

And in the following example, Prue speaks of Sarn Mere in a different mood:

> That was the best time of the year for our lake, when in the still, hot noons the water looked so kind, being of a calm, pale blue, that you would never think it could drown anybody. All round stood the tall trees, thick-leaved with rich summer green, unstirring, caught in a spell, sending down their coloured shadows into the mere, so that the treetops almost met in the middle. From either hand the notes of the small birds that had not yet given up singing went winging out across the water . . . All around the lake stood the tall bulrushes with their stout heads of brown plush, just like a long coat Miss Dorabella had. Within the ring of rushes was another ring of lilies . . . When they were buds, they were like white and gold birds sleeping, head under wing . . . So the mere was three times ringed about, as if it had been three times put in a spell. First there was the ring of oaks and larches, willows, ollern trees and beeches, solemn and strong, to keep the world out. Then there was the ring of rushes, sighing thinly, brittle and sparse, but enough, with their long, trembling shadows, to keep the spells in.
>
> Then there was the ring of lilies . . .

Another important modern theme in *Precious Bane* is the power of literacy and women's literacy in particular—an element in the plot of her previous novel, *Seven for a Secret* (1922). Literacy was rare in farming and working-class women at that date, and Prudence Sarn's ability to read and write adds to the suspicion and fear in which she is already held by her neighbors. But to Prue, learning to read and write and do sums is "like a big window opening." And it makes possible the book itself, as she tells her story retrospectively with the help of a little calico-covered journal she has kept, a story illustrative both of the repressive treatment of women in a male-dominated society and of the liberation and inner growth that literacy can bring.

Unified by her highly individual voice and vision, Mary Webb's work forms a coherent whole. Her nature essays, *The Spring of Joy* (1917), are little-known but make explicit the nature philosophy which informs her fiction. Here she communicates her clear understanding of the significance of the natural world, perspectives of particular value today. Totally at one with the Shropshire countryside, she explores her own close and passionate bond with the natural environment, sharing her discoveries, both outer and inner:

> There is nothing so restful as the perfect circle, whether seen, as in the full moon, or implied, as in the young crescent. It is a symbol of things men feel but cannot understand; so Merlin "made the round table in tokening of the roundness of the world"; so Vaughan saw eternity "like a great Ring". Nearly all essential things are round—the perianth of flowers, where the seed is, stars, the window of the eye. . . . a circle, however small, is immutable, holds infinity; because of this, and because of the implied centre, it is the most perfect symbol of Divinity.
>
> All green things that have to cleave their way come into the light like swords—grass, leaves emerging from the sheath, shoots splitting the bark—all these are pointed. In the outermost branch and the topmost twig of a tree the point sharply defines the limit of the individual form as it stands against the vagueness of air. The point is where the thought slips from the finite to the infinite, like a bird balanced on the top of a fir-tree before he trusts himself to immensity. "At the point of death" has in it something of this idea of the sudden ending of a form . . .

She celebrates nature's variety and secret orchestration, its principles of structure and growth, the suggestions inherent in its colors. And always aware of the symbolic in the real, she interprets nature's "cabalistic signs," its "occult script." In these nine related essays, her emphasis is on the spiritual ties between man and the natural world. Her senses were hyper-acute and from first-hand knowledge she conveys what William Blake calls the holiness of "minute particulars": for instance, the "curious redolence" of rock in hot weather, the faint gradations of movement in flowers, the "intrinsic structure" of snow crystals (these "complex and lovely figures, condensing upon their mysterious nucleus of cosmic dust"). Reading *The Spring of Joy* today, in our increasingly technological and synthetic age, not only sharpens but extends the reader's perception of the value and wonder of the natural environment. And Mary Webb makes clear her belief, born of experience, that when a person is "totally receptive," nature's healing power is a "spiritual healing," an influx of vitality "into those recesses of being beyond the conscious self."

Another undervalued aspect of Mary Webb's work is her poetry, which stands in close relation to her nature essays and novels. Like

Thomas Hardy, whose work she admired, she thought of herself as primarily a poet, writing from childhood onwards, tutored in traditional forms such as the sonnet, by her poet father. Rooted firmly in the countryside of Shropshire, evoking a powerful sense of place, her poems are yet rich in human interest, often deeply felt personal songs:

> Let fall your golden showers laburnum tree!
> Break the grey casket of your buds for me—
> Soon I shall go where never gold is seen,
> And who will be with you as I have been?

As Walter de la Mare noted, her poetry is "more than usually her very self's." There are many skillfully crafted sonnets among her poems, such as "Swallows":

> The swallows pass in restless companies,
> Against the pink-flowered may, one shining breast
> Throbs momentary music – then possessed
> With motion, sweeps on some new enterprise.
> Unquiet in heart, I hear their eager cries
> And see them dart to their nests beneath the eaves;
> Within my spirit is a voice that grieves,
> Reminding me of empty autumn skies.
> Nor can we rest in Nature's dear delight:
> June droops to winter, and the sun droops west.
> Beneath the dark eaves of the infinite,
> We sing our song in beauty's fading tree,
> And flash forth, migrant, into mystery.

While her dominant themes are perennial ones of love, transience, death, she has her own distinctive voice, characteristically lucid, with an emotional charge all the more effective for an artistic control which for her was second nature. In "Viroconium," for instance, describing the ruins of a Roman city in the Shropshire plain, she conveys both the atmosphere and a keen historical perspective. Here are four of the ten stanzas:

> Virocon—Virocon—
> Still the magic name rings on
> And brings, in the untrampled wheat,
> The tumult of a thousand feet.
>
> Where trumpets rang and men marched by,
> None passes but the dragonfly.
> Athwart the grassy town forlorn,
> The lone dor-beetle blows his horn.

> The poppy standards droop and fall
> Above one rent and mournful wall:
> In every sunset flame it burns
> Yet towers unscathed when day returns
>
> . . . .
>
> Grief lingers here, like mists that lie
> Across the dawns of ripe July;
> On capital and corridor
> The pathos of the conqueror.

Her poetry certainly merits wider recognition than it has been accorded. A fine nature poet, in this tradition of English poetry she stands with John Clare and Edward Thomas, her naturalist's knowledge serving her well in the choice of sharp simile and metaphor. As Walter de la Mare said, she could "seize the momentary." One example must suffice, an extract from her poem "The Wood," in which she depicts Spring Coppice, a place special to her near her Shropshire home on Lyth Hill:

> Tall, feathered birches on the tides of air
> Wash to and fro, like seaweeds fine and fair,
> And deep in leaf and blossom from all eyes
> The rope-walk of the honeysuckle lies . . .

She expresses her wish to be there forever, in all seasons:

> Like a bird, with wings
> Dusky and silent, I would flit through spring's
> Wistful, immaculate colours, through the dream
> And hush of summer; down the rush and gleam
> Of autumn . . .

Nor has she been sufficiently recognised as a woman poet, and in the literary context of her time this is particularly regrettable for there have been few English women poets of distinction (Emily Brontë, Christina Rossetti, Elizabeth Barrett Browning, Alice Meynell, Charlotte Mew). While always attentive to craft, she thought deeply about the art of poetry, making considered statements in reviews and articles. In her remarkable essay "The Core of Poetry" (*The English Review*, February 1920) she emphasizes the importance of the unconscious in the creative process:

> Poetry is the subconscious self breaking from its prison of silence and finding its way through the mazes of the written word. Very often it frees

itself from the tyranny of the word, expressing itself not through the
thing said, not even through the idea, but through a rhythm, a cadence,
or a chiming of sounds.

From her own creative experience she can speak of "the being that
dwells far within the poet's deepest self . . . quickened to some latent
memory." Elsewhere, in a review entitled "The Wing of Psyche" in the
Bookman (July 1926), she writes of the poet as "a listener on the shelving
shores of the subconscious . . . He listens; then he writes. Often he is
greatly surprised at what he writes."

Mary Webb did not fulfill her ambition to see a collection of her poems in print. A posthumous volume, *Poems and The Spring of Joy,* assembled by her husband and published in the *Collected Works* (1928), has
long been out of print. My edition, *Selected Poems of Mary Webb* (1981),
published to mark the centenary of her birth, was the first selection
drawing on the entire body of her work and arranged chronologically
to represent adequately her achievement. Now reprinted in an updated
third edition (2005), this volume is bringing the poetry of Mary Webb
to new generations of readers.

H. P. Marshall said in the *Edinburgh Review* (April 1929): "I think we
do not yet fully realise how much Mary Webb has given to the world . . .
We must be careful by what canon we judge (her) . . . she had in her gift
an understanding of the spiritual truths of life which we should be unwise to ignore." He was among the few perceptive critics who foresaw
that Mary Webb's work would be more rightly understood by future generations who would be attuned and receptive to her meaning.

While Prime Minister Stanley Baldwin's praise in April 1928 had promoted her popularity (her books were best-sellers throughout the
1930s), his recommendation of her work had an adverse effect on her
critical reputation, alienating academics and the young intelligentsia of
the day. As Arnold Bennett wrote in the *Evening Standard* on May 3,
1928: "The resuscitation of books out of a state of suspended vitality is a
fine game. Mr. Stanley Baldwin has just been playing at it—with the novels of the late Mary Webb. I receive with polite reserve the pronouncements of Prime Ministers about imaginative literature." Her work was
neglected in scholarly studies, and the post-Second World War years,
when literary tastes changed, brought the waning of her public popularity. In the decades that followed, there was little interest in her work.

Revival began with the publication of my critical biography *The Flower of Light* (1978), reviewed extensively and selected as "Book of the Year" in the *Financial Times* and the *Birmingham Post,* and adapted as a "Radio Portrait" for *BBC Radio 4*. Widely purchased by libraries, colleges, and the reading public, it was published in a paperback edition in 1998. The interest in Mary Webb generated by *The Flower of Light* accelerated after the publication of my second study, *Mary Webb* (1990, reprinted 1996), and I am frequently consulted by university and college thesis writers. Mention must also be made of the Mary Webb Society's enthusiastic support and annual program of talks and events.

I hope in this essay to have directed attention to Mary Webb as not just a modern writer but an inspirational one whose work is of immediate relevance in the twenty-first century.

How I Came to Discover, Collect, and Appreciate Mary Webb   MARY E. CRAWFORD

All my life, I have been a reader. I began collecting literature after marrying (thirty-two years ago) into the Crawford book-collecting family. We laughingly refer to our family as "idle readers of novels." Literary material in the Crawford library ranges from early seventeenth-century dramatist Ben Jonson to late twentieth-century novelist Jean Auel. There has always been an unwritten rule among Crawford family collectors: We do not collect the same authors. We do not compete for each other's books.

I began to collect Jane Austen in the early 1980s, and broadened over time to include Isak Dinesen; Mary Webb; J. R. R. Tolkien; Dorothy L. Sayers; Charlotte, Anne, and Emily Brontë; Lin Yutang; Pearl Buck; Kate Seredy; and Jean Auel. While it appears as if I collect primarily women writers, I am merely filling in gaps in the already well-established Crawford libraries. The distinct voices of these authors appealed to me, and each led an interesting personal life.

My late father-in-law, Ralph Crawford, introduced me to Mary Webb some twenty-five years ago. As I was casting about for a novel to read over a summer weekend, he suggested that I might enjoy *Precious Bane*.

I felt, upon first reading *Precious Bane*, that I had rediscovered an ancient tale, filled with collective human truths. Old countrywoman Prudence Sarn's first-person narrative about her life on the Welsh borderlands after Waterloo is told in Shropshire dialect. The cadences of her narrative echo the rhythms of the Bible. Webb's descriptive passages evoke a keen, ethereal beauty and also presage tragedy. Her language is imbued with emotional sensibility and spiced with humor. In *Precious Bane*, Mary Webb—with her distinctive vision and powerful imagination—transcends time and place to create a story of universal significance.

I determined to acquire Webb's relatively small lifetime literary output of six novels, and the collected editions of her prose and poetry. I was initially taken aback to find these first editions both difficult to locate and expensive to acquire. In studying biographies of Mary Webb's life, however, the reason soon became apparent. Webb's first editions were printed in small quantities using poor quality materials (due to materials shortages, both during and after World War I). Mary Webb was accorded a measure of recognition during her lifetime from the London literati, and slowly developed a circle of discerning admirers. Yet, despite high praise from a number of these respected authors (such as Rebecca West, John Buchan, Walter de la Mare, J. M. Barrie, Caradoc Evans, and Edwin Pugh), Webb's first editions sold poorly.

Each of Webb's six dramatic tales is set in her own intimately-known Shropshire borderland between England and Wales. Webb's strength as a novelist lies in her poetic imagination—her tales exhibit an exquisite perception of nature and are clothed in evocative prose. Webb did not write to entertain or to tell rustic tales. Neither is her creative impulse intellectual—she is not innovative with dialogue or plot. Instead, Webb gave literary form to her spiritual insights. She felt compelled to communicate her intuitive perceptions of life and human experience. Webb's novels present problems of modern living (and her answers to them) in characters who act out her insights and intuitions. Webb repeatedly returns to the same themes: good versus evil; individuality versus conformity; love and sacrifice versus lust and selfishness; physical deformity versus inner beauty; the cruelty of mankind to living things; and man's interrelationship with nature. I admire and enjoy a writer who addresses these important, universal issues.

In large measure, Webb's novels should be read as allegories. While she creates realistic accounts of rural country people, her narratives also expose visionary revelations to discerning readers. In her articles, reviews and novels, Webb shows her preoccupation with the influence of the subconscious mind. She had an intuitive grasp of many now-well-accepted psychological concepts, and would today be considered a Jungian for her beliefs. She did not have the benefit of psychiatrist Carl Gustav Jung's theories, however, as he was a contemporary (1875–1961) and his Swiss writings were inaccessible to her. Like Jung, Webb believed that the human psyche is by nature religious. As she wrote in "The Poetry of the Prayer Book," a review for *T. P. and Cassell's Weekly* for April 17, 1926, ". . . the Prayer Book is ours by divine right, because it is the folklore of the soul."

One of Mary Webb's main weaknesses (which sprang from her urgent desire to convey her deeply-held visions of life) was a tendency to shout her message over her characters. She brought her didacticism under control with the publication of *Precious Bane*, in which she successfully adopted the first-person narrative form to integrate her concepts and ideas into her story.

Prime Minister Stanley Baldwin read *Precious Bane* over the Christmas holidays in 1926, and sent Mary Webb a letter of appreciation in January 1927 (cat. 127). Webb died less than nine months later—on October 8, 1927—at the age of forty-six, poverty-stricken, estranged from her husband, and feeling largely unheard and unappreciated.

It was Baldwin's tribute to Mary Webb and *Precious Bane* at a Royal Literary Fund dinner held in April 1928—six months after her death—that secured Webb's reputation. Literally overnight, her fame was established as newspapers trumpeted Baldwin's praise under the headline "Neglected Genius." Jonathan Cape hurriedly published her work in a seven-volume *Collected Works of Mary Webb* (1928–1929) with introductions written by famous men of the day who had known her. Literary biographies were written and published. From 1928 until after the onset of World War II, Mary Webb became one of the most popular woman authors in Great Britain and Europe. Collected editions of Webb's books ran into thirty-five reprintings and were translated over the next two decades into more than fifteen languages. A number of her books were dramatized for stage. Sheet music was written using her poems. Movies were made of her most popular works. The British Broadcasting Corporation (BBC) aired radio and television series based on her novels.

Book collectors fought over scarce first editions, tidbits of literary manuscripts, and memorabilia. First editions of Mary Webb were highly prized and eagerly sought, as described in A. Edward Newton's book, *End Papers* (Boston: Little, Brown & Company, 1933):

> An English bookseller's catalogue reaches my desk. It quotes three of Mary Webb's books . . . No modern could be more attractive to the collector; her books total only six . . . all genuinely rare and of real importance. I cannot stress too strongly the difficulty of obtaining her books. Since reading *Precious Bane* three years ago I have searched consistently, and during that period I have only seen or heard of (apart from mine) four copies of *Precious Bane*, none of *Gone to Earth*, and one each of the others. I allude, of course, to good copies. Compare such a record with the flood of *Jane Eyres, Tom Joneses*, second Shakespeares, *Vicars of Wakefields*, and Boswell's *Johnson*! These are not rare—they are only expensive. (chapter 3 "Mary Webb," p. 45)

Webb's posthumous fame was primarily based on readers' admiration for her poetic and perceptive uses of language, and her depiction of the Shropshire landscape and rural people. Rather than being seen as the highly educated, deeply philosophical and complex personality that she was, Mary Webb was characterized posthumously by reviewers and biographers as a homespun mystic of the Shropshire hills. Perhaps because of the intense public enthusiasm for her works, there was a general reluctance at the time among academics to acknowledge Mary Webb as a major writer. Yet, a rereading of her novels will establish that Mary Webb was well ahead of her time and an early voice for the individual spirit. While not a modern feminist—indeed Webb felt that motherhood and wifehood were sacred callings for a woman—she characterized the ideal woman as "being in other things than sex free and equal, and in sex so mutually generous as to forget self and rights" (*The Golden Arrow*, p. 158).

The title of this exhibition and catalogue, *Mary Webb: Neglected Genius*, might seem pretentious to those unfamiliar with Stanley Baldwin's posthumous tribute in 1928. Yet in the four years that I have spent preparing for this exhibition, many lovers of literature have said to me, "Tell me about Mary Webb. I am unfamiliar with her." Despite past decades of intense popularity, Mary Webb's genius is once again little known.

Yet a writer who has fallen out of current academic or public consciousness is not doomed to obscurity. Literature is, in large part, the study of the human heart. A novel establishes a personal, one-on-one dialogue between the writer and reader. So long as a communication of interests, ideas, and heartfelt emotions exists, there is relevance—a universal connection. Past authors may come to be seen in a new light and with new relevance. Webb's specific talent for presenting the subtlest truths in the clearest of language, and her fusion of strong emotion, close observation, and precise expression deserve to be enjoyed and reexamined.

Over the past two decades, my husband and I have had the good fortune to gather together a large amount of Webb's primary literary material. Much of our archive consists of manuscripts, typescripts, and association copies that had originally belonged to Henry Webb. In the eighty years since Mary Webb's death, this material has never been publicly exhibited or made available for academic study.

The San Francisco-based bookseller Tom Goldwasser has been instrumental in helping us obtain many Mary Webb items from the dispersal of the libraries of noted collectors: Frederick Baldwin Adams, Jr. (Grolier Club member, 1937–2001 and Grolier Club president, 1947–1951); H. Bradley Martin (Grolier Club member, 1938–1988); Halsted B. Vander Poel (Grolier Club member, 1936–2003); Benjamin D. Hitz (Grolier Club member, 1939–1949); and Fred Board (Grolier Club member, 1972–2005). In an essay for this catalogue, Tom Goldwasser details the history of the early collectors of Mary Webb.

As "generational stewards" of this archive, we feel responsible for studying, enhancing, and preserving the collection. Over the past few years, we have been cataloguing Webb's manuscript and typescript materials, locating additional ephemeral and undocumented material, and updating our Mary Webb bibliography, which is available online at www.marywebb.org.

In preparation for this catalogue and exhibition, we have spent time at the British Library unearthing Webb's contributions to literary periodicals and extending the list of her known works. We have traveled annually to Mary Webb's native Shropshire (the source of her inspiration), have enjoyed meetings of the Mary Webb Society, and have regularly consulted with Webb's biographer, Dr. Gladys Mary Coles, who has contributed an essay and a foreword, and made editorial suggestions to the balance of the present catalogue.

We hope this exhibition encourages a re-examination (and a renewed enjoyment) of Mary Webb's works, and we look forward to introducing her to readers and scholars who might be unfamiliar with Webb's life and literary output. To these ends, we have collaborated with Stanford University Libraries to digitize the unique material in our Mary Webb collection so that it may be accessible online for scholarly research. By making the archive available to scholars and enthusiasts, we hope to contribute to an ongoing critical evaluation and reassessment of Webb's place in English literature, nature writing, poetry, and women's studies. The 2010 Grolier Club exhibition will travel to the Stanford University Libraries later in the same year.

A Bookseller's Retrospective on Collecting Mary Webb   Thomas A. Goldwasser

The Crawfords' Mary Webb collection is the result of a confluence of several specialized twentieth-century collectors' years of acquisition and dispersal—revealing histories of ownership and migration of the books and manuscripts—of this author whose popularity rapidly waxed and waned over a few years, and for whom the supply of collectable material has been mostly known and relatively small.

The first major dispersal of material after Webb's death in 1927 was of the collection of the books and manuscripts belonging to her husband, H. B. L. Webb, sold in the mid-1930s to the London firm of Elkin Mathews (then owned by Greville Worthington, Ian Fleming, and Percy Muir). Muir's *Minding My Own Business* (London: Chatto & Windus, 1956) recounts the purchase:

> Greville discovered that Mary Webb's husband owned, and was prepared to sell, presentation copies of all her books inscribed to him, and the thirty books which made up her pathetic library. These were nearly all cheap editions, or rather tattered copies of books she had acquired for a few pence in the market-place where she had supplemented her income by selling bunches of flowers from her cottage garden. There were also a few books given her mostly by not very highly esteemed authors.
>
> What excited Greville most, however, and what caused me most anguish of mind were two manuscripts. One was a fairy story that she wrote when she was thirteen; the other was the manuscript of the novel she left unfinished when she died, *The* [sic] *Armour Wherein He Trusted*. These two manuscripts had survived only because they were unpublished. All her published manuscripts she had used to light her cottage fire. Mr. Webb was prepared to sell everything of hers that he possessed; and I was shattered by Greville's proposal that we should blue almost our entire bank-balance in acquiring them.
>
> I tried to persuade him to make it a personal speculation, the firm to sell the material for him on commission; but he rightly said that this would not be a satisfactory scheme. Finally I said that I would waive all my objections if John Carter would take a half share in the transaction for Scribner's . . . We dealt with it jointly, and we both made a good deal of money out of it quite quickly. (pp. 199–200)

David A. Randall, long employed by the rare book department at Scribner's, in his engaging memoir *Dukedom Large Enough* (New York: Random House, 1969), devotes a chapter to Mary Webb and her collectors, noting that in 1929, when he entered the rare book business, she had "a small but devoted cult of admirers and collectors, and [he] set out to gather what [he] could for them" (p. 171). The collectors Randall names are Frederick Baldwin Adams, Jr., George Matthew Adams, and Benjamin Hitz. Others active at the same time were H. Bradley Martin, Roland Bruce Barrett, and Gustine Courson Weaver. Randall fills out the story of Worthington's purchase from H. L. Webb:

> It seemed that on Worthington's arrival Mr. Webb began examining closets, drawers and the like where such of Mary's letters, manuscripts and books which had survived were stored. The more he examined them the sadder he became: he literally wept over a copy of *The Golden Arrow*, her first novel (London, 1916) dedicated "To A Noble Lover H.L.W.," and well he should have. Her last novel *Precious Bane*, at the start no more successful than its predecessors, was also dedicated to him, though his copy was not inscribed, as she gave it to him personally. Inserted in it, however, was Baldwin's glowing letter to her on his first reading the book, dated "Downing Street, Jan. 14, 1927," well preceding his speech at a dinner of the Royal Literary Fund which struck the effective note of appreciation that led to the great demand for her work that followed.
>
> As he perused these, Webb became more and more loath to part with them, and quite understandably so. Worthington had just about given up any hope of obtaining them when the second Mrs. Webb, who had been off somewhere, appeared just at the end of teatime. When she heard that the ragged and tattered remnants of books and papers were worth the modest sum offered for them, she commanded her husband to accept Worthington's offer and "get that trash out of here before the fool changes his mind." (pp. 171–172)

Randall describes the sale of several items, as noted below, *passim*, and concludes his chapter remarking on two unaccounted-for pieces "Somewhere, on someone's shelves, rests the dedication copy of *Precious Bane* of surpassing interest. I cannot recall what happened to the fairy story she wrote when she was thirteen" (p. 174).

The Elkin Mathews Catalogue 68, "First and Last," issued in October 1936, took its title from the two manuscripts: Webb's unpublished first prose work, the fairy story entitled *Clematisa & Percival*, and her last work, the unfinished novel *Armour Wherein He Trusted*. *Clematisa & Percival* was priced at £50. It is now in the Crawford collection. *Armour Wherein*

53

He Trusted, together with a presentation copy of *The Golden Arrow*, was catalogued at the enormous price of £550. It seems to have remained unsold for some time (Muir, p. 203) but was eventually purchased by the New York rare book seller Edgar H. Wells (1875–1938) from whom it was acquired for $1,250 by Frederick Baldwin Adams, Jr.

In 1938 Elkin Mathews issued Catalogue 73, containing what they described as a "melancholy little collection of thirty volumes . . . the whole of Mary Webb's personal library with the exception of two reference books." Frederick Baldwin Adams, Jr. acquired from this list Lady Charlotte Guest's translation of *The Mabinogion* (Everyman's Library, 1906), and a copy of *The Scarlet Letter*. He had also acquired what must be the two "reference books," Charlotte Sophia Burne's *Shropshire Folk-Lore* (1883) and Georgina Jackson's *The Shropshire Word-Book* (1879). Bradley Martin bought her Chaucer (Oxford, 1906), which was described as "much underlined and annotated." Other books were acquired by George Matthew Adams, (Frederick Baldwin Adams's annotated copy of the catalogue marks as George Matthew Adams's the two-volume Robert Browning's *Poetical Works* [London, 1901] in which "the flyleaves and margins are much annotated"), and sold at Parke-Bernet in 1963. Webb's copy of James Thomson's *The Seasons and Castle of Indolence* offered for £20 in the 1938 catalogue with a typescript poem, reappeared, without the poem, in a P. H. Muir (for Elkin Mathews Ltd.) Catalogue twenty years later at £6/10/–. The Weaver collection has Webb's copy of *Pride and Prejudice* (London: Thomas Nelson, 1903), given her by her father, and not included in the Mathews catalogue.

Benjamin Hitz died in 1949 and his collection was dispersed. The most important of Hitz's Mary Webb holdings was the collection of a group comprised of 37 autograph poems; 35 typewritten poems typed by Webb between 1911 and 1917, mostly signed and corrected by hand; and seven typewritten poems not typed by her, but with some autograph corrections, purchased from Scribner's, these representing the majority of Mary Webb's extant poetical manuscripts. Of the 85 poems published in the 1928 edition of *Poems and The Spring of Joy*, which at that time were all that was known to have survived of her poetry, manuscripts existed only for these 79. Randall remarks erroneously that the collection later went to the University of Chicago (p. 174); in fact it was acquired by the Stamford, Connecticut collector and Borden executive, F. J. Board.

Randall also notes his purchase of "most of [George Matthew

Adams's, sold in 1963] Webb material for the Lilly Library for considerably less than he had paid me" (p. 174). The Lilly's manuscripts are the short stories "Antonio" and "Over the Hills and Far Away," and the poem "Reveille." Roland Bruce Barrett's collection made sixteen lots in a Parke-Bernet sale on April 24, 1962. Most of the manuscripts and letters are now in the Berg collection at New York Public Library.

H. Bradley Martin's collection was sold (Sotheby's, New York, May 1, 1990) in four lots: A complete collection of Webb's books, including two presentation copies, went to Auerbach, who also bought the second lot (works by and about) which included two books from her library (*Chaucer's Works* and *In the Day of Battle*, the latter not listed in the Elkin Mathews catalogue); all but two insignificant titles from these lots are now at Columbia. The letters (to Jonathan Cape [these had previously been sold by G. F. Sims, catalogue 55] and A. St. John Adcock) went to Woolmer, and the collection of manuscripts for the fifty-one poems published in 1946 was purchased by David Holmes, most of it (the Crawfords bought a few poems from Holmes) later sold and given by him to Smith College. A few other manuscript pieces were catalogued by Holmes and some of those are now at Denton.

In 1998, F. J. Board sold his Mary Webb collection to Thomas A. Goldwasser Rare Books. The collection also included the manuscripts of the short story "In Affection and Esteem" (acquired by Board in 1973 from Joseph the Provider Books) and the review "Glorious Apollo" (formerly in the Barrett collection and purchased by Board from G. R. Minkoff in 1978), but the *clou* was undoubtedly the long-lost dedication copy of *Precious Bane*, which has inserted in it the famous Stanley Baldwin letter. Except for one typescript poem, "The White Moth" sold to the University of North Texas, the entire collection was purchased by Kerry Payne, an American collector resident in France. Early in 2001, he added the collection of Betty M. Horton, which had the manuscript of the short story "The Chinese Lion," presentation copies to May Sinclair of *Gone to Earth* and *Seven for a Secret*, and ten letters (dated between February and October of 1925) to the editor A. St. John Adcock. (Seven of these letters had been catalogued in 1963 by H. Karnac (Books), 58 Gloucester Road; two additional letters to Adcock were in the Karnac catalogue, but their whereabouts is presently unknown. As mentioned above, H. Bradley Martin also owned ten letters to Adcock, dated from December 1925 to December 1926.)

In November 2001, when Frederick Baldwin Adams, Jr.'s collections were sold at Sotheby's, the chance to add to what was becoming a very good collection (enough to make it the best possible) proved irresistible. All ten Sotheby's lots (some of multiple volumes) were purchased. These included the dedication copy of *The Golden Arrow*, inscribed to her husband; his inscribed copy of *The Spring of Joy;* presentation copies of *Seven for a Secret* (the dedication copy) and *Precious Bane* inscribed to Thomas Hardy, both of which had been given to Adams by Mrs. Hardy in 1937; the manuscript of *Armour Wherein He Trusted;* two manuscripts on Shropshire folklore (important as source material for the novels); other manuscripts, both poetry and prose; letters; and some books from Mary Webb's personal library.

In 2004, I began discussing with Bruce and Mary Crawford their interest in having a definitive Mary Webb collection and the possibility to purchase the Payne collection, which they were able to accomplish that spring. Shortly after that deal was concluded, the last major piece came in, with the sale in one lot of H. B. Vander Poel's Mary Webb collection, in which was found the manuscript of *Clematisa & Percival*. It had been purchased from Elkin Mathews's catalogue by Bertram Rota, who had offered it in his Catalogue 55, in June 1937, for £65, whence it was successfully ordered by H. B. Vander Poel. Rota remarked in his letter to Vander Poel, "handling this has given me as much pleasure as anything which has come my way for a long time."

Mary Webb and her Work: Some Views of the Critics

"This year's discovery has been Mary Webb, author of Gone to Earth. She is a genius, and I shouldn't mind wagering that she is going to be the most distinguished writer of our generation."

    — Rebecca West, review of *Gone to Earth* in the *Times Literary Supplement*, August 30, 1917, p. 416.

"She is equipped at every point with all the talents that go to the making of masterpieces . . . she has a style of exquisite beauty which has yet both force and restraint, simplicity and subtlety . . . she can moreover tell a story and so intrigue you with its sense of inevitableness that it seems more real than reality . . . She has, in short, genius. And though she has not yet come fully into her own, the day is surely not far off when she will be acclaimed as among the greatest of living novelists."

    — Edwin Pugh, "Promise and Performance," review of *Precious Bane* in the *Bookman*, September 1924, p. 324.

"Mary Webb's rich idiom and rhythm cannot be overpraised."

    — Austin Clarke, review of *Precious Bane* in the *Nation and the Athenaeum*, August 2, 1924, p. 560.

"In all these novels she shows at times almost uncanny understanding of human character, an intense love of nature, a subtle art and imaginative power in picturing a scene, in the telling of a story, and a feeling for the magic of words, a beauty of style that none of her contemporaries surpassed."

    — Arthur St. John Adcock, *The Glory that was Grub Street: Impressions of Contemporary Authors* (London: Sampson Low, Marston & Co., Ltd., 1928), p. 324.

"Mary Webb had power; she could create beauty; and she is truthful concerning human nature."

    — Arnold Bennett, "Books and Persons" in the *Evening Standard*, May 3, 1928.

"It is by her understanding of spiritual truth that Mary Webb will stand or fall... She makes plain the motive of her writing, the desire for that subtle beauty which lies beyond the rim of the sky, and the passionate longing to share her experience of that miraculous sweetness. She was a nature-mystic, but her mysticism was no vague and formless refuge from reality... It makes clear for us the truth to which she wished above all to bear witness. For her God was expressed in natural beauty; and He was a loving God, offering strength to mankind through the earth, and made manifest in the stirring of the sap and the re-birth of spring. From this knowledge, and it is no less than knowledge, arises her intense pity for all hurt and suffering things, her passionate belief in a purposeful wisdom too deep for human apprehension, but revealed to those who listen for the voices on the wind. This mysticism suffuses her writings with a spiritual integrity and loveliness which is not often found outside the avowedly religious writings of the great mystics."

    — H. P. Marshall, "Mary Webb" in the *Edinburgh Review*, April 1929, pp. 315–327.

"Her sensibility is so acute and her power over words so sure and swift that one who reads some passages in Whitehall has almost the physical sense of being in Shropshire cornfields."

    — Stanley Baldwin, "Introduction" to *Precious Bane* (London: Jonathan Cape, 1928), p. 9.

"The light in the stories of the Shropshire Lass is a light not shining on things but through them."

    — G. K. Chesterton, "Introduction" to *The Golden Arrow* (London: Jonathan Cape, 1928), p. 8.

"Impregnated with poetry... No one of our day has a greater power of evoking natural magic... Mary Webb need fear no comparison with any writer who has attempted to capture the soul of nature in words and to 'tease us out of thought' by glimpses into our ancient inheritance."

    — John Buchan, "Introduction" to *Gone to Earth* (London: Jonathan Cape, 1929), p. 10.

"Mary Webb had that always fascinating quality of genius—imaginative energy. It is a quality so precious that when an author possesses it the waves of criticism beat against his work in vain . . . Her work is alive with the fiery genius of sympathy, pity, and awe . . . It is not too much to say that in her writings fiction becomes a branch of poetry."
> — Robert Lynd, "Introduction" to *Seven for a Secret* (London: Jonathan Cape, 1929), p. 11.

"Mary Webb, whose world was 'a place of almost unbearable wonder,' had senses almost microscopic in their delicacy. She could—most rewardful of feats—seize the momentary . . . Few writers indeed have left behind them so rich a posthumous gift."
> — Walter de la Mare, "Introduction" to *Poems and The Spring of Joy* (London: Jonathan Cape, 1928), p. 15.

". . . in the conflict between Gilbert de Polrebec's spiritual self and his earthly love for Nesta . . . the two forces of her own character—as discovered in her earlier work—were curiously blended" . . . namely "a keen consciousness of physical life mingling and merging into spiritual ecstasy . . . Mary Webb had an imagination that broke down barriers; barriers of the spirit and barriers of time."
> — Almay St. John Adcock, review of *Armour Wherein He Trusted* in the *Bookman*, March 1929, p. 332.

"Mary Webb is my subject. She is undoubtedly one of the greatest women writers in English literature."
> — A. Edward Newton, *End Papers: Literary Recreations* (Boston: Little, Brown and Company, 1933), p. 36.

"I could go on for a long time about Mary Webb. She has caused me more pangs of realization of sudden perfect beauty than almost any other writer, certainly any modern writer."
> — Greville Worthington of the London bookselling firm Elkin Mathews in an undated letter cited by A. Edward Newton in *End Papers: Literary Recreations* (Boston: Little, Brown and Company, 1933), p. 38.

"Her work is written upon a plane above that of the conventional novel . . . her books are all charged with feeling and understanding of an uncommon order."
— Frank Swinnerton, *The Georgian Literary Scene: 1910–1935* (London: Hutchinson, 1934), p. 247.

"The character of Prue Sarn [in Precious Bane] could not have been created by other than a genius . . . With Mary Webb's creatures one shares joy and sorrow as if they were our living friends."
— Paul Jordan-Smith, *For the Love of Books* (New York: Oxford University Press, 1934), pp. 78–79.

"For nothing is more characteristic of Mary Webb than lyrical joy in the beauty of the earth and a salty sense of life's comedy."
— A. R. Reade, *Main Currents in Modern Literature* (London: Ivor Nicholson and Watson, 1935), p. 207.

"As the reader of her books soon discovers, she had an eye of almost microscopic keenness for minute details—the centre of a small flower or the curve of an insect's wing . . . She could certainly detect an exquisite perfume in flowers which, for most of us, are scentless."
— Martin Armstrong, "Introduction" to *The Essential Mary Webb* (London: Jonathan Cape, 1949), p. 8.

"The sense of the mysterium tremendum, the secret that's never been told, is the essence of Mary Webb's work. It is something beyond all natural beauty and beastliness, its glory glimmering through the gloom of our mortality."
— Frank Shepherd, B.A., *Many Mansions* (Leigh-on-Sea: Citizen, 1960), p. 27.

"Mary Webb might have been a novelist of rural life and manners, for her knowledge of rural life was first-hand, her acquaintance with ancient customs and intuitive sympathy with them comparable to Hardy's; but alongside this straightforward human responsiveness there existed a fervent romanticism that knew man and nature as part of a reality greater than either. Her rejection of orthodox religion

did not, however, issue in pantheism, but rather in a clothing of the landscape with human attributes, and the belief in a spiritual presence within nature less akin to Pan than to Jesus Christ."
    — Glen Cavaliero, *The Rural Tradition in the English Novel* (London: Macmillan, 1977), p. 142.

"Every so often one discovers something which strikes a chord so personal and so sacred that, though it is unfamiliar, it seems to function as a fragment of a memory long lost. Such was my feeling when I first came across Precious Bane, *by Mary Webb."*
    — Erika Duncan, "Rediscovering Mary Webb," *Book Forum 1978*, p. 326.

Clematisa & Percival.

Once upon a time there lived a gardener and his wife, who had one little daughter, called Clematisa. Now the gardener had a garden full of lillies, roses, clematis, and mountain ash trees. Each kind of plant had its own fairy. The fairies often came and talked with him in the evenings, as he worked. He was fond of them all but he liked fairy Clematis best, so he called his daughter after her. The garden was full of lovely things and the only weed was the dandelion. Little Clematisa often knocked off the dandelions for her father, because they grew so fast. This made the fairy Dandelion very angry; and

CATALOGUE

Mary E. & Bruce J. Crawford

1 *Original photograph of Mary Webb. (Illustrated on page 12)*
6" x 4¼", signed by Webb in black ink, mounted on a leaf of thin tissue, and then on gray board. The tissue mounting is signed: "Dorothy Hickling," and the board is signed in the lower-right corner: "This was given to me by / Mary Webb and I give / it to F. B. Adams Jr. / Caradoc Evans / January 3, 1938."

Welsh writer, journalist and editor Caradoc Evans was an early friend and supporter of Mary Webb. In 1916, a reviewer for the *Times Literary Supplement* had compared Evans's novel, *My People* (1915), with Webb's first novel, *The Golden Arrow* (1916). A sustained friendship began by correspondence after Evans's own enthusiastic review of *The Golden Arrow* (Coles, *The Flower of Light*, 1978). After her move to London in 1921, Webb contributed reviews to *T. P. and Cassell's Weekly* where Evans served as editor from 1923 to 1929. With a typed letter from Evans to Adams, dated January 3, 1937 [*sic*, should be 1938], saying that he encloses a corrected proof of Mary Webb, and the photograph of her, for Adams to keep. Frederick Baldwin Adams, Jr. (1910–2001) was a distinguished collector and member of the Grolier Club for 64 years, serving as president from 1947 to 1951. Adams was also director of the Pierpont Morgan Library from 1948 until 1969.

2 Mary Webb. *Clematisa & Percival. (Illustrated on facing page)*
Prose manuscript [ca. 1894–97], thirteen leaves, 8" x 6¼", off-white laid ruled paper removed from a notebook. The manuscript is written in ink on rectos only, with a youthful hand and a few small corrections.

This story is the earliest known manuscript by Mary Webb and is now first published in the second volume of this catalogue. The adolescent Mary may have written this charming fairy tale—telling of the kidnapping of the heroine Clematisa (named after the Clematis flower) by the Dandelion Fairy, and of Clematisa's rescue from a dandelion-covered moon by a prince named Percival—in order to amuse her five siblings, who were from six to thirteen years her junior. The verso of the last leaf contains geometrical drawings. With handwritten documentation from Webb's husband, Henry Bertram Law Webb, dated 18 November 1936, confirming that it is "an authentic work . . . written in her handwriting at the age of 15 or 16." Provenance: H. B. L. Webb and H. B. Vander Poel.

3 Henry Wadsworth Longfellow. *The Poetical Works of Henry Wadsworth Longfellow.*

Edinburgh: W. P. Nimmo, Hay, & Mitchell [n.d.]. The volume is inscribed on the verso of the front free endpaper: "Mary Gladys Meredith / Prize for English. / Class II. / Longsight House / Summer 1897—M. W." The rear endpapers have two pencil sketches of a young woman's face, possibly drawn by Webb; the titles of a few poems, in the table of contents, are marked in pencil.

Young Mary was well educated by the standards of the late Victorian period "and exceptionally so for a female" (Coles, *Mary Webb*, 1990, p. 22). Her father, George Meredith, an Oxford M.A. in Classics, ran a boarding school, tutoring young boys for entry to university, and young Mary, the eldest of the Meredith children by six years, "received a solid grounding in English, Maths, French, History, Geography, Classics, Scripture, Music and Art" alongside the schoolboys. When Mary was ten, Miss Edith Lory was appointed as governess, and she tutored Mary for the next four years. Coles goes on to say that Miss Lory "was impressed by Mary's facility with language and her remarkable memory—she could quote extempore from the major poets." Mary was later sent for two years to Mrs. Walmsley's Finishing School at Southport. Mrs. Walmsley herself may have awarded this book as a prize for English to sixteen-year-old Mary. It was one of only thirty books in Webb's library at her death. Bookplate of Frederick Baldwin Adams, Jr.

4 Lady Charlotte Guest, trans. *The Mabinogion.*

London: J. M. Dent & Co., 1906. One of the Everyman's Library series (no. 97). Inscribed on a preliminary leaf: "to / Mr. G. Meredith / Xmas 1907 / B. C."

The Mabinogion is a collection of eleven medieval Welsh tales, combining Celtic mythology and Arthurian romance, first translated into English by Guest in the mid-19th century. This volume may have been a Christmas present from Beatrice Cannon (Mary's closest friend from Mrs. Walmsley's Finishing School) to Mary Webb's father, George Meredith. Mary inherited from her father his Celtic temperament, lively sense of humor, and intimate feeling for nature. George Meredith instilled in Mary his fascination with the legends, lore, and superstitions intrinsic to living in the Shropshire countryside. While writing, Webb often consulted *The Mabinogion*; Webb has annotated pages 13, 95, and 150 in black ink and written a list of related works on the rear free endpaper. This well-thumbed volume was part of Mary's small library, which was sold to the bookselling firm of Elkin Mathews by Henry Webb after her death. With the bookplates of Mary Webb and Frederick Baldwin Adams, Jr.

5 Mary Webb. *"The Wild Rose."*

Typescript poem, one leaf, 10¼" x 8", white wove watermarked paper. Fourteen lines, one correction.

George Meredith encouraged his daughter's intellectual development, and "his first love was poetry . . . He wrote every day; and discovering Mary's aptitude, he fostered it, instructing her in the writing of sonnets, rondeaus and other forms. During a long apprenticeship, she was concerned with technique, attentive to rhyme and metre. Poetry played an important part in the daily lives of father and daughter" (Coles, *Mary Webb*, 1990, p. 26). First published in the *Vineyard* in June 1913 (cat. 6 below), the poem was one of the first of Webb's to be accepted for publication. Many of Webb's poems show her fascination with bees ("The humming honey-people eagerly / Enjoy this loving cup among the green"), which both her father and her brother Kenneth kept.

6 Mary Meredith-Webb [Mary Webb]. *"The Wild Rose" and "The House Beautiful."*

Two poems in the *Vineyard,* Maude Egerton King, ed. London: A. C. Fifield, June, 1913.

In these two poems, published shortly before her marriage to Henry Bertram Law Webb, Mary fuses her naturalist's eye for precisely observed detail with her poetic imagination and creates sharp sense-impressions imbued with emotion. According to Caradoc Evans, the acceptance of these early poems for publication by a noted literary journal, and Webb's engagement as a book reviewer by the editor of the *Liverpool Post,* were important confidence-builders in her literary career.

7 Mary Webb. *"The Elf."*

Manuscript poem, one leaf, 8¾" x 6⅛", on off-white wove ruled paper, titled in pencil in another hand. Twenty-one lines in three irregular stanzas, black ink, with corrections. The third stanza ends with a comma, and lacks its conclusion.

This early poem by Webb is one of several in which she lovingly describes her Welsh borderlands and the town of Shrewsbury. Webb's early poems were largely descriptive, drawn from her impressions of Shropshire and its changing seasons. This manuscript and the typescript (cat. 8 below) show significant variations from "The Elf" published in *Poems and The Spring of Joy* (1928), and are rare examples of a poem whose composition was significantly reworked by Webb.

8 MARY WEBB. *"The Elf."*

Typescript poem, one leaf, 9¾" x 8", white wove watermarked paper. Recto: twenty-four typed lines, six corrections. Verso: sixteen manuscript lines, two corrections.

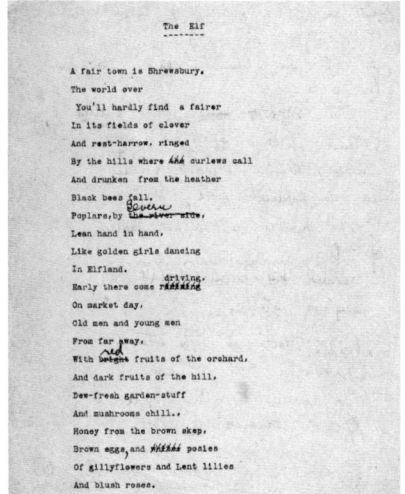

The poem on the verso, concerning an elf, has not been published in any of the four volumes of Mary Webb's poetry.

9 GLADYS MARY MEREDITH [MARY WEBB]. *"Very Early."*

In the *Vineyard*, Maude Egerton King, ed. London: A. C. Fifield, March, 1912.

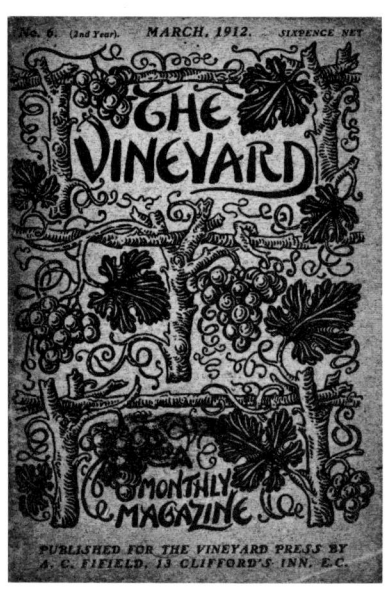

In her earliest published poems, such as "Very Early," Webb expresses her joy in life and shows the intimacy and intensity of her relationship with nature. In *The Spring of Joy* (essays written around the turn of the century but not published until 1917), Webb recalls: "As a child, I remember standing awe-struck at the strange beauty of a well known field in the magic of a June dawn." Later critics were to say that Webb's senses were "rarely delicate" (Walter de la Mare) and of "microscopic keenness" (Martin Armstrong).

10 MARY WEBB. *The Spring of Joy. A Little Book of Healing.*
London: J. M. Dent & Sons Ltd., 1917. First edition. Inscribed by Webb on front free endpaper: "H. B. L. Webb / with love from Mary. / Spring Cottage / 1917." A few passages are marked with blue pencil in the text.

Written around the age of twenty as she was recovering from her first bout of Graves' disease, but unpublished until fifteen years later (after the publication of *The Golden Arrow* [1916] and *Gone to Earth* [1917]), the printed dedication reads "TO THE WEARY AND WOUNDED / IN THE BATTLE OF LIFE / THIS LITTLE BOOK IS LOVINGLY DEDICATED." Having found her creative force during prolonged confinement by illness, Mary states in her opening essay, "Vis Medicatrix Naturae": "It does not matter how shut in we are. Opportunity for wide experience is of small account in this as in other things; it is depth that brings understanding and life." The nine essays, which explore and celebrate nature's variety, are permeated with poetry. They preview Webb's descriptive brilliance, which creates the visual power in her novels. "The essays provide an atmospheric setting for her later major work; the roots of her novels are here, a synthesis of her feeling for nature and her feeling for humanity, her close depictions of the natural world and projection of her philosophy of life" (Coles, *Mary Webb*, 1990, p. 38). However, Webb was not entirely satisfied with *The Spring of Joy*. In September 1917, she sent a copy of it with a letter to Mr. Hardress O'Grady, author and educator at the University of London. In the letter, Webb says: "Will you accept this little book? I am diffident about it, as it was written not long after leaving school. I left school at 17, to help at home, and was ill (in bed most of the time) for some years." Webb sent an extraordinary second letter to O'Grady, reading in part: "Ever since sending you my little book, on an impulse (alas! I always act on impulse) I have regretted it, being desperately afraid you would be so bored with it, that you would lose all interest in your protégé. Please dont [*sic*] read it if you haven't yet. . . . You will think me quite crazy to so bombard you with letters. I wont [*sic*] in the future, but since sending that horrid little book I have been on thorns." In 1912, O'Grady published *Matter, Form, and Style. A Manual of Practice in the Writing of English Composition*, a book intended to help school instructors improve their effectiveness at teaching English composition. (Permission to quote the O'Grady letters courtesy of the Department of Special Collections and University Archives, Stanford University Libraries). Bookplate of Frederick Baldwin Adams, Jr.

11 MARY WEBB. *The Spring of Joy. A Little Book of Healing.*
London and Toronto: J. M. Dent & Sons Ltd., 1917. First edition. Stamped at the base of the spine "E. P. Dutton and Co." (The volume is otherwise the same as the first English edition [cat. 10 above]), in the original publisher's tissue jacket. Inscribed on front free endpaper: "To F. B. Adams Jr. / from / H. Bradley Martin," and with Adams's bookplate pasted below the inscription.

Frederick Baldwin Adams, Jr. (1910–2001) was director of the Pierpont Morgan Library from 1948–1969 and served as president of the Grolier Club from 1947 to 1951. H. Bradley Martin (1906–1988) was grandson of Henry Phillips (a partner of Andrew Carnegie) and a pre-eminent book collector. Adams and Martin (also a Grolier member) both admired Webb's work and competed for important editions and manuscripts. On the front pastedown is a long (and amusing) penciled note in Adams's hand, telling how he had lost the book at auction to Martin, and how Martin had subsequently sold the book to him at cost. Adams says: "I asked him [Martin] to inscribe the book to me, as a permanent token of the generosity of one collector to another." A. Edward Newton, in *End Papers: Literary Recreations* (1933), writes: "From a book-collector's point of view, Mary Webb in first editions is difficult, almost impossible. Her books were published at a bad time; everything was bad—printing, paper, cloth, binding, everything. The editions were small and the books fell to pieces in the reading." Hence, we understand Adams's recognition of the chivalry of his rival Martin in allowing him to secure the scarce first edition of this slim volume of prose, Mary Webb's third book.

12 MARY WEBB. *"The Vagrant."*

Typescript poem, two leaves, 9¼" x 8" and 10" x 7¼", numbered (in ink) in upper-right corners, white wove paper. Forty lines in eight stanzas, two ink corrections.

Dated by Webb's biographers as composed at age 20 while recovering from her first bout of Graves' disease, "The Vagrant" depicts an elusive, mystical presence in nature that takes the form of a vague Christ-like figure. Hilda Addison says in *Mary Webb: A Short Study of Her Life and Work* (1931) that Mary Webb "always considered this poem more truly representative of her spiritual position than any other." During adolescence, Mary had moved away from orthodox Christianity to a belief that God is manifest and revealed in nature. This poem "conveys an intense yearning to grasp the elusive personality that she feels everywhere in nature" (Coles, *The Flower of Light*, 1978, p. 80). "The Vagrant" was first published in January 1915 in the *English Review* (cat. 13 below) when Webb was thirty-three.

13 MARY WEBB. *"The Vagrant."*

In the *English Review*, Austin Harrison, ed. London: 17–21 Tavistock Street, Covent Garden, January 1915.

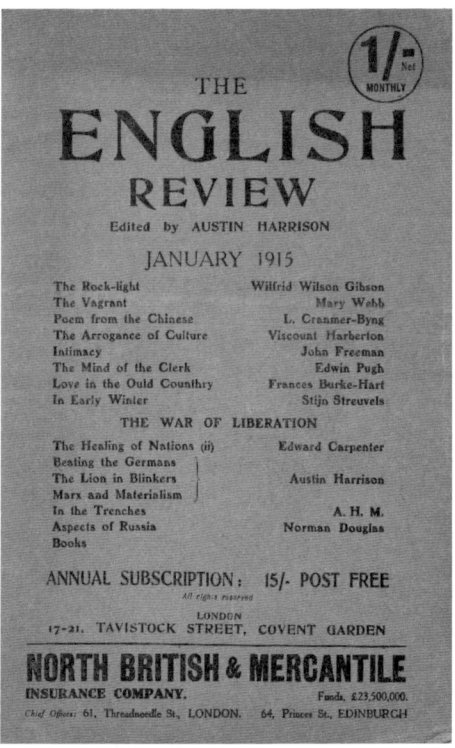

Webb's early friend Flora McLeod reminisced in a talk, "Mary Webb as I Knew Her," given to the Shropshire Women's Institute (from an undated typescript in the Shrewsbury Public Library): "Her Bible, indeed, she knew from cover to cover. . . . the churchly life in which she had been reared seemed cramping and ineffectual, and she began to build a creed of her own with Nature enthroned as God." Mary discussed with her friend "the spiritual significance of her communion with earth rather than church, . . . that nature, for her, was not 'enthroned as God' but revealed God" (Coles, *The Flower of Light*, 1978, p. 79).

14 MARY WEBB. *"Father's Path."*

Typescript poem, one leaf, 10¼" x 8", white wove watermarked paper. Sixteen lines in two stanzas, two ink corrections. Originally titled "The Father's Path"; the word "The" has been crossed out. "Mary Webb / (Mrs. H. B. L. Webb.)" is written (in black ink) at the bottom of the poem.

Devastated by her father's death at age 67 in January 1909, Webb grieved so acutely that she suffered from fever, weakness, accelerated metabolism and migraine for the next three years—a relapse of the Graves' disease that had first occurred seven years before (at age 20). Gradually, Mary worked through her grief by composing prose and poetry dedicated to her much-loved Father's memory. This early poem of rhymed, metrical lines was published in the *Vineyard* in August 1913 under the title "My Father's Path" (cat. 15 below).

15 MARY MEREDITH WEBB [MARY WEBB]. *"My Father's Path."*

In the *Vineyard,* Maude Egerton King, ed. London: A. C. Fifield, August, 1913.

Published four years after her father's death, this early poem shows the deep and abiding love that Mary had for him. The poem prefaces Webb's tribute to her father in her first novel, *The Golden Arrow* (1916), where she memorializes George Meredith as John Arden, the compassionate shepherd who thinks of God as "The Flockmaster," a leader whose ever-affirming love encompasses all.

16 MARY WEBB. *"Treasures / (For G. E. M.)."*

Typescript poem, one leaf, 8½" x 6¾", white wove watermarked paper. Eighteen lines in two stanzas. Next to the second line of the title is written in pencil: "(her father)." At the bottom is written in pencil: "Typed by Mary Webb."

"G. E. M." is Mary Webb's father, George Edward Meredith, who (as father, teacher, kindred spirit and companion) was a formative influence on her personality. This poem reveals her tender love and the spiritual anguish she suffered upon his death. George Meredith died when Mary was 28, and her grief at his passing was acute and long-standing. "The suffering extended her range of experience and ultimately had significant creative results, first in her poetry and later in her prose fiction . . . part of the motivation behind *The Golden Arrow*—creating in this first novel a portrait of her father . . ." (Coles, *The Flower of Light,* 1978, p. 93).

17 MARY WEBB. *"Winter Sunrise."*

Typescript poem, one leaf, 5¼" x 5¾", off-white wove paper mounted on white ruled paper. The title and a crossed-out notation reading: "to G. E. M." (Webb's father), are written in black ink in the top margin of the backing sheet. Fourteen lines in two stanzas, but pencil marks indicate that the two stanzas are to be read as one.

Webb conveys the mood and atmosphere of a winter's dawn, by using color imagery from an April garden. She mourns her father's absence: "Since you are not in the wintry world to love me, / How softly painted flushes Death above me!"

18 GEORGINA F. JACKSON. *Shropshire Word-Book, A Glossary of Archaic and Provincial Words, etc., Used in the County.*

London: Trübner & Co., 1879. Signed "G. E. Meredith" (Mary Webb's father) on preliminary leaf, and with a note in Webb's hand on rear free endpaper.

Mary Webb's personal library, sold off by her husband after her death, was very small. This book held both sentimental and intellectual value for Webb, as it had been part of her beloved father's library. She also consulted this reference work to verify the accuracy of the Shropshire dialect she used with her characters. "She was aware, like Thomas Hardy, of the danger of excessive localism and only occasionally employed purely dialect words, achieving her effect more subtly by idiomatic suggestion, the use here and there of a well-placed local word or turn of phrase giving widespread flavour" (Coles, *The Flower of Light*, 1978, p. 261). With the bookplate of Frederick Baldwin Adams, Jr.

19 GLADYS MEREDITH [MARY WEBB]. *Autograph letter signed to Mrs. Thomas Webb.*

May 8 [1911], eight pages on three folded leaves.

Mary Webb writes to her future mother-in-law, who has apparently praised some of Webb's poems. She discusses the prospects of having several of her poems published in periodicals, and says she is sorry not to have heard better news of Dr. Webb's illness. Webb writes that her poem "The Difference" expresses some of her feelings for her father, and regrets that Mrs. Webb had not known him. Webb further writes that she and her mother (Alice Meredith) will get up early the next day to "go bird's nesting" and says, "There are few things I love better than going out when the birds have not been awake long enough to get shy and frightened, when the world is not yet man's—when one 'knows one's place' and goes softly and just looks and listens." Provenance: Frederick Baldwin Adams, Jr.

71

20 MARY WEBB. *"The Difference."*

Typescript poem, one leaf, 4¾" x 5¾", white wove paper, mounted on white ruled paper. Twelve lines in two stanzas. The title, written in black ink, may have been added to the sheet at a later date.

Webb's mourning at the death of her father was so intense and prolonged that she suffered long spells of Graves' disease over the next three years. She turned to poetry as an outlet for her unassuaged sorrow and grief. Webb writes: "Not all the blossom on the branches left / Can fill the place of that sweet bough bereft; ..."

21 GLADYS MEREDITH [MARY WEBB]. *Autograph letter signed to Mrs. Thomas Webb.*

July 9 [1911], eight pages on two folded leaves.

Webb expresses deep sorrow at the death of Mrs. Webb's husband. She says that she went outside into the garden upon hearing the news because "... although I feel near to the unseen world and to Eternal Love in churches, I feel ten times nearer to them out of doors ..." Webb says that she has been reading William James's book, *The Varieties of Religious Experience* and, after praising James, says: "The chapter on mysticism is exceedingly beautiful I think, he gathers all mystics of every creed together and shows how much in sympathy they really are." Webb adds: "I used to think, after father died, that waking in the morning was the hardest because I had been accustomed during his illness to walk down to his room which was just below mine, to see how he was." Provenance: Frederick Baldwin Adams, Jr.

22 MARY WEBB. *"Alone."*

Typescript poem, one leaf, 7" x 8", white wove watermarked paper. Eighteen lines in two stanzas, one correction. The title is written in black ink and may have been added at a later date.

In this love poem, written to Henry Bertram Law Webb around the time of their marriage in 1912 (Coles, *Selected Poems of Mary Webb*, 1981, p. 46), Webb is already characteristically speaking of "mingled joy and pain."

23 GLADYS MEREDITH [MARY WEBB]. *Autograph letter signed to Mrs. Thomas Webb.*

September 20 [1911], seven pages on seven leaves.

Webb opens this letter by thanking Mrs. Webb for her continuing correspondence. Of herself, Webb says: "... I have a bad habit of exaggerating things—unconsciously almost—to make them suit ones idea of what they ought to be.... I try to cure myself... to say 'oh! no, there weren't thousands of butterflies, there were, to be accurate, six!'" Webb then compares her views on exaggeration to similar ones held by G. K. Chesterton. She reminisces at length about her father, and about her brothers as schoolboys. Expressing modesty about her abilities as a poet, Webb says: "... my greatest fear is lest people should take me on as a friend in hopes of that! It is just that the wonder of things gets into my head & my heart to such a degree that it must occasionally find an outlet, & being wholly un-gifted with regard to music & painting & writing, I've fixed on the unfortunate last as being the least impossible." Webb goes on to praise the author of *Thysia* (Morton Luce, a friend of the Webb family) as a fine poet, saying that after her father's death she took great comfort from the poem. *Thysia* deals with love, death, joy, sorrow, friendship, and immortality. Provenance: Frederick Baldwin Adams, Jr.

24 GLADYS MEREDITH [MARY WEBB]. *Autograph letter signed to Mrs. Thomas Webb.* (Illustrated on page 32)

July 23 [1911], twelve pages on three folded leaves. With an envelope addressed to Mrs. Webb care of A. N. C. Shelley, Esq. (the husband of her daughter, Mary) in Battersea Park, London.

In this chatty letter, Mary thanks Mrs. Webb for an issue of the *Bookman*, and mentions a recently published book by her fiancé Henry Webb, *The Silences of the Moon*. Mary writes: "Funnily enough, I had thought of writing a review for that Competition—on 'Silences' but I did not do so, not quite liking the idea of writing about a book of the kind for the sake of trying for a prize." She goes on to say: "I came across a thing of mine written a year or two ago—about this poplar, which I thought you might be interested to see, not for its intrinsic merit, but because of its very extraordinary resemblance to one of the last paragraphs of '*Silences*—'. Poplars—and especially Lombardy ones—always have had a peculiar fascination for me." Provenance: Frederick Baldwin Adams, Jr.

25 MARY WEBB. *"The Fallen Poplar."*

Manuscript poem, one leaf, 7" x 7¾", on off-white ruled wove paper. Twelve lines in three stanzas, black ink, with corrections. The final stanza may have been completed at a later time, as the last two-and-a-half lines are written in larger and darker ink script, and show signs of being partially traced over earlier writing.

This may be the poem "written a year or two ago" that Mary refers to in her letter of July 23 [1911] to Mrs. Webb (cat. 24 above). At this point in their writing careers, Mary and her fiancé Henry were both dedicated nature lovers. Yet Henry's writing was scholarly, whereas Mary's was more descriptive, sensuous and immediate. "Much that in Henry's work is made explicit discursively, in Mary's is expressed implicitly in nature imagery, is cloaked in metaphor. Where Henry explains symbol, Mary uses it" (Coles, *The Flower of Light,* 1978, p. 102).

CAT. 25

26 HENRY B. L. WEBB. *The Silences of the Moon.*
New York and London: John Lane, 1911. First edition.

Written after graduation from St. Catherine's College, Cambridge and published by the Bodley Head when Henry was 25, *The Silences of the Moon* is a book of philosophic nature essays. Henry Webb was a scholar, linguist, lover of nature, and philosopher, and later published an epic poem and historical novels. Upon Henry and Mary's engagement in 1911, Henry's mother and sisters felt that Henry was marrying down—despite the £100 per annum allowance that Mary brought to the marriage and the fact that Mary was well-educated and came from a respectable, middle-class family (as were the Webbs). "The Webbs saw only that she [Mary] was nearly five years his senior, a semi-invalid who bore the signs of her illness, an unconventional woman more interested in nature and books than in social and domestic matters" (Coles, *Mary Webb*, 1990, p. 51). The writing in *The Silences of the Moon* is classical, dry and unoriginal.

27 MARY WEBB. *"Why?"*

Typescript poem, illegible place name and the date "1910," written in ink and crossed out, in lower-left corner. "(Sphere) / 1911," written in ink and crossed out, in lower-right corner. One leaf, 5½" x 5½", white wove paper mounted on white ruled paper. Twelve lines in two stanzas. The title is written in black ink and was probably added at a later date.

The poem itself is unusually pessimistic, and alludes to an inspiring figure who has unsettled the poet. The last three lines read: "Before, I was not much unsatisfied: / but since a god has touched me and departed, / I run through every temple, broken-hearted." Coles suggests that this is a later poem to or about Henry Webb (Coles, *Selected Poems of Mary Webb*, 3rd ed., 2005, p. 102).

28 MARY WEBB. *"Ah, Do Not Be So Sweet!"*

Typescript poem, one leaf, 9" x 5¾", white wove paper (tightly crumpled, as if discarded, recovered and smoothed out). Twenty-one lines in three stanzas.

Webb invested intense energy in her relationships (first with her father and then with her husband), but her happiness was intermingled with fear of loss. "This love brought pain as acute as joy for it sharpened her awareness of transience, gave a keen edge to her happiness. . . . So the fear of loss loomed spectre-like to haunt her, and was to remain her dark companion to the end" (Coles, *The Flower of Light,* 1978, p. 105). Webb was emotionally dependent upon her "other" and haunted by insecurity, knowing that at any time he could withdraw his love or be taken from her.

29 MARY WEBB. *"The Shell."*

Typescript poem, one leaf, 10¼" x 8", white wove watermarked paper. Fourteen lines in two stanzas.

Soon after their marriage in 1912, the Webbs moved from Shropshire to Weston-super-Mare (in Somerset near Bristol) where Henry's newly-widowed mother lived, and where Henry had secured a two-year teaching position. In this poem, Webb comments that while the vast sea may hide within it many mythical and historical objects, it has washed up a small thing of simple beauty: "Pink as a baby's nail, silky and veined / As a flower petal— this casket of the sea, / One shell."

30 MARY WEBB. *"What has the sea swept up?"*

Typescript poem, one leaf, 8½" x 6", white wove paper. Twenty-four lines (typed in purple ink and on a typewriter not used for any other of Webb's typescripts in this collection), six ink corrections. Typed at the bottom of the poem: "Mary Meredith Webb." On verso, "The Shell" is written in pencil in the upper-left corner.

This poem is an early version of Webb's poem "The Shell" (cat. 29 above), first published posthumously in *Poems and The Spring of Joy* (1928). These two typescripts offer a rare opportunity to see the evolution of one of Webb's poems. Caradoc Evans wrote in the *Colophon* (Winter 1938) that Webb thought more highly of her verse than of her novels and quoted Webb as saying: "'You have no idea how hard I work over a poem. But stories—well, they just come to me and I write them without thinking and often I'm surprised at what I've written...'"

31 MARY WEBB. *Autograph letter signed to Morton Luce.*

[ca. March or April 1913]. Four pages on one folded leaf.

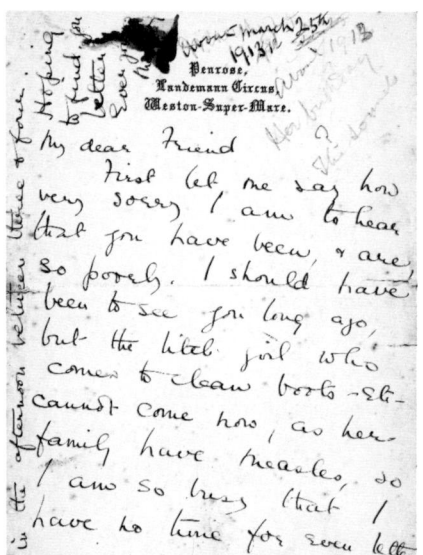

Webb says that she is sorry to hear that Luce has not been well, and that she has been busy with work at home. She thanks Luce for two sonnets that he has sent to her for her birthday, and praises his poetry: "... there is mastery of material that makes me so envious—beauty—genius." Luce (1849–1943), an accomplished late-Victorian poet and Shakespeare scholar, was a family friend of the Webbs. Mary Webb had mentioned in an earlier letter to her then-future mother-in-law (cat. 23) that she was comforted after her father's death by Luce's elegy *Thysia*, published in 1908. *Thysia*, like much of Webb's poetry, shows a sensitive affinity for nature and the outdoors. In *Thysia*, Luce writes at length of sonnets given to a lover as a birthday gift. Luce befriended the newlyweds after they moved to Weston-super-Mare, where the three resided for a time. The friendships continued by correspondence for many years and in 1925 (twelve years after this letter) Webb petitioned Arthur St. John Adcock, editor of the *Bookman*, to write a "Bookman's Gallery" (a featured review) on Luce's sonnets. See cat. 112 for the typescript of Webb's review.

32 HENRY B. L. WEBB. *Autograph letter signed.*

[n.d., but ca. September 1915], to an unnamed addressee [Morton Luce], four pages on two leaves.

Henry discusses some of his (and Mary's) literary efforts. He also mentions his recent attempts to sell insurance, and tells of Mary's activities as a "market woman," repairing men's buttonholes, and selling vegetables. In 1915, the Webbs' marriage was thriving. The two years that Henry and Mary lived at Rose Cottage in Pontesbury were among their happiest—seeking individual freedom, they lived close to nature in a quiet country house, growing their own food, and working at their writing with little intrusion from the outside world. Henry writes: "We hope to get a new typewriter soon, and make it hum. Meanwhile we are

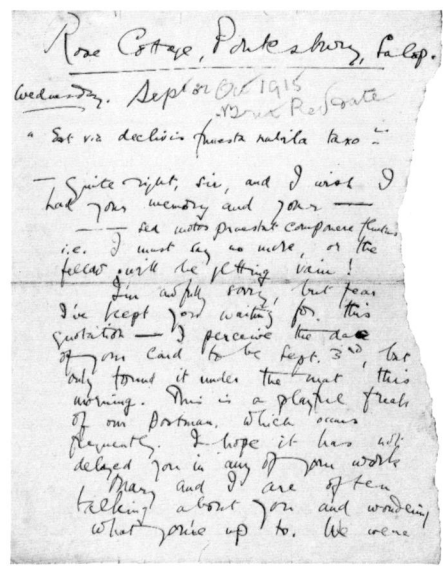

(entre nous) looking for a smaller and cheaper house, and keeping triumphantly out of the only two evils that seem to matter—being separated and 'potboiling.'" Both were pursuing literary careers, hoping to live from their writings (supplemented by Mary's £100 annual allowance from monies inherited by her mother, and by sales of extra vegetables and flowers grown in their garden). Mary was busy writing her second novel *Gone to Earth* (to be published the following year), while Henry was working on a verse epic about Gilgamesh, to be published under the title of *The Everlasting Quest* in 1917. An autobiographical passage in *The Golden Arrow* reveals Mary's contentment: "To give—to be with her man—to be so utterly at one that no explanation was ever necessary—to work, laugh, sleep and watch the splendid seasons together, being in other things than sex free and equal, and in sex so mutually generous as to forget self and rights. . . ."

33 HENRY B. L. WEBB. *The Everlasting Quest.*

London: Macmillan and Co., Limited, 1917. First edition, original dark blue cloth.

This epic poem about the adventures of the Babylonian hero Gilgamesh was published in the same month that Mary's book of essays, *The Spring of Joy,* was released by J. M. Dent (cat. 10). Henry's five-stanza dedicatory poem entitled "To Mary" is somewhat uninspired but echoes Mary's recurrent theme of the inseparable duality of experience—joy and pain, bitter and sweet—in the last two lines: "With the old delight, / The passionate war."

77

34 MARY WEBB. *"Market Day."*

"Pontesbury / May & June 1914." (but crossed out) in upper-right corner. Typescript poem, one leaf, 9" x 5¾", off-white wove paper. Forty-four lines (two of these crossed out) and two further ink corrections.

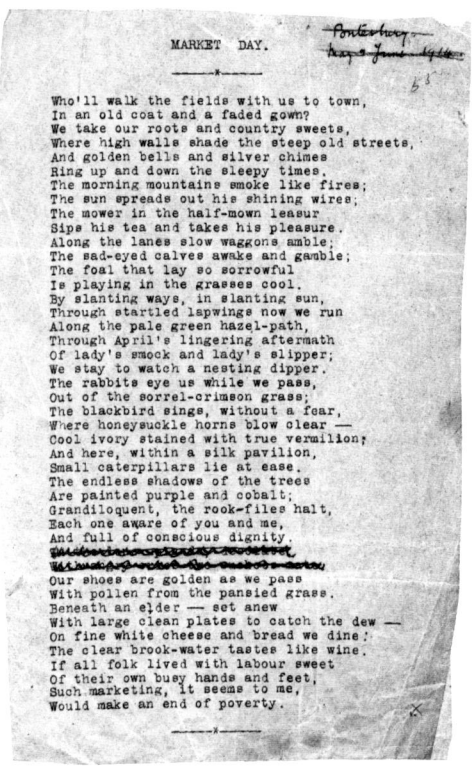

This autobiographical poem clearly shows the contentment Mary and Henry felt as aspiring writers, living among country people, and close to nature in a quiet country house. To supplement their meager earnings and to help the war effort, Mary would rise hours before dawn each Saturday, load extra vegetables and flowers in a barrow, and walk the nine miles to and from Shrewsbury market, where she rented a stall for the day. While there, Mary quietly absorbed the sights and sounds of the market, noting the local turns of phrase, and storing perceptions that she would later use to good effect in her writing.

35 MARY WEBB. *"Market Day."*

Typescript poem, two leaves, 10" x 8", thin off-white wove paper. Forty-two lines, one minor ink correction. "Mary Webb" is written in ink at the bottom of the second leaf.

In "Market Day," Webb captures the sights and sounds she encounters while walking to market. Towards the end of the piece, Webb abruptly and dramatically changes tone and direction with blunt social commentary: "If all folk lived with labor sweet, / Of their own busy hands and feet, / Marketing, it seems to me, / Would make an end of poverty."

36 MARY WEBB. *"Nature's Call to City-dwellers."*

Original printer's proof for the magazine the *Vineyard*. Crossed out in ink are four lines of the poem and the words "By Mary Meredith Webb" beneath the title.

The full publication history of this early poem is uncertain. A lament, the poem describes nature as a conscious, sentient force that regrets how few people appreciate its beauty.

37 MARY WEBB. *"Going for the Milk."*

Manuscript poem, one leaf, 8¼" x 7½", tan ruled laid paper, seventeen lines in three stanzas, brown ink, with two corrections (including one to the title).

Webb contemplates the passing of time employing the simple country task of fetching milk. In seventeen stanzas, she successively describes a toddling child, a young girl of seventeen, a new mother, and an old woman. The old woman reminisces: "It's fifty years come Easter, since that day; / The work'us ward is cold, my eyes be dim; / Never no more I'll go the flowery way / Fetching the milk. I drink the pauper's skim."

38 MARY WEBB. *"You are very brown."*

Manuscript poem, "11:30 p.m June 17th 1922" at top right (but crossed out), one leaf, 7⅞" x 7¼", on off-white laid ruled paper, twenty-one lines, black ink.

Mary and her husband Henry were both well educated but chose during the early years of their

CAT. 37

CAT. 38

79

marriage to live an outdoor country life, pursuing their writing, and growing their own vegetables, flowers and fruits. There are several possible (but uncertain) interpretations of this poem. It may reflect Webb's awareness of the unconventional choice of lifestyle and her acknowledgement that it was frowned upon by others. Both Henry and Mary had been brought up in the middle-class comfort of educated households and—because of their insistence on living a simple, subsistence lifestyle—were socially isolated. Local villagers considered their lifestyle eccentric, and the Webbs' social equals shunned them. Webb might be comparing her own coarse and unrefined appearance with the many simple beauties found in nature. With a touch of humor, she implies that brownness is a small penance to pay for living in the delights of nature.

39 MARY WEBB. *"My Own Town."*

"Spring Cottage. / Lyth Hill / Shrewsbury" in pencil, on verso of second leaf. Typescript poem, two leaves, 10" x 8", white wove paper loosely stitched together (with white thread) at upper-left corner. Forty-three lines, minor ink corrections and one typescript correction. Signed "Mary Webb" at bottom of second leaf.

Webb loved her native Shropshire and its capital town, Shrewsbury, but the meanness and pettiness of people also grieved her. "My Own Town" shows Webb's eager recognition of the goodness of her townsfolk, but also acknowledges their unkindness: "While up and down the chalice goes, / Made of a sapphire, filled to the brim / With God. I have seen them walk like kings / Pondering on majestic things. / And where the gossip gables lean / Chatting, I've met with faces mean / With meanness past all grace or cure." Webb (always self-conscious of her excessive thinness, goiter, and protrusion of the eyes, all the result of Graves' disease) found in her writing a way of reaching out to humanity with her compassionate yet shy spirit: "Shall stand the town that I have made / With golden house and silver steeple / And a strange, uplifted people, / Who in their charmed streets shall go, / Hushed with a tremendous woe / And a joy as deep and vast / As shadows that the mountain cast."

40 MARY WEBB. *"Christina Rossetti."*

Manuscript poem, one leaf, 5¾" x 7", white laid ruled paper. Twelve lines in two stanzas.

Webb studied and admired the work of Rossetti, as well as the writings of Keats, Blake, Swinburne and Browning (Coles, *The Flower of Light*, 1978, p. 74). The poem implies that Christina Rossetti was under-recognized and under-appreciated during her lifetime, and Webb may have seen a reflection of herself in the earlier Rossetti.

41   MARY WEBB. *"The Lad Out There."*

Manuscript poem, one leaf, 7½" x 5¾", on off-white laid paper, black ink. Twenty lines on recto and eight on verso, and with "P. T. O." [Please Turn Over] at the bottom right of recto. Signed on verso: "Mary Webb."

At the outbreak of World War I, Webb's eldest brother Kenneth joined the Canadian Ambulance Unit, her middle brother Douglas enlisted as a private from Liverpool (having returned as a surveyor from Canada a week before the outbreak of the Great War), and her youngest brother Mervyn enlisted from Oxford, where he was studying at Keble College. "The Lad Out There" expresses the thoughts and feelings of women for their men at war. Webb sent each of her brothers a personal letter enclosing a copy of this poem, her sisterly sympathy apparent: "Look down upon the lad I love, / (My brave lad, tramping through the mire)— / ... Let him in his long watching know / That I too count the minutes slow / And light the lamp of love for him" (Coles, *Mary Webb,* 1990, p. 70). Douglas, who rose to the rank of captain in the Royal Artillery, was to be awarded the Military Cross for his bravery in battle. Mervyn only just escaped death when part of his jaw was shot away. According to notes held at the Shropshire Archives, Castle Gates (recorded from information supplied by Mary's brother, Kenneth Meredith), Mervyn (born in 1894) "was to have been a solicitor but was badly 'smashed up' during the 1914–1918 War and died, chiefly on account of wounds, about 1935."

42   MARY WEBB. *"An Estray."*

Typescript poem, one leaf, 10" x 8", white wove watermarked paper. Sixteen lines in four stanzas, one ink correction.

Using the imagery of a domesticated animal wandering lost and alone, Webb expresses her unhappiness: "Out of a land scene, / Airy and lone, / I am come to a sadness terrene, / To a people of stone." Henry Webb attributed this poem to the spring term of 1916 while Henry taught as an assistant master for English, Latin, and History at the King's School in war-torn Chester. Mary and Henry lived weekdays with her mother and unmarried sister, Olive, in the Cheshire county capital city, returning to their Shropshire cottage, "The Nills," on weekends. The physical evidence of wartime activities in Chester, including trainloads of wounded soldiers returning to this important military base, caused Mary great distress, especially because her three brothers were then serving on the Western Front (Coles, *Mary Webb,* 1990, p. 69).

43   MARY WEBB. *"A night sky (1916)."*

Manuscript poem, one leaf, 6½" x 7⅜", on white laid ruled paper, black ink. Sixteen lines with cross-outs and corrections.

In Webb's anxiety for her three younger brothers who were serving on the Western Front, she wrote this poem alluding to the pain and bloodshed of World War I, and her hope for reconciliation through a unifying love: "The moon, beyond her violet bars, / From towering heights of thunder cloud, / Sheds calm upon our scarlet wars, / To soothe a world so small, so loud." In a letter to Arthur St. John Adcock (editor of the *Bookman*), Webb later expressed her feelings of guilt for having spent the war years "hibernated in the beauty of nature."

CAT. 43

44 Mary Webb. *Autograph letter signed to Morton Luce.*

January 27 [1921], four pages on one folded leaf. In this letter written from 46, Leinster Square, Bayswater W. 2.

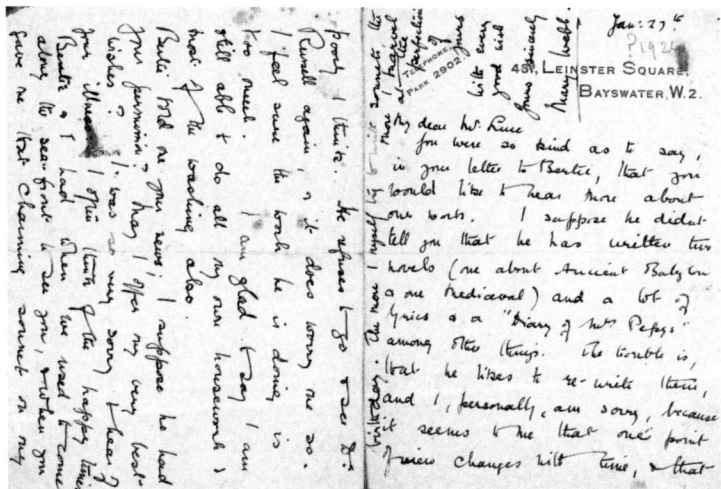

Webb describes some of her husband Henry's recent literary efforts (she refers to him as "Bertie") and then says: "For myself, I have written three novels, none of them (needless to say) as good as I should like." The three novels that she refers to are *The Golden Arrow* (1916), *Gone to Earth* (1917), and *The House in Dormer Forest* (1920). Webb says that she is homesick for Shropshire and that she is worried about her husband's health. Webb (recalling when she, Henry, and Luce all lived in Weston-super-Mare) reminisces about the time Luce "gave me that charming sonnet on my birthday" (cat. 31)

45 MARY WEBB. *Autograph letter signed to Morton Luce.*

May 24 [1923], four pages on two leaves.

In this letter, Webb regrets having missed an opportunity to speak with Luce in person, and clearly conveys the strained relationship that had developed between her and her mother-in-law: ". . . I was looking for a room on Saturday, as I did not stay at Mrs. Webbs [*sic*]. I am never invited there, and she even resented my presence in Weston at all! Though I did not have even one meal at her house, and left Bertie [her husband, Henry] free to her without troubling them at all." Webb concludes: "Bertie says he also called. I didn't know he had, as I saw very little of him & his in Weston."

46 MARY WEBB. *Autograph letter signed to Morton Luce.*

October 19 [ca. 1924], two pages on one leaf. In this letter written from 5 Grove Cottages, Hampstead N.W. 3.

Webb discusses reviews that she is writing for the *Spectator*, and comments about the beautiful country surrounding their cottage in Hampstead. She concludes: "I am working at a novel, which I do hope will be better than the others I have written." Webb refers to *Precious Bane* (1925), which in 1926 will be awarded the Prix Femina Vie Heureuse Anglais, a prestigious literary prize recognizing the best work of imagination in English published by an author whose work has not yet received sufficient recognition (presented annually by two important French magazines whose titles comprise the name of the award).

47 MARY WEBB. *"The Garden in Winter" and "Vigil."*

Manuscript poems, one leaf, 8" x 6¼", on off-white laid ruled paper, nine lines (on recto), black ink. On the verso is a poem of four lines in black ink titled "Vigil."

In the archive of poems purchased from Henry Webb in the late 1930s, "Vigil" is the only poem that was not published in *Poems and The Spring of Joy* (1928), one of the seven volumes of *The Collected Works of Mary Webb* (perhaps because it was printed on the verso of "The Garden in Winter" and missed by the publisher?). "Vigil" was first published seventeen years later, in *Fifty-One Poems* (1946), after Webb's widower, Henry, found an additional cache of poems among Mary's papers. "The Garden in Winter" alludes to a real or imagined companion who comes to share the poet's mourning. "Vigil" follows the same theme: "To stoop so low from out thy new found splendour / And watch, through all my nights of loss, with me."

48 MARY WEBB. *"The Watcher."*

[London] "Spectator / 1921," written in ink in Webb's hand. A printed copy of the poem, clipped from the magazine, and mounted on white ruled paper.

The poem was published again in *Poems and The Spring of Joy* (1928). Webb allegorizes and personifies nature: "The Watcher on the summit stands, / With a blue goblet in his hands; / He slowly drinks the glimmering years; / The sparkling laughter and the tears."

49 *The Market-place, Shrewsbury.*

Hand-colored print [English: ca. early 1900s].

50 *Shrewsbury, Salop.*

Hand-colored engraving [English: ca. early 1900s].

People from Shropshire are known as Salopians (from an old form of the name of the county town, Shrewsbury).

51 MARY WEBB. *The Golden Arrow.*

London: Constable & Company Ltd., 1916. First edition. A dedication copy, inscribed on front pastedown: "Given to me by Mary / on publication in / August, 1916. / H B L Webb." The printed dedication reads: "To a noble lover H. L. W."

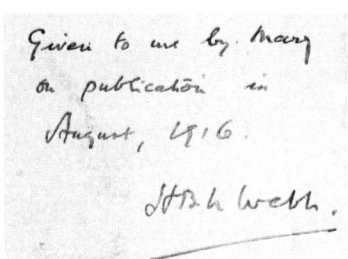

Homesick for her native Shropshire, newly-married Mary Webb pondered the plot line of *The Golden Arrow* for many months while living in the Bristol coastal town of Weston-super-Mare, where the Webbs had moved for Henry's teaching position. Mary wrote by a process of lengthy mental invention, construction, and revision, followed by rapid, inspirational composition. Henry told early biographers that, upon their return to Shropshire, Mary had completed the first draft of *The Golden Arrow* in three weeks and wrote with little revision or editing. "At such times of spontaneous composition, of sudden quickening, there was no distinction between her living self and her writing self, her conscious and unconscious, integrated in creative wholeness" (Coles, *The Flower of Light*, 1978, p. 140). With the bookplate of Frederick Baldwin Adams, Jr.

52 MARY WEBB. *The Golden Arrow.*

London: Constable & Company Ltd., 1916. First edition. Inscribed on front free endpaper: "Dr. Godson / With best wishes from / a grateful patient. / Mary Webb. / Xmas 1916."

Gladys Mary Coles identified Dr. Godson as the local physician who would arrive on his bicycle to treat young Mary Meredith for Graves' disease. While *The Golden Arrow* was widely read in Shropshire, local people were shocked by Webb's unorthodox treatment of love, marriage and sex in the novel, including: Webb's frank commentary about country women's attitudes towards pregnancy and childbirth; the pre-marital sexual relationship between Deborah Arden and Stephen Southernwood; and Lily Huntbatch's visit to the abortionist. So outraged were some Salopians that a ritual book-burning was held by readers in the Shropshire towns of Coalbrookdale and Ironbridge (Coles, *Mary Webb*, 1990, p. 68).

53 MARY WEBB. *The Golden Arrow.*

London: Constable & Company Ltd., 1916. First edition. Inscribed on front free endpaper: "Mary & Shelley / with love from the author / Spring Cottage / Lyth Hill / September 1916." The third and fourth lines of the inscription are written in different ink, and may have been added at a later time. At the bottom of the endpaper is written: "6 Mitre [?] Court Buildings. / Temple."

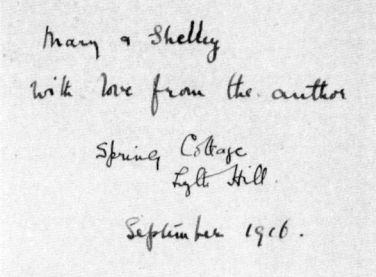

Mary Webb presented this volume to her sister-in-law and husband while family relations were still civil. Henry's mother and sisters disliked Mary's influence on their son and brother and felt that Mary's lack of class consciousness debased Henry. In their view, Henry, as a gentleman and published Cambridge graduate, was above growing his own food and selling the excess at a local market stall (Coles, *The Flower of Light*, 1978, p. 147). With the bookplate of Frederick Baldwin Adams, Jr.

54 MARY WEBB. *The Golden Arrow.*

New York: E. P. Dutton and Company [1916]. First American edition, in dust jacket.

In the character of John Arden, a Shropshire shepherd, Mary Webb portrayed her father's tenderness, humor,

85

loving affirmation and insight. The close, sympathetic understanding between Arden and his daughter Deborah is drawn directly from the central, formative relationship between Mary and her own father. Webb's mother is reflected in the character of practical, sharp-tongued Patty Arden, who chides her husband for his poor sense of time, his generosity, and his tolerance. Bookplate of Frederick Baldwin Adams, Jr.

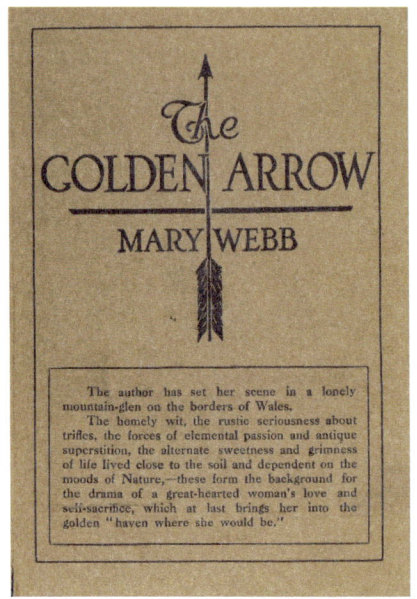

CAT. 54

55 MARY WEBB. *The Golden Arrow.*

London: Constable & Company Ltd., 1916. First edition, trial binding in blue cloth. A cataloguer's note reads in part: "One of 12 copies delivered before publication by the binders and used as travelers' samples."

Constable's prompt acceptance of Webb's first novel was significant, as wartime shortages and the high prices of materials caused publishers to cut back on their publishing lists and to favor books with war themes, then popular with the reading public (Coles, *The Flower of Light*, 1978, p. 146). Because the novel did not sell well during Webb's lifetime, copies of this publisher's sample were especially tantalizing to collectors after Webb achieved posthumous fame.

56 MARY WEBB. *The Golden Arrow.*

London: Robert Holden & Co., 1925. First Lyceum Library edition.

After the positive reception of her fifth book, *Precious Bane* (1924), Webb insisted, as part of the publishing rights agreement for her next novel, that Holden reissue her first novel, *The Golden Arrow*, which had long been out of print. Webb did not live long enough to complete that next novel, *Armour Wherein He Trusted*. Bookplate of Frederick Baldwin Adams, Jr.

57 [MARY WEBB] ANTOINETTE SIX, TRANS. *La flèche d'or.*

Paris: Nouvelle Librairie Française, 1933. Uncut and unopened.

Webb's out-of-print works were reissued in a collected edition after her death, and were quickly translated into several European languages. *La flèche d'or* is an early French translation of *The Golden Arrow.*

58 MARY WEBB. *John Ardens Tochter.*

Berlin: Dom-Verlag, 1936. Original white pebbled cloth, red label and dust jacket.

An early German translation of *The Golden Arrow,* using the German title equivalent to "John Arden's Daughter."

59 MARY WEBB. *Gone to Earth.*

London: Constable and Company Ltd., 1917. First edition, in original dust jacket. Inscribed on front free endpaper: "Miss May Sinclair / from Mary Webb. / March 18th, 1921."

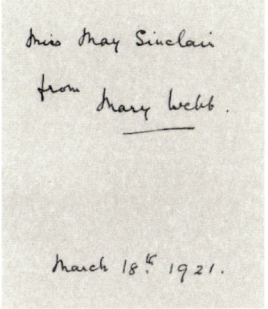

Webb's second novel, *Gone to Earth,* was written as a direct response to the carnage of World War I: "Mary Webb is expressing her own insight into the universal human condition, illustrating her view of a callous world where primitive savagery lurks within civilized man unleashing the worst evil—cruelty" (Coles, *The Flower of Light,* 1978, p. 159). While never specifically mentioning the war, Webb portrays evil as actively present in people and social institutions rather than as an abstract concept. Webb associates Squire Jack Reddin—in his need to dominate, possess and control young Hazel Woodus—with the Black Huntsman, a mythical symbol of death. A. Edward Newton in *End Papers: Literary Recreations* (1933) said of *Gone to Earth:* "Suffice to say that it is the most beautiful and tragic story I know... It has not, I think, its superior in English fiction." Rebecca West (1892–1983) in her review of the novel for the *Times Literary Supplement* (1917) unequivocally declared: "Mary Webb is a genius." In a symposium held in December 1917 by *The Times* (London), West proclaimed *Gone to Earth* "Novel of the Year." This volume is a presentation copy given four years after its publication (after the Webbs had moved to London) to fellow

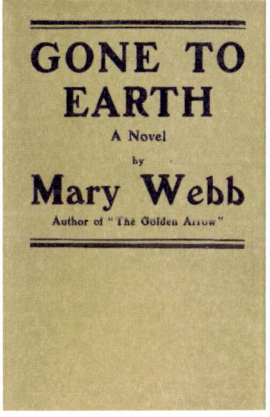

author, literary critic, and poet May Sinclair (1863–1946). Sinclair had volunteered (at the start of World War I in 1914) for ambulance duty in Belgium and was an active suffragist. Webb also presented Sinclair with an inscribed copy of her fourth novel, *Seven For a Secret,* upon its publication later in 1921 (cat. 88). Five years later, in the November 1926 issue of the *Bookman,* Mary Webb reviewed Sinclair's *Far End* (upon that novel's publication) in an article entitled "Knowest Thou the Land?" (cat. 118). The title of Webb's book review makes reference to the love poem "Kennst du das Land" by Johann Wolfgang von Goethe, which appears in *Wilhelm Meister's Apprenticeship* (first published as *Wilhelm Meisters Lehrjahre*, Berlin: 1795–96). There is no known correspondence or other documentation to determine the extent and depth of the friendship between Webb and Sinclair.

60   MARY WEBB. *Gone to Earth.*

London: Penguin Books, 1935. Third impression.

This volume is number nine in the original series of Penguin titles. Allen Lane, creator of Penguin Books Ltd., developed plans with publisher Jonathan Cape to mass-produce paperback reprints of popular works, resulting in six of the first ten Penguins coming from Cape's backlist (Michael S. Howard, *Jonathan Cape, Publisher*, 1971). In the 1930s, Cape was "publisher of the moment," having successfully published first editions of Ernest Hemingway, Sinclair Lewis, Beverly Nichols, and Mary Webb.

61   [MARY WEBB] MARIE CANAVAGGIA AND JACQUES DE LACRETELLE, TRANS. *La renarde.*

Paris: Éditions du Siècle, 1934. Uncut and unopened.

An early French translation of *Gone to Earth*, with a French title equivalent to "The Fox."

62   MICHAEL POWELL AND EMERIC PRESSBURGER, DIRECTORS. *Gone to Earth.*

Film script [United States], February 20, 1951.

Jennifer Jones starred as Hazel Woodus in the British version of this film (1950). Although he had been involved throughout the filming, executive producer David O. Selznick (who was married to Jennifer Jones), disliked the finished movie and took Powell and Pressburger's production company to court in England to obtain the right to control all versions of the film. Selznick lost the court case, but discovered that he had the right to have the movie changed for its American release. Consequently, Selznick removed almost a third of the produced film, shot extra scenes in Hollywood (under director Rouben Mamoulian), then had the film re-edited and released as the American film *The Wild Heart* (released by RKO Radio Pictures Inc. on May 28, 1952). Selznick added a prologue, new clarifying scenes (many with labels or inscriptions), and additional close-ups of his wife as the protagonist, Hazel Woodus. In this film script, the title still reads *Gone to Earth*; the Hollywood retakes and inserted lines are printed on yellow pages.

63   MARY WEBB. *Gone to Earth.*

New York: Dell Publishing Company, Inc. [n.d., but ca. 1952].

Number 436 in the Dell paperback series, issued to accompany the film adaptation of *Gone to Earth*, produced by Powell and Pressburger and released by David O. Selznick. Jennifer Jones appears on the front cover in her role as Hazel Woodus.

64   A set of eight black-and-white movie stills from *The Wild Heart.*

Directed by David O. Selznick and distributed by RKO Radio Pictures Inc., 1952. The film starred Jennifer Jones as Hazel Woodus.

65   Movie poster for *The Wild Heart.*

RKO Radio Pictures Inc., 1952. A David O. Selznick picture.

Selznick (1902–1965) is best remembered for producing *Gone with the Wind* (1939), which earned eight Oscars including Best Picture. Selznick made film history by winning the Oscar for Best Picture a second year in a row for *Rebecca* in 1940.

66   A set of seven lobby cards, each showing a different scene from the RKO Radio Pictures Inc. release of *The Wild Heart.*

67   DAVID O. SELZNICK, MICHAEL POWELL, AND EMERIC PRESSBURGER. *Gone to Earth.*

London: London Film Productions, Ltd., 1950. Digitally re-mastered and packaged digital video disc [DVD], ca 2001.

The original version of *Gone to Earth* was fully restored in 1985 by the British Film Institute's National Archive. Jonathan Coe, in a review in the *New Statesman* dated August 15, 1997, claimed that the restored film was "One of the great British regional films." Coe goes on to say that Christopher Challis, Powell's cinematographer, later praised *Gone to Earth* as "one of the most beautiful films ever to be shot of the English countryside, and in all its moods."

68   CENTRINE DE PORTHAL. *La renarde, pièce en 4 actes et 3 tableaux.*

Paris: Paris Théâtre, 1951.

A French dramatization of *Gone to Earth*, accompanied by a second play, *L'amour vient en jouant* (by Jean Bernard-Luc). With the bookplate of Frederick Baldwin Adams, Jr.

CAT. 68

69 MARY WEBB. *The House in Dormer Forest.*

London: Hutchinson & Co., 1920. First edition, first binding (green cloth stamped in gold).

The House in Dormer Forest concerns the rebellion of the four adult Darke children against the "thunderous thou shalt nots" and the "spider's web of rules, legends and customs" in their ancestral country home, Dormer Old House. This social satire, written at the close of World War I, "demonstrates the ways in which society, with its codes and creeds, its herd instinct and mass mind, can stifle or destroy the individual who is trying to find his own reality" (Coles, *The Flower of Light*, 1978, p. 185). The novel, Webb's third, was poorly received by critics, who considered it "gloomy." Coles states that Webb became depressed and suffered the first recurrence of Graves' disease since her marriage in 1912 when she realized that reviewers had missed her novel's deeper meaning, the implications of her symbolism, and her insights and perspectives ("modern man in search of his soul"). Bookplate of Frederick Baldwin Adams, Jr.

70 MARY WEBB. *The House in Dormer Forest.*

New York: George H. Doran Company, 1921. First American edition, original black-stamped red cloth with dust jacket.

Publishers in England and in the United States competed for rights to Webb's third novel. She hired a literary agent (a Mr. Dakers of Curtis Brown) to negotiate publishing rights. Hutchinson advanced £200 on royalties for the British publishing rights. Doran paid a £300 advance for American rights, and agreed to a similar amount for Webb's fourth novel (Coles, *The Flower of Light*, 1978, p. 180). Although these were considerable sums, they were soon dissipated. Hilda Addison in *Mary Webb: A Short Study of Her Life and Work* (1931) declares: "unselfishness on Mary's scale is a very expensive virtue." Webb used the money to pay off back debts, and lavishly gave what was left to the London poor. "Mary was notoriously improvident. Time and again, from friends, from her brothers, comes the comment 'She had no idea of the value of money.' Money, in her eyes, was a means of giving pleasure to others. When she had it, she spent it, though seldom on herself' (Dorothy Wrenn, *Goodbye to Morning*, 1964, p. 29). Webb's reckless generosity caused personal financial difficulties throughout her life.

71 [MARY WEBB] ODETTE MICHELI, TRANS. *Le poids des ombres.*

Paris: Éditions du Siècle, 1932. Uncut and unopened.

The House in Dormer Forest was quickly translated into French. *The House in Dormer Forest* was also dramatized by the British actor and playwright Hugh Burden (1913–1985), and was produced in 1939 at the Barn Theatre in Surrey, with eighteen-year-old Peter Ustinov in the cast. Ustinov (later knighted) went on to a distinguished stage and film career, and was awarded two Oscars for Best Supporting Actor for his roles in *Spartacus* (1960) and *Topkapi* (1964).

72 MARY WEBB. *"To a little child begging."*

Manuscript poem, one leaf, 5⅞" x 7⅜", on white laid ruled paper, black ink. Twelve lines in two stanzas, with two corrections.

After Henry and Mary moved to London in 1921, Webb found the postwar suffering there much more apparent than in the Shropshire countryside. She could not refuse any plea for help and gave to those in need from her slender resources with a passionate recklessness. Webb's lavish charity aggravated her financial distress, which in turn worsened her already fragile health.

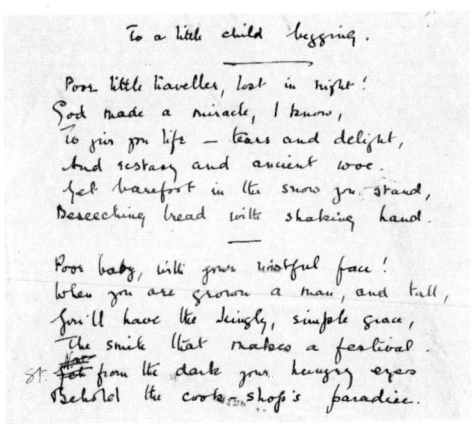

73 MARY WEBB. *Autograph letter signed to Arthur St. John Adcock.*

July 27 [1920], three pages on one folded leaf.

Webb has made the assumption that Doran (the American publisher of the *Bookman*) would have business dealings while in London with Adcock, the London editor of the *Bookman*. In this letter, Webb asks Adcock to pass an enclosure to Doran. The enclosure may have been the manuscript for Webb's short story "Caer Cariad," which was printed by Doran in the February 1921 issue of the *Bookman* (cat. 74 below). Doran had recently published the American edition of Webb's third novel, *The House in Dormer Forest*, and had also agreed to advance £300 for American rights to Webb's fourth novel. Webb also queries whether Adcock has received a copy of her new book, *The House in Dormer Forest*, and mentions that she hasn't seen it reviewed. Webb ends her letter to Adcock by offering to do literary review work. Three years later, Webb became a prolific reviewer for the *Bookman*, contributing twenty-five book reviews between December 1923 and September 1927 (one month before her death).

74 MARY WEBB. *"Caer Cariad: A Story of the Marches."*

In the *Bookman*, John Farrar, ed. New York: George H. Doran Company, February 1921.

This short love story was Mary Webb's first piece of creative writing accepted for publication by the *Bookman*. Publication coincided with the Webbs' move to London in January 1921. Publishers in England and in the United States competed for rights to Webb's third novel. Webb hired a Mr. Dakers of Curtis Brown to act as her literary agent and negotiate publishing rights. Hutchinson advanced £200 on royalties for the British publishing rights. Doran paid a £300 advance for American rights, and agreed to a similar amount for Webb's fourth novel (Coles, *The Flower of Light*, 1978, p. 180).

75 MARY WEBB. *["The Neighbor's Children."]* Untitled manuscript poem [but with this title written in pencil on the verso].

One leaf, 8½" x 6¾", on off-white ruled wove paper. Twenty-seven lines, black ink, signed at an angle at the bottom: "Mary Webb."

This emotional poem expresses the grief of a childless woman for her unconceived infant. Mary Webb desperately longed for a child of her own. Her feelings about maternity are clearly reflected in *Seven for a Secret* (1923): "For a woman's greatest career is love—spiritual and physical and the two are one and the crown of her career is a child. And whatever else she may be, and obtain, and create, she will, if she misses these, die with the knowledge of defeat. . . . A woman who has not supremely given herself is not supremely herself. Her work is halt and blind. She has not lost her life; so she has not found it."

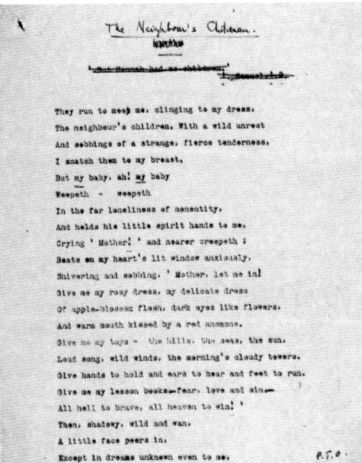

76 MARY WEBB. *"The Neighbour's Children."*

Typescript poem, two leaves, 10" x 8", white wove paper. Twenty-seven lines, seven corrections. The original typed title, "Hannah," and a typed line below it reading: "'But Hannah had no children.' / Samuel 1.2." have been crossed out, and the new title is written (above the crossed-out lines) in ink. On the second leaf, "Mary Webb" is written in ink at the bottom of the poem.

This typescript is a slightly different version from the manuscript shown (cat. 75 above).

77 MARY WEBB. *"The Ancient Gods."*

Typescript poem, one leaf, 9½" x 5½", white wove paper. The bottom has been irregularly torn off, with loss of some additional lines of verse. The typescript is accompanied by a sheet of notepaper, reading in pencil: "6 lines missing." Thirty-seven lines in nine complete stanzas, with one line of the next stanza, typed in purple ink, with one ink correction.

Using sharp sense impressions, Webb infuses her pastoral descriptions with a mythic quality: "Only I know I saw them, stately, comely / Walking along the middle of the stream. / They woke within the shallow singing water / A fading gleam. / They left no trail for any beast to follow / No track upon the moss for man to trace. / In a long silent file up-stream they vanished / With measured pace."

78 MARY WEBB. *"The Ancient Gods."*

In the *Chapbook*, Harold Monro, ed. London: The Poetry Bookshop, January 1920.

In this poem, Webb imagines seeing a stately group of men and women walking upstream in single file: "You say the sallow and the birch deceived me / But I know well that I beheld to-day / The ancient gods, unheralded, majestic, / Upon their way."

79 MARY WEBB. *"The Core of Poetry."*

In the *English Review*, Austin Harrison, ed. London: 19 Garrick Street, February 1920.

An important essay in which Webb expresses her philosophy of poetry. Webb defines poetry as: "the subconscious self breaking from its prison of silence and finding its way through the mazes of the written word. Very often it frees itself from the tyranny of the word, expressing itself, not through the thing said, nor even through the idea, but through a rhythm, a cadence, or a chiming of sounds. . . . It was because Shakespeare had so great a share of subconsciousness that he was able to express the deepest instincts of the race and something that, lying beneath them, seems to be the nearest we have yet come to a revelation of God."

80 MARY WEBB. *"Heaven's Tower."*

Typescript poem, two leaves, 8¾" x 5½", white laid watermarked paper; "Mary Webb" and "Lyth Hill" in ink at bottom of second leaf (both crossed out). Thirty-two lines in two stanzas, one ink correction.

The poem contrasts the joy of lovers within the tower with the melancholy of souls that never found a mate. The poem ends, however, by reminding the reader of impending sadness and death. "While they murmur, mouth on mouth, / The grievous bell they do not hear, / Every toll a silver tear; / Nor dream they that the mystic, tall / Tree whose leaves like shadows fall / And fill the tower with whispering breath, / Bears the purple fruit of death."

81 MARY WEBB. *"To Mother / Christmas 1920."*

Manuscript poem, one leaf, 7⅞" x 4¾", on off-white ruled wove paper, fourteen lines, pencil.

Webb's mother, Alice Meredith, maintained a stiff, brusque Victorian reserve towards her children. As a teenager, Webb had cared for her younger siblings, not only by entertaining them with stories, games and outings, but also by taking over the household during a period of five years when her mother was an invalid. Webb's relationship with her mother was never close and loving. This poem, written when Webb was nearing forty and her mother almost seventy, recalls a scene witnessed while Webb was staying with her mother in Chester prior to moving to London. Webb sees that "childish presents, bought with grave delight" held lasting sentimental value for her mother, and she recognizes (in a somewhat melancholy tone) Alice's love for her children.

82 MARY WEBB. *"To a Blackbird / Singing in London."*

"Jan: 1922" crossed out. Manuscript poem, one leaf, 7½" x 6¾", on off-white wove paper. Fourteen lines, black ink, signed at the bottom: "Mary Webb" (crossed out).

Webb's aching nostalgia for her Shropshire home, and disillusionment with life in London are evident in this autobiographical poem. She laments: "O sing me far away, that I may hear / The voice of grass, and, weeping, may be blind / To slights and lies and friends that prove unkind. / Sing till my soul dissolves into a tear, / Glimmering within a chaliced daffodil." After moving to London in 1921, Webb became desperately homesick for her native Shropshire "where the dignity and beauty of ancient things linger long." Yet the stronger her need for literary recognition became, the more she also needed London and the literary contacts she maintained there.

CAT. 82

83 MARY WEBB.
["In April, in April."]

Untitled manuscript poem whose first two lines read: "In April, in April, / My heart is set." Manuscript poem, one leaf, 11½" x 6¾", off-white laid ruled paper. Thirty-three lines, in black ink.

It was with the coming of spring each year (in April) that Webb's Celtic sensibilities quickened. "In borders dark with melted snow. / Wakening there from wintry sleep / With every bud, I sunward creep. / The empurpled crocuses, that dare, / With delicate veins the dawn-cold air."

CAT. 83

95

84 MARY WEBB. *"In April."*

"5. Grove Cottages / The Grove / Hampstead" on verso in black ink. Typescript poem, one leaf, 8¾" x 7", white wove paper. Thirty-three lines. "Mary Webb." is written in black ink at the bottom of the poem. On the verso is also written: "Mary Webb," and below is (crossed out) "46 B Leinster Square / Bayswater."

Matthew Arnold, while professor of poetry at Oxford, gave four lectures later published as *Celtic Literature* (1891). He describes the temperament of the Celt: "His sensibility gives him a peculiarly near and intimate feeling of nature and the life of nature; here, too, he seems in a special way attracted by the secret before him, the secret of natural beauty and natural magic, and to be close to it, to half-divine it. In the productions of the Celtic genius, nothing, perhaps, is so interesting as the evidences of this power."

85 MARY WEBB. *Seven for a Secret.*

London: Hutchinson & Co., 1922. First edition. The dedication copy, inscribed on the front free endpaper: "Mr. Thomas Hardy / with the greatest respect / and admiration from / Mary Webb. / Nov: 27th 1922. / 46. B. Leinster Square / London. W. 2." Webb's dedication reads: "To the illustrious name of THOMAS HARDY whose acceptance of this dedication has made me so happy."

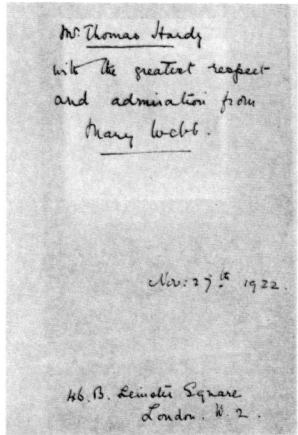

As a young woman, Mary Webb read and admired Hardy's novels of rural life in Dorset (which he renamed Wessex). Both Webb and Hardy were steeped in the traditions of their respective counties and drew upon local legends and customs for their literary material. Webb wrote to Hardy on September 5, 1922 asking for permission to dedicate her fourth novel "to the author whom I consider the greatest exponent of the wild human heart since Shakespeare." Webb subsequently sent this dedication copy to him on November 29th enclosing a letter saying, in part: "Please accept it as you would a child's stalkless daisy—valueless, but given with enthusiasm and sincerity . . . I do appreciate with intensity the rich beauty and majesty of your own interpretation of nature & humanity." Laid in are photocopies of Webb's letters to Hardy with Frederick B. Adams, Jr.'s annotation, "Original in Dorset County Museum." Thomas Hardy's widow presented Adams with Hardy's inscribed dedication copy of *Seven for a Secret* as well as Hardy's presentation copy of *Precious Bane* in 1935 (cat. 128). When asked to name the two favorite books in his library, Adams chose this volume and *Das Kapital* (Sotheby's, *The Library of Frederick B. Adams, Jr.,* 2001, p. 48). With the bookplate of Frederick Baldwin Adams, Jr.

86 MARY WEBB. *Seven for a Secret.*

London: Hutchinson & Co., 1922. First edition, in original dust jacket. Signed on the front free endpaper: "H. B. L. Webb / Oct. 1922. / Spring Cottage / Lyth Hill / Salop—."

This was Henry Webb's own copy of his wife's third novel. Later owned by William Targ (1907–1999), bookseller, publisher, and editor-in-chief of G. P. Putnam and Sons. Targ is best known for publishing Mario Puzo's novel, *The Godfather* (1969).

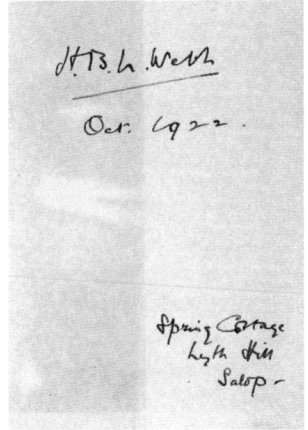

87 MARY WEBB. *Seven for a Secret.*

London: Hutchinson & Co., 1922. First edition. Inscribed on the front free endpaper: "Mary Shelley / from / Mary Webb / with love / Oct: 28th 1922. / 46. B. Leinster Square."

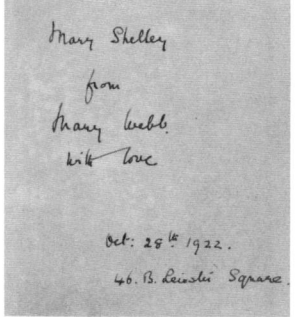

Henry Webb had two sisters (Ethel and Mary) and one brother (Tom). Biographers record that his mother and his sister Ethel disliked Henry's choice of bride and felt that Mary Webb, with her unconventional ways, was injurious to Henry's social standing. Mary Shelley was Henry Webb's other sister. The relationship between the two sisters-in-law is unrecorded, but the fact that Webb presented her first novel, *The Golden Arrow* (1916), to her sister-in-law and husband upon publication (cat. 53), and this, her fourth novel, to her sister-in-law six years later indicates at least some degree of continuing relationship and civility.

88 MARY WEBB. *Seven for a Secret.*

London: Hutchinson & Co., 1922. First edition. Inscribed on the front free endpaper: "Miss May Sinclair / from Mary Webb. / Dec: 1st 1922. / 46. B. Leinster Square / W.2."

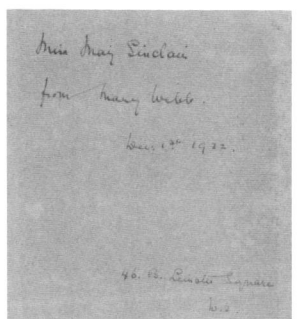

The exact extent and depth of the friendship between Webb and Sinclair (1863–1946) is uncertain, although Webb presented Sinclair with a copy of her second novel, *Gone to Earth* (1917) in 1921 (cat. 59) and reviewed Sinclair's later novel *Far End* in the November 1926 issue of the *Bookman*. *Seven for a Secret* was written in a lighter vein than Webb's previous three novels. After the lack of critical understanding for Webb's underlying themes in *The House in Dormer Forest* (1920), she hoped to generate wider popular appeal for *Seven for a Secret* by interweaving elements of love, mystery and a murder into her plot (Coles, *The Flower of Light*, 1978, p. 229).

89 MARY WEBB. *Seven for a Secret.*

New York: George H. Doran Company, 1923.

This volume is a scarce review copy of the American first edition. An inserted slip reads: "This book is not published until May 25th. It is specially requested that you do not review it before that date. George H. Doran Company." Webb could be brisk and businesslike in her relationships with publishers. Webb concurrently negotiated from Doran (through her agent, Mr. Dakers of Curtis Brown) a £300 commitment for American rights to this, her fourth novel, when she agreed to allow him to publish an American edition of her third novel, *The House in Dormer Forest* (1921) (cat. 73 and 74).

90 MARY WEBB. *Seven for a Secret.*

London: Hutchinson & Co., 1922. First edition, in a variant (pale yellow-green) binding and without the publisher's ads normally bound in at the rear.

Rare variant bindings such as this were highly prized by collectors after Webb's death and posthumous fame.

91 [MARY WEBB] MAURICE RÉMON, TRANS. *Sept pour un secret...*

Paris: Éditions du Siècle, 1933. Uncut and unopened.

An early French translation of *Seven for a Secret.*

92 [MARY WEBB] THEOBALD VERBRUGGHE AND EDUARDO ZALDÍVAR, TRANS. *Siete para un secreto.*

Buenos Aires: Editorial Sudamericana, 1947.

A Spanish translation of *Seven for a Secret* for the South American market.

93 MARY WEBB. *"The Name-Tree."*

In the *English Review,* Austin Harrison, ed. London: 18 Bedford Square, December 1921.

A short story of a young girl and her invalid father, who are forced to sell the cherry orchard where they live, and whose new owner is fascinated by the young girl's passion for her land. "'This is my name-tree,' she said. 'Do you know the old belief about name-trees? If the tree dies, you die. If you sicken, the tree withers. If you desert it, a curse falls.' . . . She had real, vital, savage passion in her fragile body. He watched her, standing slim and gauche, in her old brown dress, her soul tormented by love for something vague and mysterious, something he could not touch or name, that seemed to lie beneath the earthly beauty that she saw, like a dreaming god. . . . To possess this woman would be to ravish a forest."

94 MARY WEBB. *"Green Rain."*

Manuscript poem, one leaf, 10" x 8", off-white ruled laid paper. Fourteen lines, black ink.

This relatively short poem begins with rhymed descriptions of nature, but concludes (using dramatic imagery) with some of Webb's best lines, "Thick-set with buds, as clear and pale / As golden water or green hail— / As if a storm of rain had stood / Enchanted in the thorny wood, / And, hearing fairy voices call, / Hung poised, forgetting how to fall."

95 MARY WEBB. *"Green Rain."*

Typescript poem, one leaf, 10¼" x 8", white wove watermarked paper.

Webb found commercial success with *Green Rain*, which was accepted for publication (in mid-1923) by both the *Spectator* and the *Living Age*. Walter de la Mare selected the poem for inclusion in his anthology of poetry, *Come Hither* (1923). "Green Rain" was inspired by the dense woods near Webb's Spring Cottage, on the southern end of Lyth Hill. "The wooded isolation of Lyth Hill never ceased to beckon Mary and to inspire her poems. She responded keenly to its atmosphere: here the peculiarly compelling spell of Shropshire is intensified" (Coles, *The Flower of Light*, 1978, p. 70).

CAT. 94

96 MARY WEBB. *Autograph letter signed to Hugh Chesterman.*

April 9 [no year], two pages on one leaf.

In this letter, Webb asks if six poems that she has sent might appear in the *Girl Guide's Annual* and the *Merry-Go-Round*. Webb apologizes for a delay, saying she has had the flu, and then an accident, and as a result has "... been too exhausted to do more than 'the daily round, the common task' which the hymn says is sufficient for us." Chesterman was editor of the *Merry-Go-Round,* a monthly magazine for children.

97 MARY WEBB. *"The Prize."*

In the *Atlantic Monthly,* Ellery Sedgwick, ed. Boston: 8 Arlington Street, April 1924.

This short story was first published in the United States rather than in England because of Webb's friendship with the magazine's American editor, Ellery Sedgwick. In *The Happy Profession* (1946), Sedgwick reminisces: "Shy though she was and burdened with self-consciousness, we were old friends on the instant. Something about her compelled a sympathy . . . in herself there was something of just pride, of distrust of the world's opinion, of confidence in her own purposes; symbols of a gallant spirit going down before great odds." Sedgwick further says that Webb had left a packet of a dozen stories at his hotel in 1923, the day before his steamer sailed westward to America. He selected only "The Prize" for publication, although he admired the "complete fidelity which underlay each page of the manuscript. . . . I wrote sadly to Mary Webb that not through excellence alone can words be minted into dollars."

98   Mary Webb. *The Prize.*

Market Drayton: Tern Press, 1985. Number 16 of 24 hand-colored copies, signed by the book designers and illustrators Nicholas and Mary Parry. The paper binding decoration, lettering, and interior illustrations are all in original watercolor.

The Prize was first published in the *Atlantic Monthly* (April 1924). This fine press printing of *The Prize* is the first publication of the story in England.

99   Mary Webb. *Autograph letter signed to Arthur St. John Adcock.*

February 15 [1925], one page on one leaf.

Webb writes that she is delighted to let Adcock (editor of the *Bookman*) include some of her poems in an anthology. She states: "Perhaps the best thing would be for me to <u>bring</u> you a collection of most of my poems that I have made, hoping to get it published in volume form." She says Adcock should select the poems he prefers. Webb's poems "Foxgloves" and "An Old Woman" (cat. 147) were included in *The Bookman Treasury of Living Poets* (1925). Webb had always hoped to publish a collection of her poems. The first volume of Webb's poetry

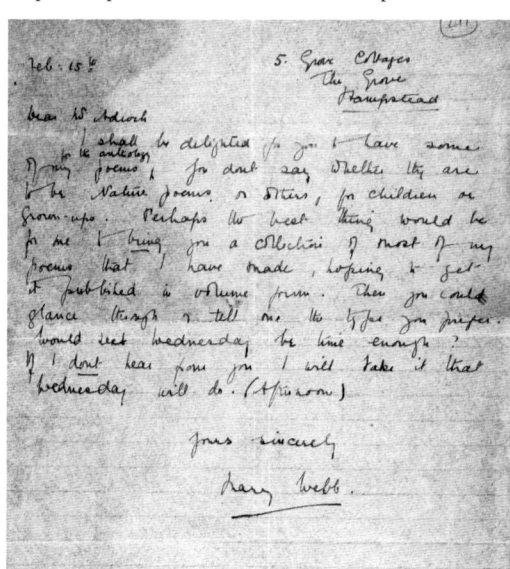

was published posthumously as *Poems and The Spring of Joy* (1928) in volume 1 of *The Collected Works of Mary Webb*. A second volume, *Fifty-One Poems* (1946), was published later from an additional cache found among her papers by Webb's husband. Two further editions of Mary Webb's poems, both edited by Gladys Mary Coles, have also been published: *Mary Webb: Collected Prose and Poems* (1977) and *Selected Poems of Mary Webb* (1981; updated third edition 2005).

101

100 MARY WEBB. *"A Gossip about Shropshire Folklore."*

Prose manuscript, twenty leaves, several different sizes of off-white laid and wove paper, black ink, rectos only, with numerous ink and pencil corrections. The title is written in pencil, and below it is written (also in pencil): "Most important. Sources of *The Golden Arrow, Precious / Bane, Gone to Earth.*"

In Webb's essay "New Year's Customs" (published December 27, 1924 in *T. P. and Cassell's Weekly*), she states: "there are many ideas of humanity expressed in books or in folklore which are immortal, shining out like lamps beyond their dark century." With original eleven-page typescript of the essay. "Mary's understanding of the growth of legend, the psychological source and significance of myth, was inherent in her mystical disposition, in the swift, intuitive apprehension which brought her to a unity with the collective past embodied in nature" (Coles, *The Flower of Light,* p. 72). Bookplate of Frederick Baldwin Adams, Jr.

101 MARY WEBB. *"Viroconium."*

Manuscript poem, one leaf, 12⅞" x 8", on off-white laid ruled paper. Forty lines in ten stanzas (on recto and verso), brown ink, signed on verso at the bottom: "Mary Webb."

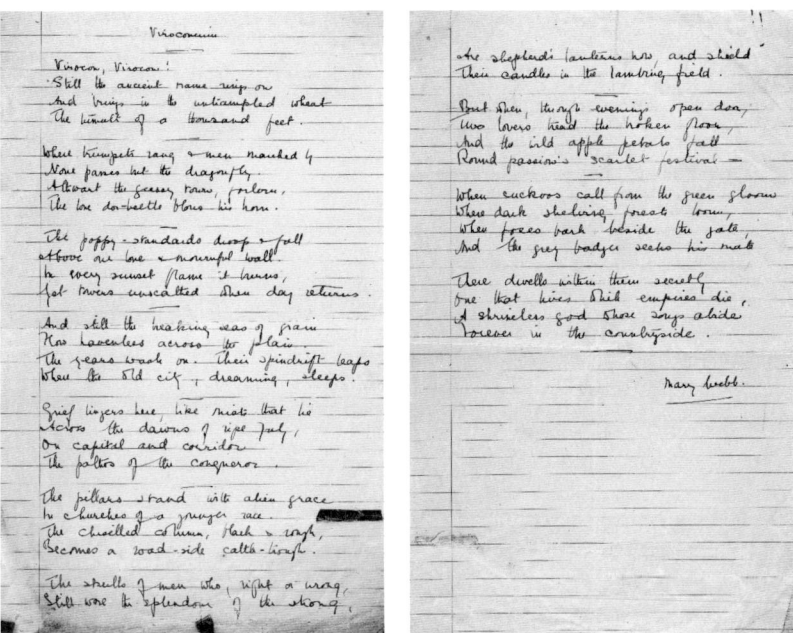

Webb frequently visited the Roman city at Wroxeter (known in the first century as Viroconium), five miles from her birthplace at Leighton. Excavations of the Roman ruin were abandoned at the beginning of World War I and recommenced in 1923. Webb also wrote of historic Viroconium in her essay "Glimpses of Old Shropshire," written for a Caradoc and Severn Valley Field Club meeting in March 1923, and published in June 1924 in the *Shrewsbury Chronicle,* and in the *Transactions of the Caradoc and Severn Valley Field Club* (cat. 104 below).

Glimpses of Old Shropshire
By Mary Webb
(A paper read before the Caradoc Field Club.)

When one comes to analyse the magic of Shropshire, or of any other place, one finds that there is something beyond the natural beauty of its woods and hills, the purity of its air, the kindness and hospitality of its people. This something is vast and mysterious, unobtrusive and yet impossible to ignore. It is the past. It is the "old unhappy things and battles long ago". It is the ancient tales of nobility and bravery. It is the love-stories laid up in lavender. All the beautiful and terrible events that have happened in a place, the lovely or ignoble lives that have been lived there, the ideals that have come into being there, give to that place its atmosphere. For thoughts and emotions do not die, any more than deeds do. Ideas are never lost. Lives once lived must leave their marks. Even if the ideas never influenced the world; even if the lives went by in seclusion, still they colour their dwelling place. We have all felt, in old houses, the sense of past inhabitants. Some houses are kind, some are dark and unhappy. And in churches that have stood for hundreds of years the wistful longings of all the forgotten worshippers seem to crowd upon us, to haunt the sunbeams like motes. It is so, it always seems to me, both in the Abbey

102 MARY WEBB. *"Glimpses of Old Shropshire. (A paper read before the Caradoc Field Club)."*

Prose manuscript, twelve leaves (numbered "2" through "13" in upper-right corners; without the last leaf containing six or seven lines), 13" x 8", off-white laid ruled paper, black ink, with a few corrections. Despite being numbered "2," the first leaf begins the paper. With an original typescript of the talk.

These two historical recreations, prepared as readings for the March 1923 meeting of the Shropshire-based Caradoc and Severn Valley Field Club, are imaginative stories set in Roman and early Christian times. Webb's interests in historical Shropshire are also reflected in her next novel, *Precious Bane* (set at the time of Waterloo), and in her unfinished fragment, *Armour Wherein He Trusted* (set at the time of the First Crusade). Bookplate of Frederick Baldwin Adams, Jr.

103 MARY WEBB. *"A Dream of Uriconium. The Return of the Romans."*

Original galley proof on a single long sheet. "Miss" deleted from author's name.

This imaginative article describes the journey of a Roman centurion, his soldiers and bullock carts from the lead mines at Snailbeach across the Stiperstones and Lyth hill to the Roman city of Viroconium. This story was part of Webb's "Glimpses of Old Shropshire" (cat. 101 and cat. 102 above) written for the Caradoc and Severn Valley Field Club. The story was later published in the *English Review* (1924), and in *Mary Webb: Collected Prose and Poems* (ed. Coles, 1977). With the bookplate of Frederick Baldwin Adams, Jr.

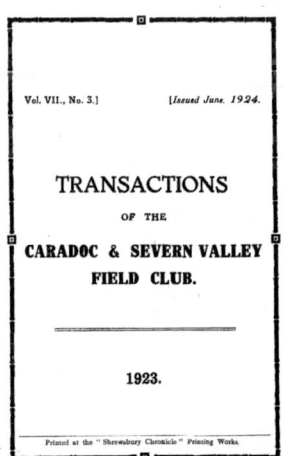

104 *Transactions of the Caradoc & Severn Valley Field Club.*

Printed at the Shrewsbury Chronicle Printing Works, vol. VII, no. 3 (June 1924).

Contains "Glimpses of Old Shropshire" with the two stories "The Return of the Romans: A Dream of Uriconium" and "Shrewsbury's Abbey Fair," which were read at the March 1923 club meeting. A scarce ephemeral pamphlet.

105 MARY WEBB. *Autograph letter signed to Arthur St. John Adcock.*

January 16 [1924] (date in pencil and possibly in another hand), three pages on one folded leaf.

In this letter, Webb thanks Adcock for sending her the proof of an article of hers for the *Bookman*. She asks Adcock for opportunities to review books, saying that she has done some reviews for the *Spectator*. Webb had been writing book reviews for the *Spectator* since 1922. Her first review commissioned by Adcock appeared in the August 1924 issue of the *Bookman*. Webb discusses arrangements for having a portrait taken. She may be referring to the photograph of herself that was published in "The Bookman's Diary" in the September 1924 issue of the *Bookman*, with a notice of a review of Webb's new novel, *Precious Bane*, by Edwin Pugh in the same issue.

106 MARY WEBB. *"Over the Hills and Far Away."*

In the *Road, A Quarterly Review*. London: The Challenge Books & Pictures Ltd., July 1925. Volume 4 (New Series), Number 22. Original green printed paper wrappers.

This short story is an example of the bread-and-butter work that Webb wrote, in addition to her review work, novels and poems, to generate income.

107 *Postcard of Mary Webb.*

[London: 1924–25.] The front of the card shows Mary Webb in Dickensian dress. Webb has also written in ink on recto: "Dickens Fellowship Christmas Party. 1924. / Mary Webb. / As Madeleine in 'Nicholas Nickleby.'"

In 1924, friend and author Edwin Pugh introduced Webb to the Dickens Fellowship. Webb made her own period gown and bonnet and was accompanied to the annual Christmas Dickens Ball at Caxton Hall by Pugh (Coles, *Flower of Light*, 1978, p. 248). Webb's short poem of tribute to Charles Dickens appeared in the *Dickensian* for January 1925. Webb's death on October 8, 1927 was noted in the December 1927 issue of the *Dickensian*, one of the few literary magazines to note her passing before Prime Minister Stanley Baldwin's eulogistic speech in April 1928.

108 MARY WEBB. *Autograph letter signed to "Dear Sir."*

April 12, 1924, one page on one leaf.

Webb says she wants to accept the addressee's terms for the publication of one of her manuscripts, in lieu of those that might be offered by another firm, if she likes the addressee's terms better. She then says: "In our present circumstances I should be ready to accept lower royalties if I could have a good advance . . . I have been offered now as much work as I can do—of the imaginative kind—by various editors or people known to them. But I am not an industrious person. Before I can work with any enjoyment I must be at peace, & being in debt is <u>not</u> peace." Webb is negotiating terms of publication for *Precious Bane*, her last complete (and best-known) novel.

109 MARY WEBB. *Autograph letter signed to Arthur St. John Adcock.*

October 19 [no year], one page on one leaf.

Webb apologizes for not having sent something earlier to Adcock, and concludes: "I trust that one day I shall wake up & find, like the bees, that I have built quite a large piece of comb & that it has honey in it—."

110 MARY WEBB. *Autograph letter signed to Arthur St. John Adcock.*

February 10 [1925], one page on one leaf. Webb discusses arrangements for articles and reviews that she may write.

Despite being always in debt, and with a reputation for hounding editors for payment, she states: "For the Morton Luce article I won't ask payment, as that is a favour <u>you</u> are granting <u>me</u>." She adds a postscript, written at a right angle in the top margin: "P. S. No telephone at present, owing to a temporary lack of 'filthy lucre,' so may I have a line as to my queries?"

111 MARY WEBB. *Autograph letter signed to Morton Luce.*

February 16 [1925], one page on one leaf.

Webb tells her friend that she has spoken to Adcock about writing a review of Luce's poetry for the *Bookman*. She asks for more copies of Luce's poems in printed or manuscript form, and for a photograph of Luce so that she and

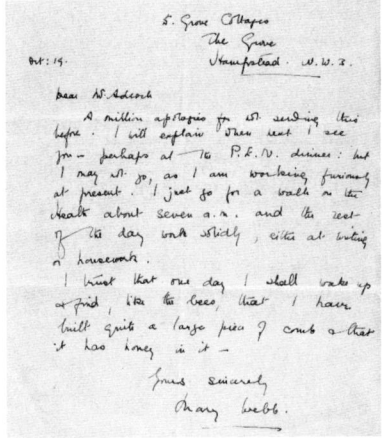

CAT. 109

CAT. 110

Henry do not have to remove from its frame the photo they own. Webb had kept in touch with her friend Morton Luce, who had lived in Weston-super-Mare since 1912, and was hoping to promote his work in London literary circles. In addition to publishing multiple volumes of poetry, Luce was a Shakespeare and Tennyson scholar.

112 MARY WEBB.
The Bookman Gallery.
Morton Luce.

CAT. 111

[London, 1925.] Typescript of the "Bookman's Gallery" (featured) review in the June 1925 issue of the *Bookman*. Six leaves, 10" x 8", off-white wove watermarked paper, ink corrections on each leaf. Typed at the bottom of the last leaf: "MARY WEBB. (Mrs. H. B. L. Webb.)."

Webb shows herself as a knowledgeable enthusiast of Luce's four published volumes of poetry: *Thysia*, *Idyllia*, *Threnodies* and *New Idyllia*, and comments that the sonnet sequences favored by Luce are a severe poetic medium, where spontaneity and emotion are often sacrificed to perfection of form. Despite this, Luce demonstrates metrical perfection and emotional power and "can create, from what to some minds would be a commonplace stroll over a dull bit of marshy land, so keen a loveliness that it cuts one to the heart." Webb compares Luce's poetry favorably to that of Wordsworth and Tennyson, and says that he is under-recognized and under appreciated—in part because of his retiring nature and the fact that he lives "remote from London, between the blue sea and the purple hills . . ." She quotes a few lines of Luce's poetry and says: "What a marvelous line that last is, and how we should all quote and requote [*sic*] and go crazy over it if Tennyson had written it! And what fools we are to let fair souls live unheeded among us just because their names do not happen to have been said or shouted a sufficient number of times for us to dare to commit ourselves." With a hand-written bibliographic note by Frederick Baldwin Adams, Jr. reading: "A carbon copy of this critical essay, with the same MS corrections, was sold to Indiana University in the

George Matthew Adams sale, Oct./63 at Parke Bernet." G. M. Adams (no relation), a Grolier Club member from 1947 until 1961, also collected Mary Webb.

113 MARY WEBB. *Autograph letter signed to Morton Luce.*

July 28 [1925], one page on one leaf.

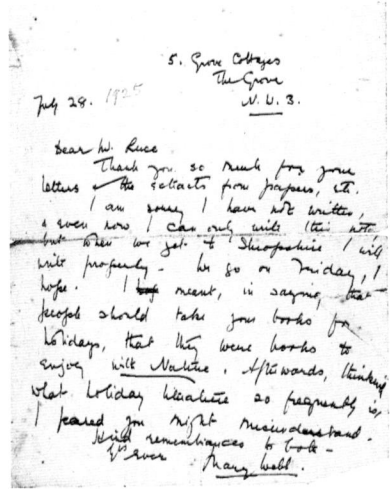

In this short letter written a month after her review "Morton Luce" in the *Bookman*, Webb clarifies one of her comments: "I meant, in saying that people should take your books for holidays, that they were books to enjoy <u>with Nature</u>. Afterwards, thinking what holiday literature so frequently is, I feared you might misunderstand." Webb reveals her sensitivity to words, particularly when critiquing the creative work of fellow-writers.

114 MARY WEBB. *"A Carol for Peace."*

Typescript poem [1925]. One leaf, 5" x 4½", white wove watermarked paper. Twelve lines in three stanzas. The title is written in pencil and may have been added at a later date.

This typescript differs considerably from the printed poem with the same title (cat. 115 below), as there are minor differences in the first two stanzas, and the third stanza is substantially changed. The verses deal with one of Webb's recurrent topics—recovery from the grief and savagery of World War I. This poem was written when Webb was at the height of her creative power. In February 1925, she had been awarded the prestigious Prix Femina Vie Heureuse Anglais for *Precious Bane*, and had been successfully writing and reviewing for the *Bookman, T. P. and Cassell's Weekly,* and the *Spectator*.

115 MARY WEBB. *"The Thornless Rose. A Carol for Peace."*

Hampstead [n.d., but "1925" is penciled at the bottom of the recto page]. A single folded sheet, printed as a Christmas keepsake. The front bears the gold design of a rose, and reads: "With all Good Wishes / for / Christmas and the New Year." On the inside upper-left corner, Mary Webb has written: "May be in Weston / next week—& shall / hope to see you."

The poem consists of three four-line stanzas. Morton Luce lived in Weston-super-Mare, on the Bristol coast, as did Henry Webb's mother. The Webbs may have been planning a holiday visit there, as Mary indicates in this card to Luce that she hopes to see him shortly.

109

116 MARY WEBB. *"Glorious Apollo."*

Prose manuscript [1926]. Four leaves, 8¾" x 6⅞", pale lavender laid ruled paper, black ink, with numerous corrections. With ink manuscript notations "488" and "New Books" (presumably written by the editorial staff at the *Bookman*) at the top of the first leaf.

On one level, this work is a review of E. Barrington's book by the same name published under the heading "The Bookman's Diary" in the March 1926 issue of the *Bookman*. Webb expresses her opinion that Byron "would have been saved" had he found the proper woman: "For lack of one woman, he insulted, destroyed, froze all with black-ice disdain." Webb later says that she is "surprised to find so able a biographer as E. Barrington [pseud. of Elizabeth Louisa Moresby], with her genius for psychology, siding with that self-conscious little icicle, Lady Byron, who prayed for Byron's soul when she should have been fainting in his arms." Humorously, Webb later says that "although E. Barrington thinks otherwise, I have thoroughly enjoyed her book . . ." Provenance: F. J. Board, Kerry Payne.

CAT. 116

117 MARY WEBB. *Autograph letter signed to Arthur St. John Adcock.*

April 27 [1926].

In this one-page letter, Webb writes about business, and also says that she is sending Adcock's daughter [Almay] some flowers, and wishes that she could ". . . also include the birdsong—so loud & sweet morning & evening." Webb also mentions that May Sinclair would like

CAT. 117

Webb to review her forthcoming novel. Webb's review of Sinclair's novel *Far End* appeared in the November 1926 issue of the *Bookman* (cat. 118 below). May Sinclair was a champion of women's rights, and joined a volunteer ambulance corps at the beginning of the First World War.

118   MARY WEBB. *"Knowest thou the Land?"*

Prose manuscript [1926]. Five leaves, 9" x 7", off-white ruled paper. Signed (on the last leaf):"Mary Webb. / (Mrs. H. B. L. Webb.)," and with a few corrections. Ink notations in Webb's hand in the top margin of the first leaf indicate that this piece is a review of May Sinclair's book *Far End* (London: Hutchinson, 1926) which was published in the November 1926 issue of the *Bookman*.

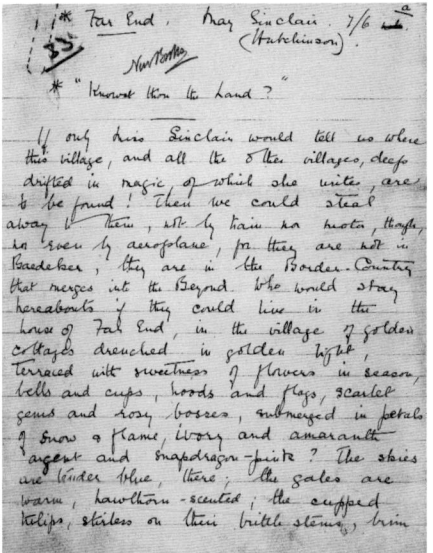

There is no known correspondence or other documentation to determine the extent and depth of the friendship between Webb and Sinclair, but Webb presented Sinclair inscribed copies of *Gone to Earth* (1917) after the Webbs had moved to London in 1921 (cat. 59), and *Seven For a Secret* (1921) upon its publication later that year (cat. 88). *Far End* is the story of a man who comes back to his wife after straying for physical passion. Webb says: "The strange woman only loves him for what he can give her. His wife loves him for what she can give to him. Therefore it was decreed from all time that the wife would be the victor. Love unspoken is the most tremendous force in the world. . . . The great lovers of the world, in silence, rule the world." The title of Webb's book review echoes Goethe's famous poem beginning "Kennst du das Land" from *Wilhelm Meister's Apprenticeship* (first published as *Wilhelm Meisters Lehrjahre,* Berlin: 1795–96). In the poem, the young girl Mignon describes a beautiful and romantic world, and begs her guardian/father-figure Wilhelm (with whom she is in love) to join her there. In her review of *Far End,* Webb suggests similarities among the worlds described by Mignon and Sinclair. The review begins: "If only Miss Sinclair would tell us where this village, and all the other villages, deep drifted in magic of which she writes, are to be found! Then we could steal away to there, not by train nor motor, though, nor even by aeroplane, for they are not in Baedeker, they are in the Border-Country that merges into the Beyond. Who would stay hereabouts if they could live in the house of Far End, in the village of golden cottages drenched in golden light, terraced with sweetness of flowers in season, bells and cups . . . submerged in petals of snow & flame, ivory and amaranth argent and snapdragon-pink?" Provenance: H. Bradley Martin.

119   MARY WEBB. *"Many Mansions."*

Hampstead (but crossed out). Prose manuscript, seven leaves, 9" x 7", thick off-white ruled paper. Numerous publisher's editorial marks in blue and red pencil throughout. In the upper-right corner of leaf one reads (crossed out with blue pencil): "From Mrs. Webb / 5. Grove Cottages / The Grove / Hampstead." In the upper-left corner of leaf one, there is another notation: "About / 950 words." At the end of the manuscript, the signature "Mary Webb. / (Mrs. H. B. L. Webb.)" is crossed out with red pencil. With a four-page typed transcript of the story.

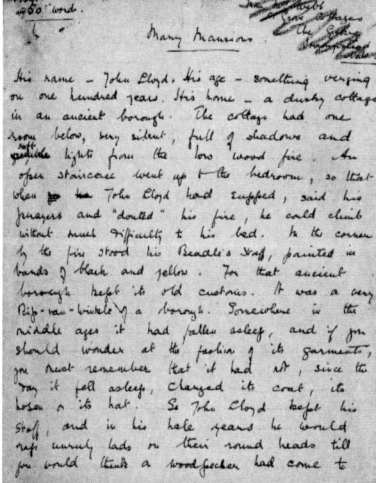

Despite the appearance of having been prepared for publication while Webb was living in London, this short story remained unpublished until after Webb's death, when it was included with her unfinished fragment, *Armour Wherein He Trusted*, in the seventh and final volume of her collected works. This autobiographical sketch shows Webb's sharp and vivid recollections from when she was ten years old and made weekly visits to an old villager. He had never learned to read and was too feeble to come to church. Old John Lloyd always asked Webb to read the same Bible passage—"many mansions"—from Luke xiv. "The child's subconscious mind retained these vivid impressions, so that, years afterwards, the writer could bring them out and use them, like coloured silks rummaged from the recesses of an old attic" (Wrenn, *Goodbye to Morning*, 1964, p. 12). Provenance: Frederick Baldwin Adams, Jr.

120 MARY WEBB. *"In Affection and Esteem."*

5. Grove Cottages / The Grove / Hampstead / London N.W.3 (these lines all crossed out). Prose manuscript, eleven leaves, 10" x 8", thin off-white wove paper, two corrections. On the first leaf "(Mrs. H. L. Webb)" is crossed out, and a pencil annotation in the top margin reads: "1 change on / last page."

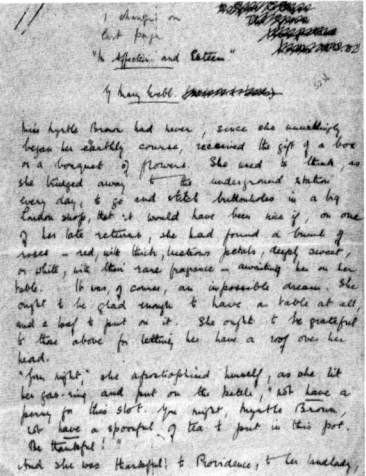

"In Affection and Esteem" is a short story about Myrtle Brown, a girl who makes buttonholes. Her great wish is to receive a beautiful box of flowers as a gift. Feeling old and lonely, Myrtle saves enough money to send herself this present. She orders the flowers, accompanied by a card that reads "In affection and esteem." On the day of delivery, Myrtle's landlady intervenes. Certain that such a beautiful gift could not be meant for her shabby little lodger, the landlady redirects the delivery boy: "There did come a parcel for Miss Brown. But it was a great expensive box with 'Cut Flowers' on it, so I knew it wasn't for you and I sent it on straight to Miss Elvira Brown, the actress, who was used to lodge here. *She* was always getting stacks of flowers, so I knew it was for her." First published in volume seven of *The Collected Works of Mary Webb* (1929), along with the unfinished novel, *Armour Wherein He Trusted,* and nine other short stories. Provenance: F. J. Board, Kerry Payne.

121 MARY WEBB. *Autograph letter signed to Arthur St. John Adcock.*

August 30 [no year], one page on one leaf.

In this friendly letter to the editor of the *Bookman*, Webb says: "I fear that I have erred and strayed from the reviewers [*sic*] straight path lately. When I think of the things I have done—been late, written too much, & so on—I am whelmed in remorse & terror!" At the bottom, Webb adds: "Would Mrs. Adcock like some blackberries for jam? There is 'God's plenty' here."

122 MARY WEBB. *"Our Immortal Jane."*

Prose manuscript, fourteen leaves: the first nine, 10" x 8", thin off-white wove ruled paper; the last five, 9" x 7", pale rose wove ruled paper. Written on rectos only, with numerous ink corrections. Signed at the bottom of last leaf: "Mary Webb. / (Mrs. H. B. L. Webb.)." Written in pencil at the top of the first leaf (in another hand): "For February [next word illegible]," and "By Mary Webb / (Mrs. H. B. L. Webb)."

113

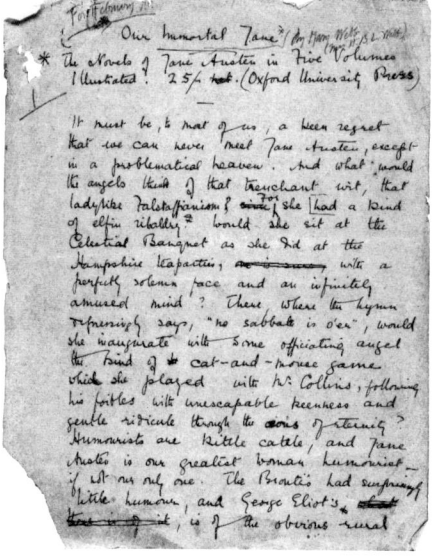

CAT. 122

This work by Webb is a review of the scholarly and authoritative edition of *The Novels of Jane Austen*, edited by R. W. Chapman, and published by Oxford University Press (1923). Published in the February 1927 issue of the *Bookman*. Webb observes: "... Jane Austen is our greatest woman humourist—if not our only one. The Brontës had surprisingly little humour, and George Eliot's is of the obvious rural type" (a surprising comment, given Webb's use of the pastoral novel form). Further on, Webb writes with her characteristic poetic imagery: "To read her [Austen] is like turning home in darkness, leaving the planetary systems wheeling on unknown ways, finding fire and candles alight, curtains drawn and supper ready. When we are afraid, after excursions into mystery with the poets, Jane Austen will comfort us." Impressed by Austen's charm and wit, Webb concludes: "Perhaps no eight words could express her so well as those on the facsimile title page 'Sense and Sensibility / A Novel / By a Lady.'" Provenance: Frederick Baldwin Adams, Jr.

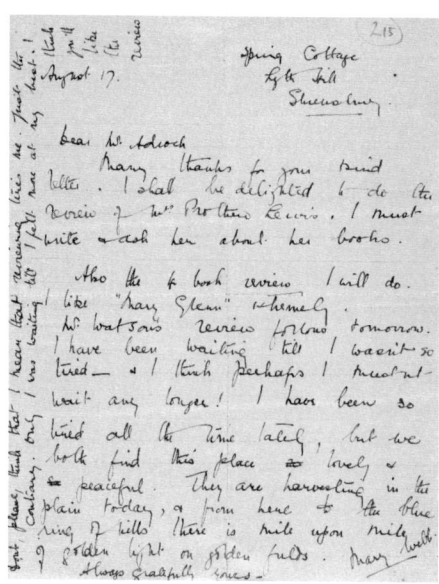

123 MARY WEBB.
Autograph letter signed to Arthur St. John Adcock.

August 17 [1925], one page on one leaf.

Webb discusses several reviews for the *Bookman*. She laments: "I have been waiting till I wasn't so tired . . . I have been so tired all the time lately, but we both find this place lovely & peaceful." Webb adds at a right angle in the left margin: "Don't, please, think that reviewing tires me. Just the contrary. Only I was waiting till I felt more at my best. I think you'll like the review." Intense mental effort and persistent undernourishment caused Webb to suffer from migraine headaches, unsteady balance, nervousness, sleeplessness, and depression. This letter was written in the summer of 1925 from Spring Cottage, when Webb's already frail health was in serious decline. Graves' disease led to deterioration of the thyroid gland, and the toxins released gradually undermined her health. Unknown to Mary (but known to Henry), pernicious anemia (then incurable) was developing and weakening Webb's resistance. (Wrenn, *Goodbye to Morning*, 1964, p. 86). Ultimately, collapse of the heart and deterioration of the spinal cord would lead to Webb's early death in 1927 at age forty-six.

124 MARY WEBB. *The Chinese Lion.*

"Mrs. Webb / 5 Grove Cottages / The Grove / Hampstead / London N.W.3." written

(and crossed out) in the upper-right corner of the first leaf. In the upper-left corner of the first leaf is written (and crossed out) "About 3000" [indicating the word count of the story]. Prose manuscript, fourteen leaves: the first ten, 10" x 8", thin off-white ruled wove paper, brown ink; the last four, 10½" x 8", heavier white ruled laid paper, black ink. With a few corrections in the text. Signed at the bottom of the last leaf: "Mary Webb."

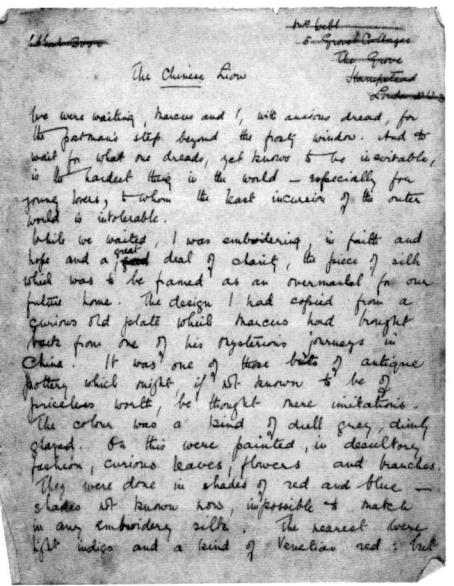

This story, one of Webb's lesser works, is about two lovers who are separated and then reunite. Published in 1937 (cat. 125 below). Provenance: Betty M. Horton, Kerry Payne.

125 MARY WEBB. *The Chinese Lion.*

London: Bertram Rota, 1937. First edition, in original slipcase. Number 16 of 350 copies. Inscribed on the front free endpaper: "For my friend / F. B. Adams Jr. / with all good wishes / Bertram Rota / London. January, 1937."

The antiquarian bookseller Bertram Rota was the first to publish this short love tale by Webb (the manuscript was found amongst her papers after her death and sold by her widower to eager enthusiasts). The story was later reprinted in *Mary Webb: Collected Prose and Poems* (ed. Coles, 1977). Bookplate of Frederick Baldwin Adams, Jr.

126   MARY WEBB. *The Chinese Lion.*

Market Drayton: Tern Press, 1989. Number 1 of 100 copies, signed by the book designers and illustrators Nicholas and Mary Parry. A pencil note on the rear blank page reads: "1 of 10—signed." Bound in beige, red and blue patterned paper and in a matching box.

The illustrations for copy number one are hand-drawn in pencil, rather than being woodblock illustrations (as indicated in the colophon). A unique copy.

127   MARY WEBB. *Precious Bane.*

London: Jonathan Cape Ltd., 1924. First edition, in original dust jacket. The printed dedication reads: "to my dear H. B. L. W." The dedicatee's copy, inscribed by him on the front free endpaper: "H. B. L. Webb / 5 The Grove / N.W.3. / 1924."

With:

BRITISH PRIME MINISTER STANLEY BALDWIN. *Autograph letter signed to Mary Webb.*

January 14, 1927, on 10 Downing Street, Whitehall stationery, two pages on one leaf, with the original envelope.

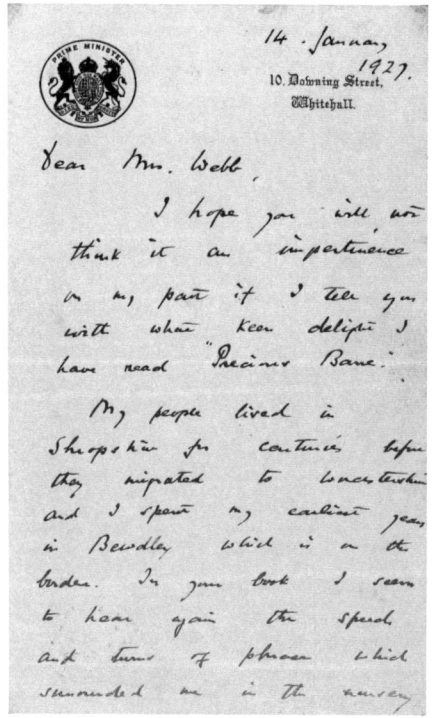
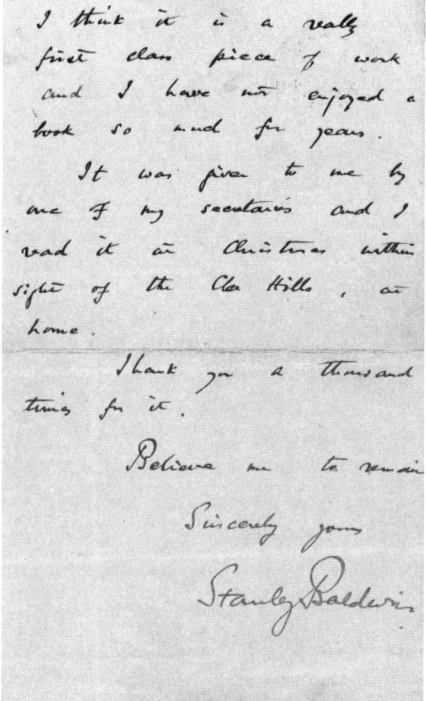

In this letter, Baldwin says: "I hope you will not think it an impertinence on my part if I tell you with what keen delight I have read "Precious Bane".... I think it is a really first class piece of work and I have not enjoyed a book so much for years.... I thank you a thousand times for it." This singular copy of Webb's masterpiece was purchased by Greville Worthington from widower Henry Webb. The purchase is recounted in David A. Randall's *Dukedom Large Enough* (1962): "It seemed that on Worthington's arrival, Mr. Webb began examining closets, drawers and the like where such of Mary's letters, manuscripts and books which had survived were stored. The more he examined them the sadder he became: he literally wept over a copy of *The Golden Arrow*, her first novel (London, 1916) dedicated 'To A Noble Lover H.L.W.' [cat. 51] and well he should have. Her last novel, *Precious Bane,* at the start no more successful than its predecessors, was also dedicated to him, though his copy was not inscribed, as she gave it to him personally. Inserted in it, however, was Baldwin's glowing letter to her on his first reading the book, dated 'Downing Street, Jan. 14, 1927,' well preceding his speech at a dinner of the Royal Literary Fund which struck the effective note of appreciation that led to the great demand for her work which followed.

"As he perused these, Webb became more and more loath to part with them, and quite understandably so. Worthington had about given up any hope of obtaining them when the second Mrs. Webb, who had been off somewhere, appeared just at the end of teatime. When she heard that the ragged and tattered remnants of books and papers were worth the modest sum offered for them, she commanded her husband to accept Worthington's offer and 'get that trash out of here before the fool changes his mind.'"

128   MARY WEBB. *Precious Bane.*

London: Jonathan Cape Ltd., 1924. First edition. Inscribed on the front free endpaper: "To Mr. Thomas Hardy / from the authoress. / Sep: 1924."

With:

MARY WEBB. *Tipped-in autograph letter-card signed to Thomas Hardy.*

November 19, 1923.

Webb writes that she has seen a notice that Hardy is to produce one of his plays in Dorchester. She says: "And I thought how lovely it would be if my husband & I could come over to Dorchester for the day when it

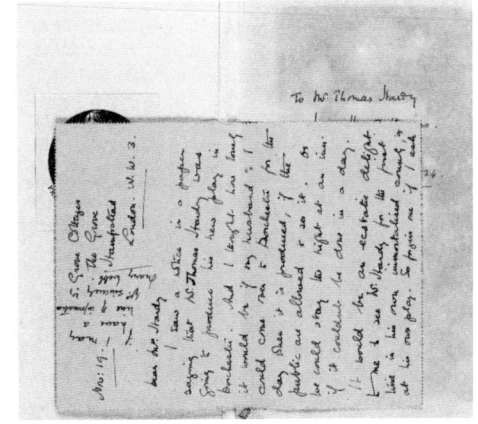

is produced, if the public are allowed to see it. . . . It would be an ecstatic delight to me to see Mr. Hardy for the first time in his own immortalised country, & at his own play." The Sotheby's auction catalogue for November 6, 2001 states that this presentation copy and the dedication copy of *Seven for a Secret* were given to Frederick Baldwin Adams, Jr. in 1937 by Hardy's widow, Mrs. Florence Hardy, in appreciation of his visit to her in 1935. Laid in is a penciled note from Adams reading: "The first performance of *The Queen of Cornwall* was scheduled for Dorchester 28 November 1923. There is no indication of an answer to this letter [i.e. Webb's letter card to Hardy] but I found it pasted in to *Precious Bane* when the volume arrived." Provenance: Thomas Hardy, Florence Hardy, Frederick Baldwin Adams, Jr.

129 CHARLOTTE SOPHIA BURNE, ED.
Shropshire Folk-Lore: A Sheaf of Gleanings.

London: Trübner & Co., 1883. Inscribed on preliminary leaf: "Mary Webb / 9 Nov. 1925." Page 184 contains a marginal annotation in Webb's hand.

Mary Webb grew up steeped in the traditions of her native Shropshire. Her father, George Meredith, was a great teller of tales and local legends. Webb believed that traditional beliefs, customs and superstitions were timeless expressions of human truths and emotions, and she integrated them into her novels—most particularly *Precious Bane, Gone to Earth,* and *The Golden Arrow*. Webb "wove more than 200 instances of lore, legend, custom and superstition into the fabric of *Precious Bane*" (Coles, *The Flower of Light*, 1978, p. 264). Webb, in her foreword to *Precious Bane*, thanks the authors of *Shropshire Folk Lore* [*sic*] for two rhymes and "the verification of various customs which I had otherwise only known by hearsay." With bookplates of Frederick Baldwin Adams, Jr. and John Symonds Udal (a friend of Thomas Hardy and the author of *Dorsetshire Folklore*, 1922).

130 MARY WEBB.
Autograph letter signed to Arthur St. John Adcock.

September 25 [no year].

In this one-page letter, Webb thanks Adcock for giving Edwin

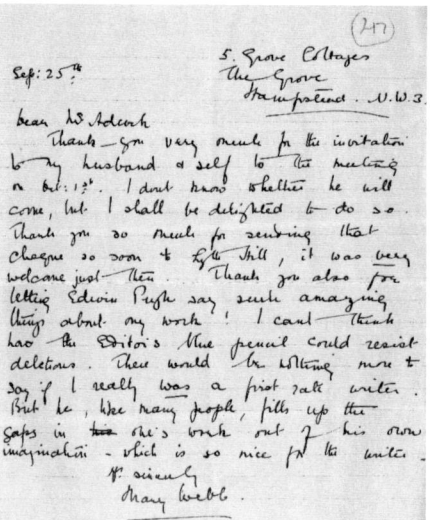

CAT. 130

Pugh the opportunity to "say such amazing things about my work." It is unclear whether the letter was written in response to Pugh's overview of her first four novels in the April 1923 issue of the *Bookman,* or in response to Pugh's review of Webb's fifth novel, *Precious Bane,* in the September 1924 issue. In his review for April 1923, Pugh declares: "To pass from the work of the average modern novelist to the work of Mary Webb is like stepping out of a stuffy room into the fresh air. . . . She has the full dower of poet and seer; wit and wisdom, humour and fancy, the twin senses of tragedy and comedy." In his review of *Precious Bane,* Pugh amplifies his praise: "She has a style of exquisite beauty which yet has both force and restraint, simplicity and subtlety; she has fancy and wit, delicious humour and pathos of the finest and most delicate, almost subliminal gifts of characterization and visualization—she sees and knows man aright, as no other English woman novelist does; she can moreover tell a story and so intrigue you with its sense of inevitableness that it seems more real than reality. She has in short genius. And though she has not yet come fully into her own, the day is surely not far off when she will be acclaimed as among the greatest of living novelists." Pugh was one of the first and most vocal of Webb's admirers. Adcock was later to write in his memoir, *The Glory that was Grub Street* (1928), that Pugh's praise of Mary Webb had been "very much a voice crying in the wilderness" and that he had "courageously and persistently" proclaimed her genius while Webb was struggling to gain serious critical attention and public recognition.

131 [Mary Webb] Jacques de Lacretelle and Madeleine T. Guéritte, trans. *Sarn.*

Paris: Bernard Grasset, 1930. Uncut and unopened. A pencil note on the front free endpaper reads: "Publicity copy for the press: S. P."

An early French translation of *Precious Bane.*

132 Edward Lewis. *Precious Bane, A Play in a Prologue and Three Acts. Adapted from the Novel of Mary Webb.*

London and New York: Samuel French, 1932.

Webb's best-loved novel, *Precious Bane,* was quickly adapted for the theater and translated into many languages. *The Times* (London) reported that the Swanage Repertory Company opened Lewis's dramatization of *Precious Bane* on August 11, 1930. A dramatized version of *Precious* Bane starring Robert Donat as Gideon Sarn and Donald Wolfit as Beguildy was staged in January 1931 at the Embassy Theatre in London (Wrenn, *Goodbye to Morning,* 1964, p. 106). This copy was used for a later performance, as an ink stamp on the verso of the title page reads: "The fee for each amateur performance of this play is reduced now to two guineas" [from the original five].

133 [MARY WEBB] BOLESŁAWY KOPELÓWNY, TRANS. *Miłość Prudencji Sarn.*
Warsaw: Powszechna Spółka Wydawnicza, 1934.

An early Polish translation of *Precious Bane.*

134 MARY WEBB. *Precious Bane.*
London: Jonathan Cape, 1948. Original green-stamped beige cloth and dust jacket.

This Sarn edition reprint shows (on the verso of the title page) how often this best-selling novel was reprinted by Cape: forty-eight impressions of the Sarn edition were printed over the nineteen years from 1929 to 1948.

135 MARY WEBB. *Precious Bane.*
New York: E. P. Dutton & Company, Inc., 1940.

Twenty-first printing. A humorous inscription on the front free endpaper begins: "I heard last week of a man who collected twenty [of Webb's] first editions (or printings, or something)."

136 Photograph of Shrewsbury, *Old Market Hall 1891.*
Salisbury: The Francis Frith Collection [n.d., but a later reproduction].

137 MARY WEBB. *"On receiving a box of spring / flowers in London."*
Manuscript poem, one leaf, 8½" x 5½", on off-white ruled paper. Twelve lines on recto and two on verso.

Webb's yearning for Shropshire was keenest in spring, when London's greening parks reminded her that she was exiled from her beloved county. This poem reflects Webb's pleasure upon receiving spring flowers from her cottage garden in Shropshire. She expresses delight in violets,

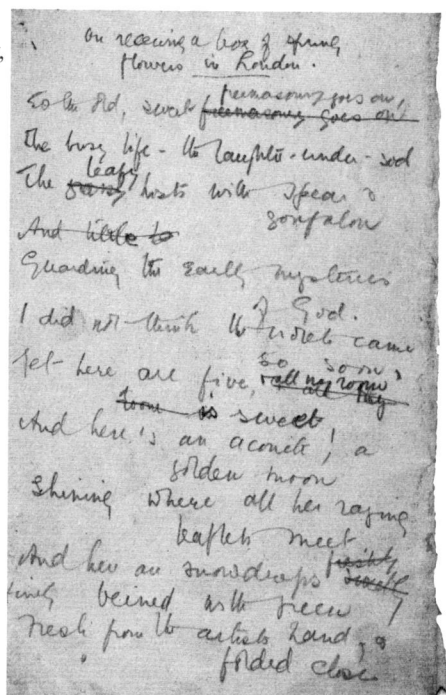

CAT. 137

aconites and snowdrops. Mrs. Thorne, a Lyth Hill neighbor, recalled: "She was always very fond of flowers. Later on, when she went to London, I used to send her boxes of them from her garden" (Wrenn, *Goodbye to Morning*, 1964, p. 66). In contrast with her earlier manuscripts—written in a small, neat and firm hand—this manuscript poem has scrawled letters, uneven lines, and numerous cross-outs and corrections.

138   Mary Webb. *"The Land Within."*

"Mrs. Webb / 5 Grove Cottages / The Grove / Hampstead / N.W.3." in ink (and with an illegible address in N.2. crossed out) on verso of last leaf. Typescript poem, three leaves, the first 10" x 6¼", the second and third leaves 10" x 8", off-white wove paper loosely stitched together (with blue thread) at upper-left corner. Forty-six lines in two stanzas, eight corrections. Signed at the bottom: "Mary Webb."

An autobiographical poem, "The Land Within" is a sad consideration of Webb's life and her failed relationship with Henry: "This is a land of forests, and of meres / Stirless and deep, replenished with my tears. / Here the pine harps, and many voices moan / Within the cedar, crying, 'Lone! Alone!' . . . And that brown woodman, where and whence was he— / That woodman, with the eyes that dazzled me / Far more than rosy fire or golden gleams / Of April? O, in dreams, my soul! In dreams."

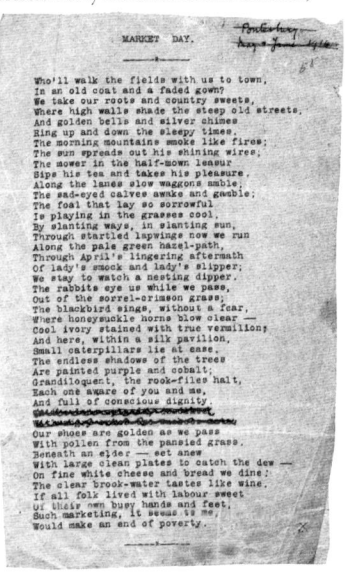

CAT. 138

139   Mary Webb. *"Swallows."*

Typescript poem, one leaf, 5¼" x 5½", off-white laid paper, mounted on white ruled paper of slightly larger size. Fourteen lines in two stanzas, but pencil marks indicate that the two stanzas are to be drawn together as one. The title is written in black ink, and appears to have been added at a later date.

One of Webb's best poems, "Swallows" reflects a muted pathos and Webb's sense of the impermanence of human life: "Within my spirit is a voice that grieves / Reminding me of empty Autumn skies. / . . . We sing our song in beauty's fading tree, / And flash forth, migrant, into mystery."

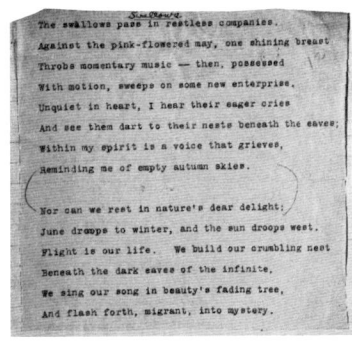

CAT. 139

121

140 MARY WEBB. *"A Will-O'-The-Wisp from the Steppes."*

In the *Bookman, Christmas Number 1925*. London: Hodder & Stoughton, Ltd., 1925.

A review of C. A. Nicholson's *The Dancer's Cat*. Webb gives a balanced but positive review of Nicholson's novel about a young Russian dancer and her tragic love affair. After Webb's death, the *Evening Standard* (on July 18, 1928) published a remembrance of Mary Webb written by Nicholson. She states that she admired Webb's writing and had on one occasion spoken to Webb expressing concern for Webb's clearly declining health, and suggesting a remedy for one of her ailments. According to the article, Webb took offense at Nicholson's apprehensions, saying: "You have intruded into a poet's reserve and sorrows. In that wilderness you have no guide—and there you are lost." Shortly thereafter, Nicholson received a letter from Webb (cat. 141 below).

141 MARY WEBB. *Autograph letter signed to an unnamed addressee [C. A. Nicholson].*

December 4 [1926], four pages on one folded leaf.

In this impassioned (indeed, remarkable) letter, Webb insists that she cannot be friends with Nicholson, as "the fact of your saying what you did to a complete stranger shows that we have <u>nothing</u> in common." Webb says of herself: "When

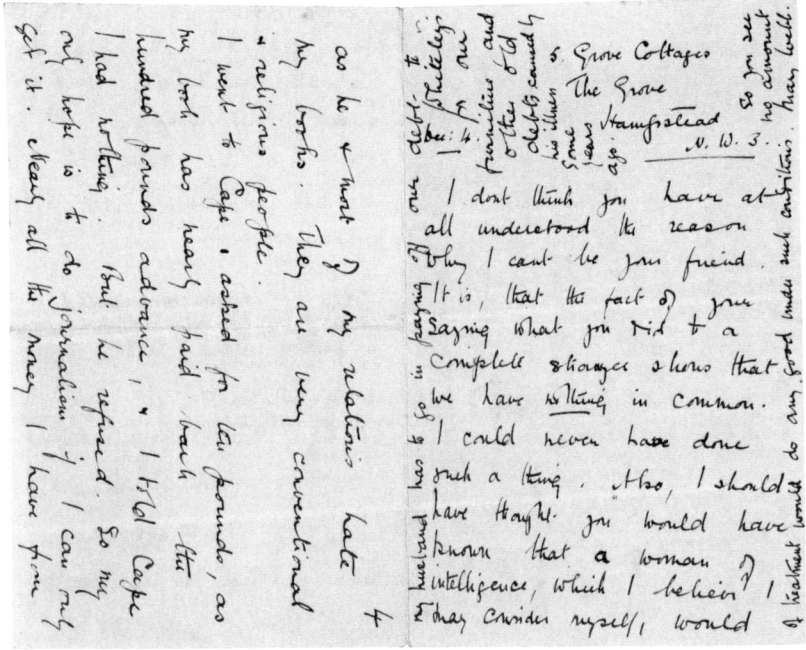

I have succeeded in getting paid fairly by the British public for my work, I shall naturally have the best treatment I can get. But not till then. Also, it is less treatment that I want than ordinary good food and a suitable amount of rest and exercise. I have this week existed on bread & scrape & tea." Webb then complains that her late mother's executor is trying to defer payment of trust money owed to her because "he <u>wants</u> me to stop getting on as he & most of my relations hate my books. They are conventional & religious people." Webb writes in a postscript at a right angle in the letter's margin: "You'll think it strange that I have a telephone when I am poor, but it is my only help, if I didn't have it I couldn't go on." In his memoir, *The Glory that was Grub Street* (1928), Arthur St. John Adcock, editor of the *Bookman* (for whom Webb wrote more than twenty-five reviews between 1923 and 1927), describes Webb: "Her manner fluctuated between shyness and a sort of hesitant self-confidence; she was very highly-strung, worried terribly about trifles, and so sensitive that she was often deeply wounded by wholly imaginary slights, and would come and complain to you of these with a childishly desperate seriousness at which it was at times impossible to refrain from laughing, and as soon as you began to laugh she would see the absurdity of her agitation over such a trifle and laugh at herself, and the trouble was over." This letter and Nicholson's article (cat. 140 above) certainly support Adcock's opinion of Webb's high-strung temperament.

142   MARY WEBB. *"Colomen."*

Manuscript poem, five leaves, first three leaves 10" x 8", final two leaves 8" x 6", on thin, off-white wove ruled paper, fifty-seven lines in four stanzas, brown ink, with one correction.

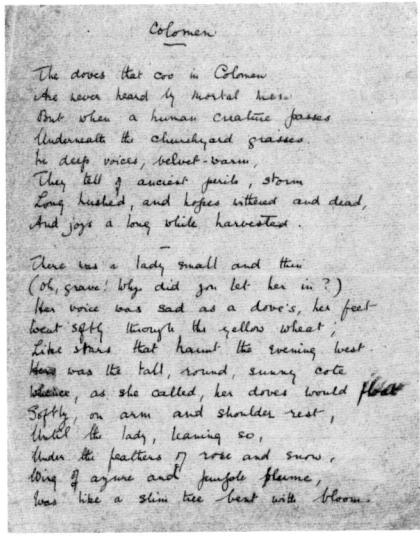

Colomen is the Welsh word for "dove." The poem tells of the love between a lady and a wandering portrait painter, his subsequent forced departure by her "proud and haughty" family, and the lady's suicide beside the portrait he had painted of her. Webb was only in her mid-forties but increasingly suffered from attacks of vertigo, migraine headaches and depression. Webb uses the imagery of doves in this poem to symbolize her sadness and grief. "She would be free of the distress / That men call joy, the littleness / That men call life — as birds are free. / So in the dewy morning hour / She hanged herself within the tower." This narrative poem allegorizes the breakdown of Webb's relationship with Henry, who had become infatuated with Kathleen Wilson, a student, twenty-three years his junior, whom he was tutoring and would marry in September 1929, twenty-three months after Webb's death (Coles, *Mary Webb*, 1990, p. 144). Henry discovered "Colomen" among his wife's papers after her death.

143   MARY WEBB.   *"'Their being is to be perceived.'"*

With an illegible pencil annotation to title. Manuscript poem, one leaf, 10½" x 8", off-white laid paper. Recto: twenty lines in five stanzas plus another seven or eight lines (with substantial corrections) written sideways in the left-hand margin, black ink. Verso: twenty-six lines in three stanzas, plus another eight lines in two stanzas (all with substantial corrections), written sideways in the left-hand margin, blue ink.

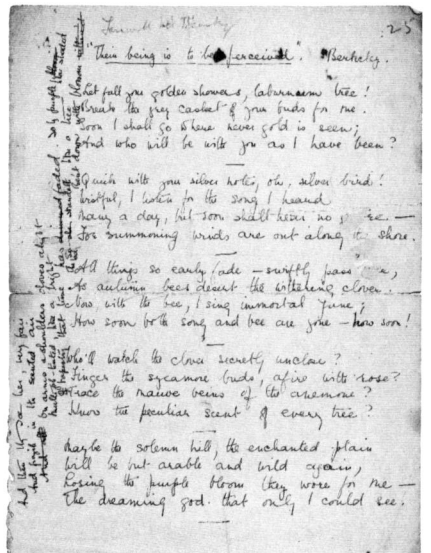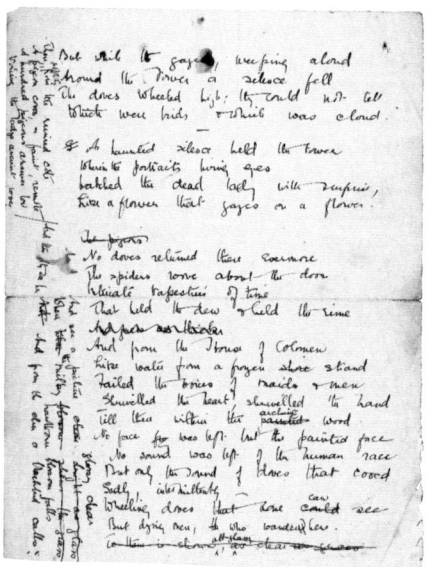

The five stanzas in fair-copy manuscript are of one of Webb's last poems, later to be titled "Farewell to Beauty." The entire verso and two stanzas on the recto margins of "Farewell to Beauty" (all with substantial alterations) are the final verses to the poem "Colomen," described in cat. 142 above. This manuscript offers a rare opportunity to see the preliminary composition of an important poem by Webb.

144   MARY WEBB.   *"Farewell to Beauty."*

Typescript poem, one leaf, 9" x 6", off-white wove paper. Twenty lines in five stanzas, eight ink corrections. The title has been altered in manuscript from its original reading, which was: "A Farewell." Below the title is a typed line reading: "'Their being is to be perceived'. Berkeley."

The first and last stanzas in this poem contain some of Webb's best poetry: "Let fall your golden showers, laburnum tree! / Break the grey casket of your buds for me— / Soon I shall go where never gold is seen, / And who will be with you as I have been?" and "Maybe the solemn hill, the enchanted plain / Will be but arable and wild again, / Losing the purple bloom they wore for me— / The dreaming god I could so clearly see." A chill presentiment has touched Webb, and there is a sense of pathos and sorrow in her later poems. As Graves' disease and pernicious anemia continued to weaken her resistance and sap her strength, Webb wrote more than ever about the transience of life.

145 MARY WEBB. *"The Birds will Sing."*

Typescript poem, one leaf, 5¾" x 6", white wove watermarked paper. Twelve lines in two stanzas, one correction. Titled in black ink and typed in blue ink. An ink notation in the upper-right corner is crossed out, but reads: "(Sunday Pictorial)."

Webb was slowly dying from pernicious anemia and Graves' disease. She suffered from migraine headaches, vertigo and depression. The prevailing mood of this poem (one of Webb's last) is of imminent separation from the beauty of an indifferent nature. Her illness would ultimately lead to her death at age forty-six.

CAT. 145

146 MARY WEBB. *"Safe."*

Manuscript poem, one leaf, 7" x 4⅜", on off-white wove watermarked paper, eleven lines in pencil with ink corrections.

Webb's uneven, scrawled handwriting—as much as the poem's content—shows her declining health and despair toward the end of her life. Written on the verso in pencil is "Nation / Adelphi Terrace / Saturday Review /

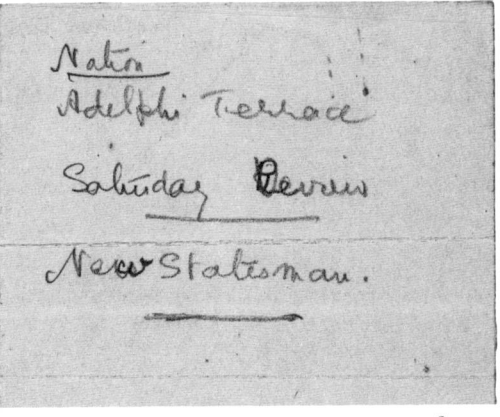

CAT. 146 verso

New Statesman." The title (compared to the other lines of the poem) is in a slightly different handwriting style. As Webb's health declined, her poetry took on an urgent, yearning undertone. Webb saw the beauty of the physical world with greater clarity, and her words took on a haunting sense of impermanence. Acknowledgement and appreciation for her writing was important to the very end of her life, as demonstrated by Webb's continuing efforts, despite her failing health, to have her poems published in literary magazines and newspapers.

CAT. 146 recto

147 MARY WEBB. *"An Old Woman."*

Typescript poem, one leaf, 10" x 6", off-white wove paper mounted on white ruled paper. Twenty-four lines in three stanzas, one ink correction. An ink notation in the upper-right corner is crossed out, but reads: "(English Review)." Signed in the lower-right corner (and crossed out): "Mary Webb."

Initially published in *The Bookman Treasury of Living Poets* (1925), "An Old Woman" tells of extravagant flowers, clothing, love, and praise bestowed on a woman who has lately died, and how pleased she would have been by these things, which now come too late to enjoy. Webb says: "They give her tears— affection's frailest flowers— / and fold her close in praise and tenderness: / She does not heed. Yet in those empty hours / If there had come, to cheer her loneliness, / But one red rose in youth's rose-loving day, / A smile, a tear, / It had been good. But now she goes her way / And does not hear." Ironically, Webb was to achieve recognition, fame and wealth beyond her wildest dreams—six months after her death—with Prime Minister Baldwin's praise of Webb's "beautiful and almost inspired mind, noble, with a very high degree of art" during his speech at the Royal Literary Fund anniversary dinner (*The Times* (London), April 26, 1928, p. 18). Two lines from this poem ring true: "This would have pleased her once. She does not care / At all to-night."

AN OLD WOMAN.

English Review

They bring her flowers — red roses heavily sweet,
White pinks and Mary-lilies and a haze
Of fresh green ferns; around her head and feet
They heap more flowers than she in all her days
Possessed. She sighed once — "Posies aren't for me;
They cost too much."
Yet now she sleeps in them, and cannot see
Or smell or touch.

Now in a new and ample gown she lies —
White as a daisy-bud, as soft and warm
As those she often saw with longing eyes,
Passing some bright shop window in a storm.
Then, when her flesh could feel, how harsh her wear!
Not warm nor white.
This would have pleased her once. She does not care
At all to-night.

They give her tears — affection's frailest flowers —
And fold her close in praise and tenderness:
She does not heed. Yet in those empty hours
If there had come, to cheer her loneliness,
But one red rose in youth's rose-loving day,
A smile, a tear,
It had been good. But now she goes her way
And does not hear.

Mary Webb

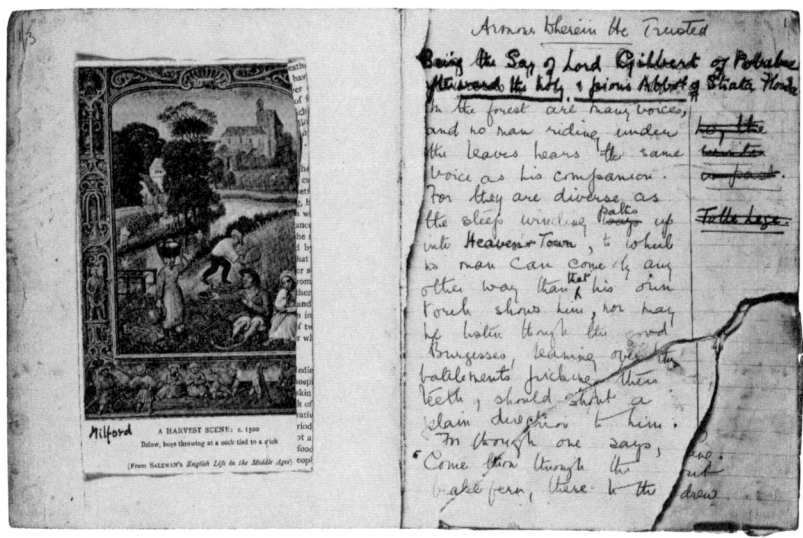

148 MARY WEBB. *Armour Wherein He Trusted.*

[n.d., but 1925–27]. Prose manuscript, one hundred and ninety-four leaves. The first eighty-six leaves, 8" x 6¼", white ruled laid paper, written in black and blue ink, and pencil. These leaves are in a notebook, bound in coarse rose-colored cloth. The last 108 leaves, on widely varying sizes and types of paper, written in black and brown ink and pencil. The manuscript has been corrected throughout, and the leaves are worn and show indications of fire damage on some of the upper edges. The first four leaves are torn, and roughly repaired. On the inside back cover of the notebook, below a pasted-in reproduction (taken from Owst's *Preaching in Medieval England,* ca. 1350–1450) of a preacher in a churchyard, Webb has poignantly written: "My child I said, I see that you have not-yet-learned what alone-ness is. But I know it, & it is that stark silence, grey, absolute, clear of all created things, in which I was when I took thee. I had like to have died—But then God came in, with flowers & a retinue of stars, & since that time He hath filled all the place, & so there is no sorrow for thee."

Mary Webb had formally expressed her belief in God and biblical teachings in an earlier review, "The Poetry of the Prayer Book," in *T. P. and Cassell's Weekly,* 17 April 1926. In that review, she stated: ". . . the Prayer Book is ours by divine right, because it is the folklore of the soul." As she felt her life-force ebbing away, Mary Webb's wistfulness for earth's beauty was never greater than in her last unfinished novel. She allegorizes her own life's conflicts in the story of Sir Gilbert Polrebec's struggle to renounce the material world, and especially to leave his wife Nesta (who symbolizes earthly love and loveliness) to follow Peter the Hermit in the First Crusade. In his memoir, *The Glory that was Grub Street* (1928), Arthur St. John Adcock, editor of the *Bookman,* relates that a publisher had readily signed an agreement in 1925, giving Webb liberal terms sight-unseen for her next novel. Webb told Adcock in early 1927 that, after two years, she (uncharacteristically) had completed barely half of the new book. A few days after his conversation with Webb, Adcock recalls: ". . . she called me on the telephone in evident distress, began saying how unwell she had been, then interrupted herself to say abruptly, 'I have destroyed all I had done of the new novel.' There was no immediate reply to my surprised, 'Good lord, whatever made you do that?' and I have seldom heard anything more piteous than the subdued, broken sound of her crying at the other end of the line. Presently, when she could speak again, she blamed herself miserably, said she had felt so dissatisfied, felt that she could not finish it, and would never write any more, so, on a sudden impulse, had torn it and put it on the fire."

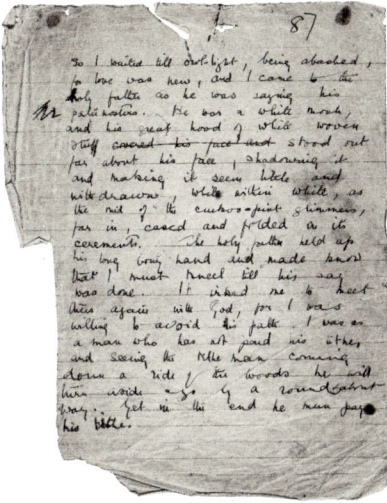

Henry Webb saved the manuscript of *Armour Wherein He Trusted* from the fire (Wrenn, *Goodbye to Morning,* 1964, p. 100). This is the only extant manuscript of any of Webb's six novels. An article, "Mary Webb's Pathetic Little Library Sold, Shabby Volumes Now Rare Pieces" (in the *News Chronicle,* April 28, 1938) reads in part: "Henry Webb told antiquarian bookseller Elkin Mathews (to whom he later sold this manuscript and the books in Mary's small library): 'All the other manuscripts were burnt. They took up too much room in the tiny cottage, and, besides, they made a splendid fire which lasted a long time.'" Bookplate of Frederick Baldwin Adams, Jr.

149 MARY WEBB. *Armour Wherein He Trusted.*

London: Jonathan Cape, 1929. First edition, with an introduction by Martin Armstrong. The last half of this volume contains ten short stories by Webb. Original gold-stamped green cloth and dust jacket. With a rare green printed slip surrounding the dust jacket, commenting on the content and literary interest of the volume.

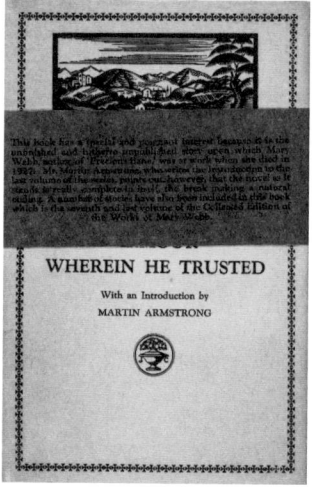

Bookplate of Paul Jordan Smith. Smith (1895–1971) was an American journalist, editor, and bibliophile who lived in Los Angeles, California. In *For the Love of Books* (1961), Smith devotes five pages to his appreciation of Mary Webb's novels and says: "I congratulate myself that I began collecting Mary Webb before Mr. Stanley Baldwin's testimony sent her first editions skyward!"

150 MARY WEBB. *Armour Wherein He Trusted.*

New York: E. P. Dutton & Company, Inc., 1929. First American edition, original bright orange cloth and dust jacket.

Webb (in her usual method) had worked out in her mind the entire plot and characterization of this story before beginning to write. Although she did not live to complete the novel, we know (from allusions in the fragment) that Nesta will be sought after by many men (during the seven years when Sir Gilbert is away on Crusade) and that Sir Gilbert's arch-enemy Ranulph Jorwerth will woo Nesta. (The fragment, in fact, ends when Sir Gilbert receives a letter from his mother while in the Holy Land with disquieting news of Nesta and Jorwerth.) We also know from early intimations in the novel fragment that Sir Gilbert (in spite of his hatred for Jorwerth) will do for this man's benefit some good deed which will lead to Sir Gilbert's harm, and that Nesta will die an early death (Coles, *Mary Webb,* 1990, p. 136).

151 [MARY WEBB] MARIE CANAVAGGIA, TRANS. *Vigilante armure.*

Paris: Nouvelles Éditions Latines [n.d.]. Uncut and unopened.

A French translation of Webb's unfinished novel, *Armour Wherein He Trusted.*

152 MARY WEBB. *Poems and The Spring of Joy.*

London: Jonathan Cape, 1928. First edition, in original dust jacket.

One volume in *The Collected Works of Mary Webb.* With an introduction by Walter de la Mare. Laid in is a newspaper clipping from the *New York Times*, December 31, 1944, with a review of *The Spring of Joy.* Bookplate of Frederick Baldwin Adams, Jr.

153 MARY WEBB. *Poems and The Spring of Joy.*

New York: E. P. Dutton & Company, Inc., 1929. First American edition.

With an introduction by Walter de la Mare.

154 EDWIN PUGH. *"Mary Webb."*

In the *Bookman,* John Farrar, ed. London: Hodder & Stoughton Limited, July 1928. Front cover features a photograph of the late Mary Webb.

There was intense public interest in Webb after Prime Minister Stanley Baldwin's tribute to her at a Royal Literary Fund dinner in April 1928. Speaking of *Precious Bane,* Baldwin stated: "I thought that, whether this book is known or whether it is not, it seems to me, so far as I am able to judge, a book of absolutely first class quality. . . . her characters really are the creation of the country, and they spring out of her love of nature, which

131

is the parent and dominating factor" (*The Times* (London), April 26, 1928, p. 18). Edwin Pugh was a long-time supporter of Webb's literary genius, and had written a review of Webb's first four novels in the April 1923 issue of the *Bookman*. Pugh also wrote a glowing review of Webb's fifth novel, *Precious Bane* (referred to by Baldwin above), in the September 1924 issue of the *Bookman*. Pugh's posthumous remembrance of Webb's oeuvre is complimentary, but his review is overly-effusive.

CAT. 154

155 HENRY B. L. WEBB. *Autograph letter signed.*

August 18, 1928, to an unidentified addressee, two pages on one leaf, to a literary agent negotiating terms for film rights to Mary Webb's novels.

Henry Webb declares that £2,000 is a reasonable price for a seven-year lease of one of the novels. Henry had written a letter to Mary's siblings in the same month, in which he states "the management of her [Mary's] literary estate has become my chief interest in life recently and it would be a satisfaction to me to feel that I had quite a free hand in dealing with it" (Coles, *The Flower of Light*, 1978, p. 324). In the same letter quoted by Coles, Henry disingenuously assures Mary's brothers and sisters that "there is obviously nothing of a goldmine in Gladys' copyrights." (Their sister, Mary Gladys Meredith, had been known as "Gladys" before her marriage to Webb in 1912.) Two thousand pounds was more than double Mary Webb's £936 estate at her October 1927 death, and represented a tremendous amount of money (especially for a teacher) in 1928!

156 HENRY B. L. WEBB. *Autograph letter signed.*

August 26, 1928, to unidentified addressee, one page on one leaf.

Henry Webb, during a hotel stay in France, continues negotiations with literary agents for the film rights to Mary Webb's novels. As administrator of Mary

Webb's estate, he is bound to "take rather a long view in the interests of other beneficiaries." He concludes by saying that if *Precious Bane* is the story wanted by a film company, then £500 "is definitely not nearly enough." Mary's mother (Alice Meredith) had died in 1924, and she had arranged in her will for almost all of her £4,000 estate to be put into a fund for Olive (her only unmarried daughter). The five other Meredith siblings were each to have a 20% reversionary interest in case of Olive's death. Henry apparently recognized the value of Mary's work and planned to profit from it. Henry wrote a letter to Mary's siblings in August 1928, proposing that a deed be drawn up in which he would relinquish his rights as widower to Mary's 20% reversionary interest in family money if the siblings would grant Henry full ownership of the copyrights to Mary's books (Coles, *The Flower of Light*, 1978, p. 324).

157   Henry B. L. Webb. *Autograph letter signed.*

Paris, September 8, 1928, to unidentified addressee, two pages on one leaf.

In this letter, Webb asks for help in securing American film rights for Mary Webb's novels. He adds that he has some short stories by Mary Webb, and that he wants to: ". . . get these out—immediately in England, and later on in America, to coincide in each case with the publication of her *Collected Works*."

158   Henry B. L. Webb. *Autograph letter signed.*

September 15, 1928, to unidentified addressee, three pages on two leaves.

Webb says that he will send copies of Mary Webb's novels ". . . as they come out in the new edition, for film purposes." He instructs the addressee to place some short stories for serial rights in England and America, and discusses other publication arrangements that he is making with the publishers Jonathan Cape and E. P. Dutton.

159   Henry B. L. Webb. *Autograph postcard signed to Messrs. J. B. Pinker & Sons.*

October 17, 1928, address: "Talbot House / Arundel St. / Strand W. C. 2."

Webb says that he has sent copies of Mary Webb's five novels to the addressees' representative in Hollywood. The literary agent James Brand Pinker (1863–1922) represented many well-known British and American writers, including: H. G. Wells, Jack London, James Joyce, Stephen Crane, Arnold Bennett, Henry James, and Joseph Conrad. After Pinker's death in 1922, his firm continued under the direction of his two sons, Eric and James Ralph, with whom Henry dealt in 1928. Jonathan Cape's seven-volume *Collected Works* (1928–29) was reprinted six times from 1928 to 1929; each volume became a best seller in its own right. In managing Mary's literary estate, Henry rapidly became quite wealthy.

160   Henry B. L. Webb. *Autograph letter signed.*

November 9, 1929, to unidentified addressees, two pages on one leaf.

Webb leaves the negotiation of film rights for *Precious Bane* in the hands of the addressees, subject to his approval of any deal. He acknowledges a caution previously received from them, on "the 'talkie' development" (presumably some new profits associated with sound films). Webb concludes by saying that he wants to be able to entertain any offer for film rights which may come to him directly from Jonathan Cape, the publisher of *Precious Bane*. Two months earlier, in September 1929, forty-four-year-old Henry had married his former student, now twenty-one-year-old Kathleen Wilson. Henry first met and taught Kathleen (in 1921) at King Alfred School in London. By 1925, he was privately tutoring Kathleen at her home for entrance to London University. In the summer of 1926, when Henry brought then-eighteen-year-old Kathleen for a visit to Shropshire, Mary Webb was seized by doubt, fear and jealousy, and a major rift developed in their marriage. The newly-married Henry was wealthy enough from royalties received from Mary's novels to retire permanently from teaching by December 1929.

161   H. P. Marshall. *"Mary Webb."*

In the *Edinburgh Review,* Harold Cox, ed. London: Longmans, Green, & Co., Ltd., April 1929.

Prime Minister Baldwin's posthumous tribute in April 1928 at the Royal Literary Fund dinner created an immediate demand for Webb's writings. Coincident to the publication of Jonathan Cape's seven-volume *Collected Edition of Mary Webb,* H. P. Marshall published an extensive appreciation of Webb's oeuvre that helped to define Webb's particular appeal. Marshall writes: "There is no need to labour the fact that Mary Webb wrote great prose, though it is never easy to trace the pattern which produces in a sequence of words the most lovely music, for the instinct which arranges the pattern lies deep in the personality of the writer. Prose is governed by no laws; it has an inevitability of form which proceeds from a depth of emotion intuitively expressed. It is almost possible to feel the pause, when the writer waits in silence for the slow emergence of the thought-form, almost possible to see the image rising through passionate conviction to take certain shape. All we can know, and we know it instinctively, is that we could alter or move no work without destroying the whole, and that as we read we are in direct contact with an actual personality." Marshall goes on to state: "I think we must be careful by what canon we judge Mary Webb. . . . it is by her understanding of spiritual truth that Mary Webb will stand or fall. . . . mysticism suffuses her writings with a spiritual integrity and loveliness which is not often found outside the avowedly religious writings of the great mystics. . . . she had in her gift an understanding of the spiritual truths of life which we should be unwise to refuse."

162   W. REID CHAPPELL. *The Shropshire of Mary Webb.*

London: Cecil Palmer, 1930. First edition, brown pictorial cover.

In 1928 enthusiasts began making pilgrimages to see "Mary Webb Country." Chappell's topographical review features Shropshire locales, and contains reminiscences of Mary Webb by local county people who knew her. In the preface, Chappell thanks Henry Webb for inspiration and guidance.

163   GRACE CHAPMAN. *"Mary Webb."*

In the *London Mercury,* J. C. Squire, ed. London: 229 Strand, W. C. 2, February 1931.

Grace Chapman reviews *The Collected Works of Mary Webb,* published in 1928–29 by Jonathan Cape. Each volume is introduced by a notable personality of the day who had known Webb during her lifetime: Prime Minister Stanley Baldwin, G. K. Chesterton, John Buchan, Robert Lynd, Martin Armstrong, H. R. L. Sheppard, and Walter de la Mare. Chapman comments upon the almost cult-like following for Webb's work: "It is as impossible to explain the comparative apathy with which her earlier novels were received as to justify the extravagant chorus of praise which broke out in 1927 [*sic,* should be 1928] after the then Prime Minister had publicly testified to his reading and appreciation of *Precious Bane.*"

164   HILDA ADDISON. *Mary Webb: A Short Study of Her Life and Work.*

London: Cecil Palmer, 1931. First edition.

Henry Webb was charming and cooperative to writers preparing the first biographical studies of Mary Webb. Gladys Mary Coles (who knew Hilda Addison) says that Henry gave Addison information about Mary's life "on the condition that nothing was said which would upset his 'new young wife.'" Addison became aware—by speaking with Miss Edith Lory (Webb's former governess and long-time friend), and with Mrs. Ethel Wicksteed (the wife of the headmaster of King Alfred School, in London, where Henry Webb taught)—of the unhappiness of the Webbs' marriage in its later years. However, Addison's sense of honor was strong, and she did not "break confidences" (Coles, *Mary Webb,* 1990, p. 151). Bookplate of Frederick Baldwin Adams, Jr.

165   ANONYMOUS. *A Quotation Calendar from Mary Webb.*

London: The Medici Society [1931–32].

The Medici Society was founded (in 1908) to bring artists' work to the attention of a wider public, and at low prices. This calendar of folio sheets, tied together at the top with ribbon, contains quotations from Webb's writings illustrated by Roland Hilder, whom Cape would later hire for the illustrated edition of Webb's *Collected Works* (1937). Today, the society makes stationery, calendars, greeting cards, reproduction prints, and children's books.

166   THOMAS MOULT. *Mary Webb: Her Life and Work.*

London: Jonathan Cape, 1932. First edition, in original dust jacket.

Jonathan Cape commissioned Moult to write the official biography of Webb, and Henry influenced the biographer to portray Mary and Henry's marriage as happy and supportive. Douglas Meredith (who had supplied information to Moult about his sister) wrote an angry letter to Moult after publication: "As regards the latter part of her married life, I suppose you considered that it was a question of less said the better, although I consider that it had a lot to do with her inability to write and her early death. The latter part of her married life was not happy, and I am sorry you thought it—found it—necessary to say the opposite" (Coles, *Mary Webb*, 1990, p. 151). Bookplate of Frederick Baldwin Adams, Jr.

167   A. EDWARD NEWTON. *End Papers: Literary Recreations.*

Boston: Little, Brown and Company, 1933. Number 29 of 1,351 copies of the Dream Children Edition.

Newton has inscribed this copy: "Mary Webb's best novel, in my opinion, is 'Gone to Earth.' A. Edward Newton." The frontispiece, "The Book-Collector Masquerading as Master of Hounds," is further inscribed: "To John Howell from H. J. Brothers." Brothers created the frontispiece, and his dedication was to the proprietor of John Howell Books, a well-known antiquarian bookshop in San Francisco.

168   MAGDALENE M. WEALE, M.A.
Through the Highlands of Shropshire on Horseback.

London: Health Cranton Limited, 1935. First edition, in dust jacket.

Weale devotes the final chapter, "The Country of the Mary Webb Novels," to describing the physical localities of her books. Weale states: "True, she is no mere guide-book author, but a creative artist, claiming the right to take liberties with her material whenever necessary. . . . her descriptions will be found to be extraordinarily accurate and the literary jigsaw puzzle capable of being worked out with a good measure of success."

169 MARIANNE TIEMANN. *Naturbetrachtung und Weltanschauung in den Werken von Mary Webb.*

Greifswald: E. Danzig & Co., 1936. Original printed paper wrappers.

The title of this dissertation can be roughly translated as "Contemplation of nature and world-view in the works of Mary Webb." Webb's popularity led to scholarly study until World War II turned Europe's attention to matters of war and survival.

170 E. MOORE DARLING. *Seeing Shropshire.*

Shrewsbury: Adnitt & Naunton, Ltd., 1937. First edition, original silver-stamped green cloth and dust jacket.

On the rear endpaper, a Mary Webb enthusiast has written in ink a brief chronology of Webb's life, and has penciled Shropshire place-names cited in the book.

171 W. BYFORD-JONES. *The Shropshire Haunts of Mary Webb.*

Shrewsbury, Wilding & Son, Ltd. [n.d., but with a foreword dated November 1937]. First edition, in dust jacket.

This volume was written for "Mary Webb Pilgrims" wishing to visit Shropshire and experience the magical environment that inspired Webb to write her fiction. Tucked into the book is a 5" x 3½" advertisement for the book; the verso reads: "GREETINGS from Shrewsbury to The Friends of 'The Gustine Courson Weaver Mary Webb Shrine' located in State Historical Museum, Teachers' College, Denton, Texas, U.S.A." Also in the book is a reprinted newspaper article from the *Campus Chat*, North Texas State Teachers College, Denton, Texas, and dated (in ink) "April 14–[19]38." Henry Webb had reportedly referred to Gustine Courson Weaver, an early collector and Mary Webb enthusiast, as "The Cotton Dolly from the States." With the bookplate of Frederick Baldwin Adams, Jr.

172 HENRY B. L. WEBB, ED. *A Mary Webb Anthology.*

London: Jonathan Cape, 1939. First edition, in original dust jacket, and illustrated by Norman Hepple and Rowland Hilder.

This one-volume anthology of Webb's works is the first to contain excerpts from her novels, short stories, essays and poems (some published for the first time). Henry Webb selected the material to appear in this anthology just prior to his death in 1939 at the age of fifty-three, caused by a fall from the pinnacle of Scafell Pike in the Lake District (cat. 184). A publisher's note states that the selection "is not intended to represent the cream of her work, for there is material enough in her writings for a dozen such anthologies." Rather, the purpose of this anthology was to serve as an introduction to Mary Webb for the new reader and as a miscellany for those who already knew and appreciated her work.

173 MARY WEBB. *Fifty-One Poems.*

London: Jonathan Cape, 1946. First edition, in original dust jacket. At the bottom of the contents page, an early collector (Benjamin Hitz) has written: "Only 'Vigil' is not to be found among my copies of MSS and TSS, made before sale in 1937."

All that were known of Mary Webb's poems had been published posthumously in *Poems and The Spring of Joy* (1928). Printed here for the first time is a cache of poems by Webb that was discovered among the papers of the late Henry Webb. Ostensibly, these had been set aside by him for publication at some later date.

174 MARY WEBB. *Fifty-One Poems.*

With wood engravings by Joan Hassall. New York: E. P. Dutton & Co., Inc. [n.d.]. Apparently the first (undocumented) American edition. The verso of the title page reads "Printed in Great Britain." Original gold-stamped turquoise cloth and dust jacket.

Except for the preliminaries, the contents appear virtually identical to the first British edition, suggesting that some copies were uniquely bound up in Britain for release in America in this turquoise cloth, with the E. P. Dutton title page, preliminaries, and dust jacket. A rare item.

175 MARY WEBB. *The Essential Mary Webb.*

London: Jonathan Cape, 1949. With an introduction by Martin Armstrong, and illustrations from drawings by Norman Hepple and Rowland Hilder. In original dust jacket.

Martin Armstrong served as associate literary editor for the *Spectator* from 1922 to 1924, during the period that Webb was contributing book reviews and poems to this literary magazine. By virtue of his editorial position, Armstrong was well-positioned to "give a bird's eye view of all sides of Mary Webb's genius." He cites

Webb's ability to convey her feelings about nature in a precise yet delicate style, and to recreate country characters with a sympathetic yet sharply penetrating eye. This single volume presents: extracts from Webb's six novels; essays from *The Spring of Joy;* and reprints of a dozen of her poems. Armstrong says: "In each of her books the reader is made to see and feel the little tract of England which it so vividly conjures up, with such intensity, that he inhabits it, under all its changing weathers." Also notable (on the verso of the title page) is the listing of the numerous editions issued for each of Webb's six published novels, including the number of impressions printed of each edition (through 1949).

176   SUSAN TWEEDSMUIR. *A Winter Bouquet.*
London: Gerald Duckworth & Co. Ltd., 1954. First edition. A chapter is devoted to a remembrance of Mary Webb.

Susan Tweedsmuir was the wife of John Buchan (prolific Scottish author and member of Parliament for the Scottish Universities). Upon reading *Gone to Earth,* Lady Tweedsmuir wrote a letter of appreciation to Webb, and a friendship developed between them. Recalling Webb's posthumous fame, Lady Tweedsmuir writes: "That Mary Webb should have died before fame came to her, and have reaped so few of the fruits of literary success, is a melancholy reflection upon the taste and discrimination of her fellow-countrymen, who apparently could only recognize merit when underlined to them by their Prime Minister." In 1937 Lady Tweedsmuir wrote the article on Mary Webb for Webb's first appearance in the *Dictionary of National Biography.* Gladys Mary Coles was later commissioned by Oxford University Press to write a new biographical entry for Mary Webb, published in 2004.

177   DOROTHY P. H. WRENN. *Goodbye to Morning.*
Shrewsbury: Wilding & Son Limited, 1964. First limited edition, number 31 of 100 copies on handmade paper and signed by the author on the title page.

This third book-length biography of Mary Webb was published more than thirty years after Hilda Addison's *Mary Webb: A Short Study of Her Life and Work* (1931), and the official biography (commissioned by publisher Jonathan Cape), Thomas Moult's *Mary Webb: Her Life and Work* (1932). Wrenn, a local Shrewsbury teacher and historian, writes in her preface that she was inspired to write the biography when she was collecting material about Mary Webb for a series of lectures she was to give and discovered (despite Webb's great posthumous fame) that "in her own countryside, often Mary Webb was a name and nothing else."

178   CHRISTOPHER LE FLEMING. *"The Hills of Heaven."*
(Illustrated on page 143)

A one-page manuscript musical score, signed by Le Fleming, and setting the beginning of Webb's poem of the same name to music.

Le Fleming, educated at the Royal School of Church Music, was a writer, schoolteacher, railway enthusiast, and (in 1971) the chairman of the Composers' Guild of Great Britain. Le Fleming also set several of Beatrix Potter's stories to music.

179   GLADYS MARY COLES, ED.
Mary Webb: Collected Prose and Poems.

Shrewsbury: Wildings of Shrewsbury, Ltd., 1977. Signed by Coles on the title page. Published on the fiftieth anniversary of Webb's death.

In this collection, Coles has included some of Mary Webb's hitherto uncollected essays and book reviews (written in the 1920s for literary magazines), as well as short stories and a selection of Webb's poems, some of them published here for the first time.

180   GLADYS MARY COLES.
The Flower of Light: A Biography of Mary Webb.

London: Gerald Duckworth & Co. Ltd., 1978. First edition in the original dust jacket. Laid in is a review (from the *Times Literary Supplement*, September 22, 1978), together with a published response to the review by Coles.

This fourth book-length biography of the author, written more than fifty years after her death, is now recognized as the seminal critical study and biography of Mary Webb. In it, Coles shows unusually keen empathy and insight in her interpretation of Webb's life and work. *The Flower of Light* was selected as "Book of the Year" in the *Financial Times* and the *Birmingham Post*, and was adapted as a "Radio Portrait" for BBC Radio 4. The book was reprinted in a paperback edition by Headland Publications in 1998. Like Webb, Coles is an author and poet of Celtic heritage. Bookplate of Frederick Baldwin Adams, Jr.

181   CAROL SNAPE. *"My Wife Did a Bit of Scribbling."*

Dinham: [No publisher] 1980. A printed copy [ca. 2007] of a 39-page stage or radio production.

The two characters are Mary [Webb] and Henry [Webb]. In a personal email, Carol Snape-Barker recalls that she was asked to write a play about Mary Webb for the centennial of her birth in 1981. This dramatization was performed at the Ludlow Festival in 1982 and later made into a radio production. Ms. Snape-

Barker says that she raised her family in Shropshire, and learned much about Mary Webb's life from Webb's brother, Kenneth Meredith, whom she met when attending school in North Wales. The title is taken from an anecdote after Mary's death, after Henry had leased Spring Cottage to Raymond Poynton, a young man in publishing. When Poynton later offered to buy the cottage, Henry initially refused, using the excuse that "this was where my wife did her little bit of scribbling." Coles also relates this anecdote in *Mary Webb* (1990), p. 152.

182   ERIKA DUNCAN. *Unless Soul Clap Its Hands.*

New York: Schocken Books, 1984. In dust jacket.

Contains a chapter entitled "Rediscovering Mary Webb" that begins: "Every so often one discovers something which strikes a chord so personal and so sacred that, though it is unfamiliar, it seems to function as a fragment of a memory long lost. Such was my feeling when I first came across *Precious Bane* by Mary Webb. . . ." Erika Duncan has been a contributing editor to *Book Forum*, has taught English composition at New York University, and also wrote the introductory essay to *Precious Bane*, reprinted by the University of Notre Dame Press (1980).

183   GLADYS MARY COLES. *Mary Webb.*

Bridgend: Seren Books, 1990. In dust jacket, signed on title page by Coles. Inscribed on half title "All good wishes Frances— / Gladys Mary Coles / 25 March '91."

This clear and factual biography of Mary Webb is one of the Border Lines series of short biographies published with the financial support of the Welsh Arts Council. The book complements Coles's more detailed biography, *The Flower of Light* (1978). It includes new biographical material (especially dealing with the later years of marriage after Henry and Mary had moved to London), fresh critical assessments of Webb's novels, and a selection of previously unpublished Webb and Meredith family photographs.

184   GLADYS MARY COLES. *The Echoing Green.*

Hexham: Flambard Press, 2001. Signed on the title page by Coles, and inscribed on the half-title: "For Mary and Bruce / in Mary Webb Country / 6 June '06— / Gladys Mary / with 'warmship.'"

Gladys Mary Coles creates a long sequence of poems entitled "The Land Within," detailing the tragic life of Mary Webb with explanatory notes. An additional poem, "Henry Webb," along with the final chapter ("Afterwards") in *Mary Webb* (1990), suggest that Henry's fall from the pinnacle of Scafell in 1939, which resulted in his death, may have been suicide. This volume is a personal association copy, given to the Crawfords on the day spent with Coles, visiting Spring Cottage on Lyth Hill and walking on God's Little Mountain, the setting of *Gone to Earth*.

185 PATRICIA A. EVANS. *Poetical Landscapes: Watercolour Paintings by Patricia A. Evans.*

Pennerley: Tankerville Gallery, 2002. Foreword by Gladys Mary Coles. With quotations from the work of Mary Webb. Original illustrated paper covers.

Patricia Evans pairs her watercolor landscapes with extracts from twenty-nine of Mary Webb's poetry and prose works.

186 LINDSAY DUGUID. *"Maid in Shropshire."*

An article, clipped from the June 11, 2004 issue of the *Times Literary Supplement*, reviewing Helen Edmundson's adaptation of *Gone to Earth*. With a flyer announcing the performance of the play at the Lyric Theatre, Hammersmith.

187 GLADYS MARY COLES, ED. *Selected Poems of Mary Webb.*

Wirral: Headland Publications, 2005. Third edition, enlarged. Signed on the title page by Coles, and inscribed on the half-title: "To Mary and Bruce / —memories of Lyth Hill / and the Mary Webb Country / Gladys Mary / 6/June/06."

Although Mary Webb had occasional success publishing her poems in literary magazines and anthologies, she never realized her lifetime ambition of publishing a volume of her poetry. After Prime Minister Baldwin's posthumous tribute brought Webb's writing into vogue, her known poetry was hurriedly gathered together and published in *Poems and The Spring of Joy* (1928). A second volume, *Fifty-One Poems* (1946), was later published from an additional cache found among the papers of Webb's late husband. Gladys Mary Coles edited a third volume, *Mary Webb: Collected Prose and Poems* (1977). In *Selected Poems of Mary Webb*, Mary Webb's poems are for the first time arranged in rough chronological sequence to show the development of Webb's technique and imagery.

188 RICHARD MOULT. *The Secret Joy.*

France: Cynfeirdd [ca. 2005]. Compact disc recorded live at the Church of St. Mary Magdalene, Bleddfa, Wales.

This contemporary album is dedicated to Mary Webb, and sets a number of her poems to music.

"PRECIOUS BANE"

Synopses of the Six Novels, and a Selection of Poems   Mary E. Crawford

THE GOLDEN ARROW

Webb wrote her first novel in a burst of inspiration—in the space of just three weeks—after the she and Henry had returned to Shropshire from coastal Weston-super-Mare. *The Golden Arrow* (1916) was published when Mary was thirty-five by Constable & Company Ltd. On its surface, this is a simple rural tale of young lovers broken apart, and then made whole through suffering, a crisis of faith, and ultimate reconciliation. Yet, beneath the simple story, Webb wrote on a symbolic level to communicate her vision of the struggle of opposites, and the need for the individual to reconcile polarities into blended components of a whole.

The Golden Arrow is based upon an old Shropshire legend in which lovers earn good fortune by finding a mythological arrow—said to bond couples together if found on Palm Sunday on nearby Pontesford Hill. Webb uses the golden arrow of the legend as a metaphor to illustrate that true spiritual love both wounds and heals, and intermingles acute happiness and intense pain.

Webb creates a closely-knit, self-contained world in *The Golden Arrow*, made real through her poetic imagination and her evocative depiction of the Shropshire borderlands. The Devil's Chair—an ever-brooding granite mass that portends evil and ill luck—dominates the story. Webb contrasts the peaceful folds of the Wilderhope Range (where shepherds graze their flocks) with the jagged outcroppings of Diafol Mountain (home to the Lostwithin lead mine.)

John Arden, a shepherd, and his practical, sharp-tongued wife Patsy live with their daughter Deborah and son Joe on the slopes of Wilderhope Valley. Eli Huntbatch, a mean-spirited widower who preaches fire and brimstone, lives nearby with his shallow and self-absorbed daughter, Lily.

The plot centers on the relationship between sensitive, sweet-tempered Deborah and the dynamic young preacher, Stephen Southernwood, who desires and pursues Deborah. Stephen is an unconventional "free thinker" who now rejects the institutional religion in which he was raised. Stephen abandons his ministry and takes a job as foreman of the Lostwithin mine on Diafol Mountain.

Deborah cares for Stephen with a self-giving love:

> Deborah's love was the sweetest flowering of which humanity is capable, because it was primitive and spiritual. To give—to be with her man—to be so utterly at one that no explanation was ever necessary—to work, laugh, sleep and watch the splendid seasons together, being in other things than sex free and equal, and in sex so mutually generous as to forget self and rights—such was Deborah's idea of love. This idea, though vague, made her feel glorified and not lowered by giving herself to a lover.

Impulsive, immature, and suspicious of commitment, Stephen convinces a reluctant Deborah to live with him outside of marriage. Deborah risks local censure and moves with Stephen into the cottage he has restored beneath the shadow of the Devil's Chair. From the start, the massive outcropping casts an ominous shadow on their relationship.

A secondary story revolves around Deborah's kind but simple brother, Joe Arden. Joe is spiritually incapable of the passionate intensity of his sister's love for Stephen. He wants to marry Lily Huntbatch and father a brood of children. Lily consents to marry Joe, not because she loves him, but to escape her abusive father. Lily is also attracted by Joe's physical strength and flattered by his devotion to her. Yet Lily resents Joe's desire for a large family and dreams of being known as "pretty little Mrs. Joe Arden" with a trim figure and soft hands.

The novel incorporates a loving portrayal of Mary's late father (George Meredith) as John Arden, the compassionate father, shepherd, and mystic. John tells Stephen Southernwood about the golden arrow:

> "It's an old song, Stephen, and it's about an old ancient custom . . . And it was said that if two as were walking out found the arrow they'd cling to it fast though it met wound them sore. And it was said that there'd be a charm on 'em, and sorrow, and a vast of joy. And nought could part 'em, neither in the flower of life nor in the brown winrow."

John Arden acts as the moral center of the novel, around which the interwoven, contrasting stories of the two couples illustrate Webb's themes of spiritual love (with its requirement for self-sacrifice and suffering) versus profane (selfish and self-centered) love. Many incidents in the novel are designed to illustrate the difference between love and lust, givers and takers, and love and self-interest. To John Arden, God is "The Flockmaster," a personification of love, whose fold encompasses all. John believes in a love "that gives and asks naught," neither judging nor denying.

Deborah later persuades Stephen to marry her, not telling him that she is pregnant with their child. Stephen detests the idea of being tied down. On her wedding day, there are no good omens for Deborah's happiness. The wind rages and the surrounding environs are bleak and unforgiving. Disliking the desolate landscape when winter sets in, and feeling pressured by Deborah's clinging dependence, Stephen comes to feel that "a blight" has fallen on his love for her. Summer is over, and the symbolic drabness of autumn in the countryside around the cottage depresses Stephen.

> He was thinking how dull the country was getting, how forlorn. For the colours were withdrawing with what seemed to him the terrible leisureliness of fatality. They would soon be gone as the willow-wrens were gone from the woods below Lostwithin, as the cuckoos had long been gone from field and hill. The density was gone from the shadows, scent dwindled daily, the stars were like scimitars instead of silver flowers.

Stephen begins to loathe the countryside. His depression increases and (in his agnosticism) he faces the horror of emptiness—negation. Stephen's dread of nothingness is symbolized by the Devil's Chair.

> Any god—however mutable, however cruel—he thought, would be better than this nullity. Suddenly the whole thing was summed up and symbolized for him in the Devil's Chair—an empty throne. There it was; no devil, no angel, no god ever was there, ever would be, nothing . . . just vacancy and the insect-like lives of himself and the other millions in the world, all going nowhere for no purpose except extinction. He shuddered at the appalling picture. He could not get the look of the empty throne of black rock from his mind.

Stephen attempts to destroy the Devil's Chair with explosives, but fails to cause even the slightest damage. He has neither the strength of character to endure his situation, nor the shallowness to be indifferent to it. Stephen abandons Deborah (on the longest night of winter, St. Thomas' Eve), still unaware that she is carrying their child. Deborah believes the local legend that warns of ghosts collecting around the Devil's Chair on St. Thomas' Eve to elect a king. In panic and near-madness, Deborah piles their belongings in a heap and sets the cottage ablaze. In the darkness, Deborah stumbles across to Wilderhope to her parents' home. She finds her way by the lantern that John Arden has left alight, as a loving beacon on the longest, darkest night of the year.

With her father's patient love and understanding, Deborah eventually returns to health and gives birth. With the coming of summer (although she is still broken in spirit by Stephen's betrayal), Deborah begins to find spiritual peace. ". . . [B]ehind light and shadow, under pain and joy she felt a presence—too intangible for materialization into words, too mighty to be expressed by any name of man's. . . . only a conception as vague and volatile as light or scent . . . She was content with the balance of life as she found it, being dimly aware that the terror and the beauty intermingled in something that was more wonderful than beauty." At this moment, Stephen returns a changed man. Deborah rebuffs him kindly but firmly. Ultimately, John Arden helps to reunite the young lovers. "His [Stephen's] love for Deborah made him impregnable to terror, gave him a grasp of truth deeper than reason. He had found the golden arrow, to his own agony and ennobling."

GONE TO EARTH

Written in 1917, when all three of Mary Webb's younger brothers were serving in the trenches of the Western Front, *Gone to Earth* denounces the callous inhumanity of "civilized" man. Webb's second novel is a work of high imagination that reflects her horror at the slaughter of young soldiers, yet she never mentions the war that was devastating Europe at the time. Webb clothes her message in the setting and characters she knows best—Shropshire—and translates her anguish and compassion into poetic images.

The title of the book is taken from the hunter's cry, "Gone to Earth!" when the fox has fled into its underground den. Webb cries out through this allegorical story: why do men, seeing something innocent and beautiful, seek to destroy it? At its most basic, *Gone to Earth* is the melodramatic tale of a country girl's tragedy. Yet it is also a timeless, placeless morality tale of inhumane cruelty.

Gone to Earth tells of eighteen-year-old Hazel Woodus who lives in intuitive harmony with the creatures of wood and field. Hazel's Welsh gypsy mother has died years earlier, leaving adolescent Hazel ignorant of the ways of the world. Hazel exists as an emanation of her landscape. She lives with her aimless father, Abel, and her pet fox, Foxy, in a tiny hovel far removed from regular human contact. Along with her mother's book of spells, Hazel has inherited her deep kinship with the land.

Hazel Woodus feels infinite love and pity for persecuted and hunted wild creatures and a burning hatred of all forms of cruelty. Local superstitions and legends have a powerful hold on her mind (as they do for most country dwellers in Webb's novels). Hazel particularly dreads the Black Huntsman and the death pack, legendary beings who prey forever on the trail of the defenseless. She is doomed from the outset, destined to be hunted, a victim of the savagery of man.

Abel Woodus, Hazel's father, is a man without ambition and untroubled by convention. He is an aimless coffin maker, harpist, and beekeeper. When a village child dies, Abel is happy because he can then meld his three skills into a show of purpose: coffin making, mournful and melancholy harping, and the construction of new beehives from the leftover coffin wood.

Hazel's spontaneity, loveliness, and innocence attract two men —representing the opposing spiritual and physical sides of her nature—who compete for her attentions. Neither of them understands Hazel's spirit:

> She wanted neither. Her passion, no less intense, was for freedom, for the wood-track, for green places where soft feet scudded and eager eyes peered out and adventurous lives were lived up on the tree tops, down in the moss.

After her father threatens to kill Foxy for disturbing the chickens in their hen house, Hazel vows to marry the first man who asks her. Reverend Edward Marston asks for her hand in marriage. He respects the naïve young girl, and marries Hazel to protect her innocence. Out of mistaken chivalry, the simple preacher does not consummate his marriage, and fails to perceive that his new bride might hunger for physical intimacy as well as spiritual communion.

Responding only too willingly to Hazel's puzzled yearnings, the dissolute Squire, Jack Reddin, overpowers Hazel and takes by force what Reverend Marston does not take by right. The sexually awakened Hazel now becomes a divided being, torn between her conflicting spiritual and physical needs. Hazel loves her husband's kindly, tender, and sympathetic nature and she detests Reddin's cruelty and savagery. Hazel is nevertheless torn—the innocent victim of passion—feeling that she belongs more to cruel Reddin than to Marston.

Hazel is finally repelled by Reddin's brutality and returns to Marston, now pregnant with Squire Reddin's child. In spite of shocked protest from his mother and from his congregation, Marston shields Hazel from their scorn. Yet Marston's good intentions cannot protect his young wife in a world dominated by savagery. When Squire Reddin and his hunting party approach the rectory, Hazel mistakes them for the

Black Huntsman and the death pack. In a panic, Hazel shields Foxy in her arms and runs in terror. However, pregnant Hazel cannot run fast enough to protect her pet from the pursuing hounds. Unwilling to allow Foxy's dismemberment by the pack, Hazel leaps with her beloved pet over the quarry's edge—to their deaths.

Mary Webb offers no vision of hope or peace in *Gone to Earth*, only "shivering echoes." Her protest of man's inhumanity to man, implicit throughout the novel, becomes at the last a cry of primeval fear that encompasses all—"a voice, awful and piercing, deep with unutterable horror . . . clutched the heart of every man and woman." Webb's description of Hazel's tragic end is a masterpiece of word economy: "She was gone with Foxy into everlasting silence."

With the publication of *Gone to Earth*, Mary Webb gained the attention of critics and secured an admiring, if small, following in the literary world. John Buchan appreciated *Gone to Earth*, caught by its "beauty of phrase and exquisite perception of nature," the style "impregnated with poetry." Reviewers commented: "Mary Webb is unquestionably a poet" (Robert Lynd); *Gone to Earth* is "a book rich at once in beauty and excitement" (*Daily News*); "the passionate beauty" of the novel "conceived in a mood of poetry and mysticism" (Gerald Gould); "it is as a poet Mary Webb must be judged. Her narrative is strange, fantastic, symbolical" (*New Statesman*); and "*Gone to Earth* is the most impressive novel since Thomas Hardy gave us *Tess of the D'Urbervilles*. It has many points of resemblance to *Tess*. The chief of these is its possession of the great secret of tragedy, mastered by the Greeks and lost and reconquered in these later years only in a few solitary instances" (New York *Sun*).

Rebecca West, in her review for the *Times Literary Supplement* (August 30, 1917) declared, "This year's discovery has been Mary Webb, author of *Gone to Earth*. She is a genius, and I shouldn't mind wagering that she is going to be the most distinguished writer of our generation." Later in the same year, West proclaimed *Gone to Earth* as "Novel of the Year."

THE HOUSE IN DORMER FOREST

The House in Dormer Forest (1920), Webb's third novel, revolves around the ill-fated Darke family, whose members live together in uneasy proximity and are repressed by the atmosphere of their ancestral country mansion. Dormer Old House is described by Webb as "a mansion to the majority, a prison to the few."

Although *The House in Dormer Forest* is the most populated of Mary Webb's novels, Dormer Old House is the primary focus in this novel. Landscape takes on symbolic significance, and becomes the controlling background of the story. The opening chapter, which describes Dormer Old House in its setting, can be compared to the description of Egdon Heath at the beginning of Thomas Hardy's *The Return of the Native*. Both novels vividly convey a sense of place, and an awareness of the influence that landscape can exert over human endeavor. The fact that Webb doesn't introduce a human personality until the second chapter is an indication of the importance of setting to action.

Dormer Old House exerts an unwholesome influence on its inhabitants. The needs of the individual are subservient to convention and stifled by a demand for conformity:

> All these things you could see in clear weather, but when it was misty—and mist lingered here as of inalienable right—the house was obliterated. It vanished like a pebble in a well, with all its cabined and shuttered wraths and woes, all its thunderous "thou shalt nots." At such times it did not seem that any law ruled in the valley except the law of the white owls and the hasty water and the mazy bat-dances. Only those who slept there night by night could tell you that the house was overspread with a spiders-web of rules, legends and customs so complex as to render the individual soul almost helpless.

Against this backdrop, the Darke family acts out its drama: the rebellion of the four grown children of Solomon and Rachel Darke—Amber, Jasper, Peter, and Ruby. Grandmother Hannah Velindre (Rachel's mother) and distant cousin Catherine Velindre also form part of the Darke household, along with four servants—Sarah Jowel (kitchen maid), Mrs. Gosling (upstairs maid), Marigold (housemaid), and Enoch Gale (Dormer's earth-mystic handyman). Lively, ironic, sharp, and humorous, *The House in Dormer Forest* is more social satire than rural novel, with the action centered on human relationships.

Jasper Darke's rebellion is his refusal to accept religious dogma, which he perceives as "the idiotic hotch-potch of the churches." Dismissed by the Theological College where he has been studying, Jasper feels alienated by the hostile reception he receives from his parents and grandmother. Jasper works as a farm hand upon his return to Dormer Old House. In his spiritual loneliness, he is ensnared by his cousin, Catherine Velindre. Ultimately, the lovely but heartless Catherine spurns Jasper as an infidel when he refuses to "make the truth in himself a lie."

Peter Darke rebels against Dormer's moral class-code. Peter also desires his cousin Catherine, but is rebuffed by her and turns instead to the young housemaid, Marigold. Peter's passionate love for Marigold leads to Marigold's upbraiding and dismissal by Mother Rachel Darke. The headstrong and impulsive Peter defies his elders and marries where his heart lies.

Ruby Darke's materialistic nature leads her into a marriage to Ernest Swyndle, the clergyman (second only to Jane Austen's Mr. Collins in his bigotry and hypocrisy). The match is thoroughly approved by the elder Darkes, but Rachel soon realizes that marriage for ease rather than for love can be a loathsome trap.

The eldest child, Amber Darke, is a self-portrait of the young Mary Webb before her marriage. Amber has been a silent rebel all her life. Early on, she learns from handyman Enoch Gale how to survive the repression of Dormer House. Amber spends each dawn in the Bird's Orchard and forest far from the house. Unmarried at thirty, she is a failure in the eyes of her family. Amber loves "maternally, protectively, perceptively" and is spiritually sensitive:

> For Amber Darke was something of a mystic, though not exactly a religious mystic, nor that wilder, sadder creature, an earth-mystic. Sometimes she was deeply stirred by the beauty of Nature, but she did not live for it alone, as does the true child of the weeping god. Sometimes it was music that stirred her, or a stray sentence from the Bible, or the stars, or poetry; but most often it was the sudden rapture or the sudden pain of loving. Love would leap up in her at a chance touch of pathos in the most unpromising people. At these times she left the shallows of beauty that is heard and seen, and slipped out into the deep sea where are no tides of change and decay, no sound, no colour, but only an essence. In those waters nothing is but the spirit.

Amber has, however, paid a physical price for her intensity of feeling. Plain and sallow, she believes that "perceptiveness and emotional beauty, even the gift of humour must be paid for to the last drop of vitality."

Behind Old Dormer House is the Beast Walk, a steep avenue of fantastical animal shapes fashioned from primeval yew and holly trees by ancestors of the Darke family. In *Mary Webb* (1990), Gladys Mary Coles says: "the Beast Walk is one of Mary Webb's most extraordinary imaginative creations, a powerful symbol of the dark unconscious, and particularly of man's tendency to revert to the beast when dominated by 'herd instinct' or in upholding the 'isms' he has created." Jasper goes to the Beast Walk, tormented by his hopeless love for Catherine and miserable at his family's harsh treatment of him since his crisis of faith:

> He [Jasper] was realizing that there are depths of savagery in the human heart deeper than that of killing; that when law is put before love and the material before the spiritual there is nothing left wherewith to combat evil.

Amber, modest and graceful, finally finds true love when Jasper's idealistic and intelligent friend from Theological College, Michael Hallowes, comes to Dormer Valley to visit his friend. The calculating but beautiful Catherine Velindre tries but fails to snare Michael. Amber is then no longer "the honeyed flower that no bee visits."

The House in Dormer Forest is the most modern of Webb's novels. In it, she is preoccupied with the collective tyranny that dominates society and the need for the individual to discover and fight for the integrity of the self. Webb uses Amber Darke to express her beliefs about the unconscious mind:

> ... within, deep in the tenebrous recesses of sub-consciousness, man hopes to find God. Not in churches, not in his fellows, not in nature will he find God until he has seen all these things mirrored in that opaque and fathomless pool lying within his own being, of which, as yet, we know nothing.

Despite its range of characterization, humor, irony, and sureness of touch, *The House in Dormer Forest* is less of an artistic success than her first two novels. Webb is so eager to get her message across that she sometimes intrusively shouts over her characters instead of conveying her ideas through the drama of her story. In spite of her didacticism, most contemporary reviewers did not respond to the symbolized truths embodied in this novel. The reviewer for the *Bookman* (September 1920) recognized the "all-pervading humour. The description of the house and of people are touched with an agreeable wit," but "there is much of gloom in the story and a little of tragedy." The reviewer for the *Times Literary Supplement* (July 22, 1920) was less complimentary, saying that the world Webb creates is "a very gloomy place" and the impact of "so much unrelieved intensity is to produce not only gloom but monotony."

Mary Webb felt a fierce necessity to transmit her intuitions to the world through her writing. As Webb's convictions deepened, her literary ambitions increased. Webb was so distressed by the reviews of *The House in Dormer Forest* that she became ill, and suffered her first serious attack of Graves' disease in eight years (since before her marriage).

SEVEN FOR A SECRET

Webb's fourth novel, *Seven for a Secret* (1922), is set in the heavily-forested region where Shropshire merges into Wales, "the country that lies between the dimpled lands of England and the gaunt purple steeps of Wales—half in Faery and half out of it." The primary characters inhabit isolated farms and inns. Gillian Lovekin, the pampered, only child of a wealthy local farmer living at Dysgwlfas-on-the-Wild-Moors, is a self-absorbed, immature young woman who craves excitement and attention, her ultimate ambition being to go to London. Gillian's interferences and flirtations bring pain and suffering to herself and to others. *Seven for a Secret* contrasts Gillian's sensual infatuation with the wealthy but sordid innkeeper, Ralph Elmer, with her romantic love for her father's high-principled, devoted, and honest cowman-shepherd, Robert Rideout.

Gillian, considering that living in the county's capital city will be her first step towards eventual fame and fortune in London, persuades her prim Aunt Fanteague to invite her to stay with her in Silverton. Gillian gets her wish, and Robert Rideout is ordered to drive her on the farmer's cart to catch the train to Silverton. Robert is in love with Gillian. Gillian in her immaturity finds the moors lonely, whereas Robert cannot live away from them. Robert is of the land—almost a part of it—and, as with the land, Gillian scarcely notices him except to flirt—both because she enjoys making Robert confused and angry, and because she can get away with her misbehavior.

While in Silverton, Gillian lives with her Aunt Fanteague and spinster Aunt Emily. Aunt Emily's elderly gentleman-friend, Mr. Gentle, has been calling and courting fortnightly for years by reading to Emily and singing to her on the pianoforte. On a lark, Gillian entices Mr. Gentle into taking her rowing on the River Severn. The results are tragic: Mr. Gentle catches a chill and dies. Poor Aunt Emily loses her mind, and Gillian is blamed for the whole affair.

Gillian makes plans to escape to London during Mr. Gentle's funeral, and is prevented from doing so only by Robert Rideout (who had heard of the death and considered what Gillian's next move might be). Robert intercepts Gillian on the train platform, and then forces her back to Dysgwlfas, where he compels her into writing letters of apology to her aunts and making a mourning wreath for the late Mr. Gentle.

While Gillian is away at Silverton, Ralph Elmer comes to Dysgwlfas with his manservant, Fringal, and his mute housekeeper, Rwth. Ralph moves into the Mermaid's Rest, a recently-vacated inn, near a lonely and dreary stretch of land known as "the unket place" where evil seems to lurk. Isaiah Lovekin has earlier warned Robert Rideout: "you'll bear in mind as my girl's for none but a farmer, or higher." Isaiah encourages Ralph, a man of sufficient wealth to deserve Gillian, and hopes that Ralph's interest in her will help to take his undeserving cowman-shepherd's mind off his daughter.

> "She's with her aunties," he vouchsafed. "And there she'll stop for a while. Plenty of young fellows there, seemingly, as likes a slim waist and a fresh colour."
> "Is she walking out with anybody?"
> "She knows better. She'll bide at home till her dad says 'walk out.'"
> Elmer laughed softly. In the laugh was the secret glee of youth in its own freemasonry. This middle-aged man might be the best sheep breeder anywhere round, he might be a terror for making money, but with regard to his own daughter, Elmer judged him a fool. He'd soon see whether old Lovekin's daughter would bide at home if he—Ralph Elmer—said "walk out."
> "But you're not a marrying man," said Isaiah slowly; and Elmer blushed up to his hair at the implied discovery of his inmost thoughts.
> Isaiah was pleased with him for blushing—it was a confession of his own power. And what a foil for Rideout! Once those sparks were well lit in Elmer's eyes, Isaiah judged that most things—cowmen-shepherds included—would go down before his eagerness in attaining his desire.

As Robert Rideout feared she might, Gillian falls in love with Ralph after she returns from Silverton. To Gillian, Ralph represents excitement and passion, just as Silverton had. Gillian accompanies Ralph Elmer to the county fair at Weeping Cross even though, deep inside, she is beginning to realize that she would rather be with Robert Rideout.

At Weeping Cross, the dissolute Ralph seduces Gillian. Mary Webb is forthright in her treatment of the physical aspects of love, yet she handles the subject with great simplicity and naturalness. Webb's description of Ralph and Gillian's physical lust is highly charged:

> In the sifting moonlight brilliant eye met brilliant eye. A vitality greater than their own rushed through their veins and pounded in their breasts. They could no more help themselves than slaves bound for sacrifice on Druidical altars. They were bound for sacrifice on an altar older than mythology: the altar of one who reigns in fold and field, in town and village, in the castle and the hut, who is merciless and arrogant; at once lovely and hideous; who wears the garb of every creed and sect, but belongs to none; who hates virginity; who will be worshipped as long as there remain in the world maids and men; but whose worship is mysterious as the forest, and whose name is unacclaimed of any worshipper—for her name is unknown. She has lust in her treasury as well as love; yet, because of her deathless, keen, miraculous vitality, she is clean. And such is her witchery that those who have lived and loved without having known her feel cheated. But those who die in her arms are content as if they already lived in Paradise.

The morning after her tryst with Ralph, Gillian wakes to the awful realization that she loves Robert Rideout, not Ralph Elmer. Yet, when Robert and her father arrive in Weeping Cross, Gillian pretends that she loves Ralph knowing that otherwise Robert would kill Ralph for his transgression, and would then be hanged for murder. Ralph Elmer is coerced into marrying Gillian, even though he is already married to his housekeeper Rwth (a secret known only to his manservant, Fringal).

In time, Gillian finds that mere physical love loses its attraction. The struggle between egoism and unselfishness rages fiercely within Gillian. As Robert begins to have suspicions about Rwth's background, he persuades the unsuspecting Gillian to teach the mute servant to write so that she will be able to communicate. Rwth eventually reveals in writing to Robert (in the presence of Ralph and Fringal) the story of her abduction as a girl by Fringal, her marriage to Ralph Elmer, and his violence after she had given birth to their child. The baby was stillborn, and the shock caused Rwth to become mute. Thereafter, Ralph degraded Rwth and treated her as a slave-housekeeper. Because Robert still believes that Gillian loves Ralph, these revelations bring him no joy.

The next day, while coming home from rabbit hunting, Ralph sees Rwth gathering firewood in the lonely and dreary unket place. A malevolent impulse overcomes Ralph and he murders her, knowing that he can bury Rwth's body and—with it—the secret of his sordid past. Robert, hearing the gunshot and meeting a now-cheerful Ralph (who tells him that Rwth has left that afternoon for the city), is suspicious. Premonition causes Robert to return to the meadow late that evening:

> When he reached the gyland he heard a sound of digging. Frantic, hurried, yet careful digging. But before he had time to go over it stopped. He waited . . . An hour went by—more. Not till two hours had gone was there any sound. Then across the bridge, very stealthily, went Ralph. And as if in an ironic jest, the moon swam out and revealed every feature—every haunted, terrified feature of his face . . . And Robert knew, as surely as he had ever known anything in his life, that Ralph had murdered Rwth, had crept here to bury her, and had waited afterwards till enough snow had fallen to conceal his work.

Even though Robert Rideout hates the dissolute Ralph Elmer and wants Gillian for himself, Robert unselfishly wants Gillian's happiness more than revenge or his own contentment. Believing that Gillian loves Ralph, Robert prepares to take the blame upon himself. Knowing that the only way to save Ralph's life is for someone else to confess to Rwth's murder, Robert is prepared to make the ultimate sacrifice and die for the sake of Gillian's happiness. He agonizes over his confession note and plans to shoot himself, waiting only until the thaw so that his poor farm animals won't starve.

Gillian discovers Robert's intention, then learns the truth of Rwth's past and her murder, and throws herself at Robert's feet. Gillian's life—with sex, death and murder in its wake—eventually chastens her into a grateful lover. At the close of the story, she is ready to take her second chance at love with the devoted Robert Rideout, who has waited and suffered through Gillian's false marriage with Ralph Elmer.

Seven for a Secret was written in the year after the Webbs had moved to London. The interruptions and personal difficulties that Mary Webb experienced in adjusting to her life in London affected the evenness of her writing. This novel contains some of Mary Webb's worst and her best writing. The major characters (Gillian, Robert, Ralph and Rwth) are less real than symbolic—like the characters in an allegory or a morality play. Webb employs melodramatic exaggeration, and relies on coincidence to further the plot. Yet her descriptions of the moorlands are evocative, and suffused with a distinctive atmosphere. The minor characters in the novel are vividly drawn: irritating Aunt Fanteague, whose bonnet "seemed to have been built of bricks and mortar, not merely sewn"; influential farmer Isaiah Lovekin, "the legend of whose acumen is about them, like the protecting leaves of winter broccoli"; maternal Mrs. Makepeace who "saw all men as so many children, to be cared for and scolded, and, because

Jonathan Makepeace was the most helpless man she had ever met, she married him."

Mary Webb's most memorable minor character in *Seven for a Secret* is the helpless rustic, Jonathan Makepeace—always mildly surprised to be in trouble with inanimate objects. Webb depicts him with humor, affection and sympathy:

> If he gathered fruit, a heavy fire of apples poured upon his head. If he fished, he fell into the water. Many bits of his coat, and one piece of finger, had been given to that Moloch, the turnip-cutter. When he forked the garden, he forked his own feet. When he chopped wood, pieces flew up into his face like furious birds. If he made a bonfire, flames drew themselves out to an immense length in order to singe his beard. This idiosyncrasy of inanimate nature (or of Jonathan) was well known on the moors, and was enjoyed to the full.

Robert Lynd, in his introduction to the novel in the *Collected Edition of Mary Webb,* suggests that *Seven for a Secret* can be read as "a tale of the conflict between light and the powers of darkness," and describes Webb's "imaginative energy" as the characteristic feature of her writing. The novel was dedicated with permission to Thomas Hardy. Webb's dedication reads: "To the Illustrious Name of Thomas Hardy whose Acceptance of this Dedication has Made Me so Happy." The dedication copy of this work (cat. 85) has the following presentation inscription: "Mr. Thomas Hardy / with the greatest respect / and admiration from / Mary Webb. / Nov: 27th 1922. / 46. B. Leinster Square / London. W. 2."

PRECIOUS BANE

Webb's fifth novel, *Precious Bane* (1924), is set in rural Shropshire at the time of the Napoleonic Wars. The title refers to a passage from John Milton's *Paradise Lost:* "Let none admire / That riches grow in Hell; that soyle may best / Deserve the pretious bane" (I. 690–692). In *Precious Bane,* the story of Gideon Sarn (whose curse is his lust for gold) is interlaced with that of his sister Prudence (whose blight is her disfigurement from birth by a harelip). *Precious Bane* is a story of the triumph of the human spirit. It is told with the grace and simplicity that marks Mary Webb's fervent, romantic writing at its best. Webb makes adept use of Shropshire folklore, customs, and religious beliefs of the early 1800s, deftly weaving these into her tale.

Precious Bane is retrospectively narrated by Prudence Sarn who, as a "very old woman and a tired woman, with a task to do before she says good night to this world," recollects the incidents and tragedies of her early life at Sarn Mere (Sarn Pool). Using local dialect, Prue tells "the story of us all at Sarn, of Mother and Gideon and me, and Jancis (that was so beautiful), and Wizard Beguildy, and the two or three other folk that lived in those parts . . ." With a lyrical (almost biblical) rhythm, Mary Webb conveys her philosophical views through Prudence Sarn's homely and moralizing digressions. Prue's warm, rich personality—her simplicity and innocence, droll observations of human nature, and her "merry ways and her mocking ways"—permeate the book. The first-person narrator is intuitively sensitive to nature and its changing seasons. The environment of Sarn Mere dominates and pervades the story. Webb's descriptive prose evokes sound, smell, sight, taste, and texture in an unusually intimate and personal way.

For centuries, the Sarn family has farmed the land around Sarn Mere. Superstitious locals are afraid of Sarn Mere after dusk, because they hear church bells toll on the wind, and believe the sounds come from a village drowned in the mere's depths. Locals also believe that the dark and sullen Sarn men have had "lightning in their blood" since the time (during the religious wars nearly two hundred years earlier) when Timothy Sarn was twice struck by lightning. Growing up on an isolated farm with a loving nature—and unaware that her cleft palate is considered the physical manifestation of a curse, Prue gradually becomes painfully conscious of the locals' conviction that she is a witch who changes into a hare at midnight.

Gideon Sarn, Prue's brother, has rare gifts of physical and mental energy. However, Gideon is consumed by an obsession for wealth. When Father Sarn dies of a stroke (in a fit of anger at his son), seventeen-year-old Gideon ignores the superstition that Sin Eaters are irretrievably doomed. He eats bread over his father's coffin (thus ritually taking on the sins of his father in the tradition of the Sin Eaters of old) in exchange for his mother's promise of undisputed possession of the farm. Gideon intends to make "a mort of money" out of Sarn by working the land. With his fortune, Gideon plans to purchase a fine house in Lullingford, and to pursue both ambition and power among a wider circle of men.

Gideon extracts an oath of service from his sister: "I promise and vow to obey my brother Gideon Sarn and to hire myself out to him as a sarvant, for no money, until all that he wills be done. And I'll be as biddable as a prentice, a wife, and a dog. I swear it on the Holy Book. Amen." In exchange, Gideon promises an operation to repair Prue's hairlip: "I swear to keep faith with my sister, Prue Sarn, and share all with her when we've won through, and give her money up to fifty pound, when we've sold Sarn, to cure her. Amen." So that she may keep the farm accounts, Gideon arranges for Prue to learn to read, write, and cipher from the Wizard Beguildy. Prue joyfully learns to write and practices each Sunday by chronicling the week's events at Sarn Mere in her handmade, calico-covered book.

Gideon spares neither himself, his sister, nor his mother in his obsessive drive for material prosperity. After a few years of hard labor and thrift, their barn begins to fill with corn. Gideon has fallen in love with his childhood neighbor Jancis, the lovely daughter of Wizard Beguildy. Jancis returns Gideon's affections, and the two are betrothed. It is at a "love spinning" (where neighborhood women gather to donate a day's work to the bride-to-be) that Prue first meets the itinerant weaver, Kester Woodseaves. Prue immediately recognizes him as "a man to die for" but, with her harelip, never considers that he could return her love.

Prue Sarn's fervent love for Woodseaves is the secondary theme of *Precious Bane,* and contrasts with Gideon's fanatical pursuit of riches. Prue, although she is painfully shy, is as generous and self-giving as her brother is grasping. She is a fine, upstanding woman who does a man's work in the fields. When Wizard Beguildy (as part of his "Raising Venus" trick) orders his daughter Jancis to appear naked in front of a local squire, Jancis recoils, being afraid that Gideon will disown her if she does so. Prue kindly takes Jancis's place, and is "crucified in nakedness" as she is made to hang by ropes in the rosy light of Beguildy's room. Prue is mortified to see that both Squire Camperdine and Kester Woodseaves are in the room for the Wizard's demonstration:

> Did ever Fate play such a trick? Here was the one man out of all the world that I must hide from, since already I loved him so dear, and so must never hurt him with my grief. And there he was, so close in the small place that two strides would have fetched him to me. He was leaning forrard like the young squire, and he made to hold his arms out and then drew back and gave a sigh, and I know now that the desire of woman was stirring within him. It came on me then with a great joy that it was my own self and no other that had made him hold out his arms. For in that place he could not see my curse, he could only see me

gleaming pale as any woman would . . . And as I saw the squire's shoulders stooped forrard with the weight of his longing I knew for the first time that, whatever my face might be, my body was fair enough. From foot to shoulder I was as passable as any woman could be. Under the red light my flesh was like rose petals, and the shape of me was such as the water-fairies were said to have, lissom and lovesome . . . I hadna cared so much nor been so dismayed, at playing this foolish game afore a stranger. But now I was all one blush from head to foot, and cold as ice as well. Every second was an hour, and I was shamed as if I had gone whoring. Yet I couldna but rejoice to have given my body in this wise to the eyes of him who was maister in the house of me for ever and ever.

When life events become too difficult to bear, Prue finds a place of refuge in the attic among the stored apples. Kester Woodseaves uses the same attic as the place to do his weaving. It is in the attic, where Prue comes weekly to write in her journal, that she experiences a mystical intuition:

. . . a most powerful sweetness that had never come to me afore. It was not religious, like the goodness of a text heard at a preaching. It was beyond that. It was as if some creature made all of light had come on a sudden from a great way off, and nestled in my bosom. On all things there came a fair, lovely look, as if a different air stood over them . . . I cared not to ask what it was. For when the nut-hatch comes into her own tree, she dunna ask who planted it, nor what name it bears to men. For the tree is all to the nut-hatch, and this was all to me.

Prue recognizes that her harelip is her "precious bane," and realizes "how all this blessedness of the attic came through me being curst."

Gideon sacrifices his fiancée to his ambitions and, despite her protests, puts off marrying Jancis. Gideon maintains that Jancis and any babies would be more mouths to feed, delaying his goal of becoming wealthy. Encouraged by the newly-enacted Corn Laws, Gideon places even more of his land under cultivation. Wizard Beguildy apprentices Jancis as a dairy maid, and sends her away for three years to a remote farm. Prue writes love letters—ostensibly sent from her illiterate brother Gideon to his equally-illiterate but lovely fiancée Jancis. Jancis seeks out the weaver to read these letters to her, and Kester Woodseaves comes to appreciate Prue's lovely spirit. Unknown to Prue—and caring little about her cleft palate—he grows to love her.

Eventually, Jancis is so miserable in servitude that she runs away and throws herself upon Gideon's mercy. Forgiving Jancis her sin of forfeiting her wages, Gideon agrees to marry his fiancée a week after the upcoming harvest—so long as the harvest yield is good. As the golden stalks are gathered in, it seems as if Gideon's fortune is made. Contented at last, and choosing not to wait the few days until his wedding, Gideon takes Jancis to his bed. Tragically, in the hour of his apparent success, the prize for which Gideon had sacrificed so much is snatched from his grasp. Jancis's enraged father, the Wizard Beguildy, punishes Gideon by setting fire to his newly-harvested crop. All is lost.

Incensed, Gideon rejects Jancis:

> All he'd felt for her had died in the fire that night of September, and the sin of the father was visited upon the poor girl. For when Gideon's eye fell on her, he saw his burning ricks, and in her blue glance there were the red reflections of fire, as you will see on some clear morning the last wild smoulderings of the thunderstorm. That was all she meant to him now.

While the Wizard Beguildy is in prison in Silverton for arson, awaiting trial, Mrs. Beguildy and Jancis are turned out of their house. Impoverished and reviled, they have no choice but to follow the Wizard Beguildy to the county seat.

In the dark winter months that follow, Mother Sarn (who lives with Gideon and Prue) becomes increasingly enfeebled and can no longer work for her keep. Prue seeks the help of a local girl to watch over their mother while she and Gideon replant their blighted fields. Unbeknownst to Prue, hard-hearted Gideon secures poisonous foxglove tea. He sees to it that the local girl serves a strong brew of the lethal tea to his mother, who is fatally poisoned by it.

The following summer, Jancis returns to Gideon with their love child. Even after the birth of his son, Gideon remains unrelenting. In her grief, Jancis drowns herself and the infant in Sarn Mere.

Prue comes to learn of Gideon's poisoning of their mother, and confronts him. He does not deny it, but tries to hold Prue to her vow: "'You swore to do as I said.' 'Murder cancels all vows,' I answered." In scenes reminiscent of *Macbeth*, Gideon becomes haunted by the ghosts of his mother, his lover, and his child. A broken man, Gideon finally kills himself in the same deep mere where his hardness of heart had led brokenhearted Jancis to drown herself and their illegitimate child.

Even after his suicide, Prue cannot find the heart to fully condemn her brother:

> The whole of that great stretch of water wasna too much to make the grave of a man as strong as that one. The mile-long mist that lay upon the place wasna too grand a shroud. For though he was wrong, and did evil, and hurtid folks with his strength, yet he never did meanly, nor turned out bad work, nor lied.

Determined to leave Sarn Mere but concerned about the fate of the farm animals, Prue arranges to have them auctioned off at the next day's fair. While she is there, the superstitious fair-goers turn on Prue, condemning her for the deaths at Sarn Mere; for the fire; for the drownings; and for Gideon's suicide. The only cause the locals can see for these misfortunes is the curse of God, and Prue's hare-shotten lip is proof to them that she is cursed. As a mob, they tie her to the ducking stool to drown her—a fitting end for a witch. Only the sudden appearance by the weaver prevents Prue's death. Kester Woodseaves proves his love for Prue by saving her from death and then marrying her. The pair achieves "the peace to which all hearts do strive."

Gideon Sarn's bane—his single-minded lust for gold—costs him love and life. His physically deformed sister, who gives all she has out of love and loyalty, gets all that is worth having. Through the immense power of the written word, Prue gains the husband and the love that she thought could never be hers. Although childless, Prue is still happy, many years later, when she writes her story at the Parson's bidding, in order to tell the truth about herself:

> Ah! Those be the ways grouse laugh, and that was how I laughed in those days. But now I sit here between the hearth and the window, with the tea brewing for one that will be home afore sundown, and the clouds standing upon the mountains, and when I laugh, I laugh easy, like the woodpecker in spring. He was ever a laugher, was the woodpecker, and a right merry laugher too. He'll fly into an ellum tree, and laugh to see it so green. And he'll fly into an ash, and laugh to see it so bare, with only the black buds and no leaves. And then he'll fly into an oak, and laugh fit to burst to see the young brown leaves. Ah, the woodpecker's a good laugher, and the laughter's sweet as a sound nut. If we can laugh so at the end of long living, we've not lived in vain.

Precious Bane was awarded the Prix Femina Vie Heureuse Anglais for 1924–1925, given annually for the best work of imagination in prose or verse (descriptive of English life) by an author who had not attained sufficient recognition. Upon reading the book over the Christmas holidays in 1926, Prime Minister Stanley Baldwin sent a letter of appreciation to Mary Webb. (cat. 127 is Henry Webb's dedication copy of *Precious Bane* containing Baldwin's letter on 10 Downing Street stationery.) Baldwin's tribute to the neglected genius of Mary Webb (paid six months after her death, at a Royal Literary Fund dinner held in April 1928) brought Webb posthumous fame. This recognition led to the publication of the seven-volume *Collected Works of Mary Webb*, each volume of which became a best seller and was reprinted many times throughout the 1930s and 1940s, bringing wealth to Webb's publisher, Jonathan Cape, and to her husband, Henry Webb, and his new wife.

ARMOUR WHEREIN HE TRUSTED
[Fragment, published posthumously]

Armour Wherein He Trusted was unfinished at the time of Mary Webb's death, at age forty-six, in October 1927. This surviving fragment of a novel is a medieval romance set in the Welsh border country in the eleventh century, just after the Norman Conquest. The narrator is Sir Gilbert de Polrebec, now the Holy and Pious Abbot of Strata Florida. Sir Gilbert recounts his early life as a young knight, and his struggle as a young man to renounce his carnal and material desires in order to follow the spiritual callings of Christ.

As in *Precious Bane*, Mary Webb uses the first-person narrative form in *Armour Wherein He Trusted*. Webb expresses her own thoughts and attitudes through Sir Gilbert, and convincingly portrays the young knight's carnality and religious devotion. Webb's use of retrospective narration creates a sense of direct contact with the personality of Sir Gilbert—his relationship with his parents, his tortured love for his young wife, Nesta, and his struggle to give up hearth and home to follow Peter the Hermit on the First Crusade. Through her use of archaic diction and antiquated language, Webb evokes the spirit of the early Middle Ages in much the same way that—by her careful use of regional dialect, folklore, and superstition—she was able to convey a sense of rural Shropshire in her other novels. She deals with medieval themes, such as damnation versus salvation, flesh versus spirit, and good versus evil.

Webb also completely controls the authorial philosophizing that sometimes intruded in her earlier novels, and speaks instead through the mind of her protagonist and the action of the story:

> For if a thing is too near us, so that we cannot get the measure of it proper, and if it is too dear, so that no word is bright enow, then it is best to tell of some other thing, and in telling of that we shall tell of the dearest thing, though in roundabout fashion, for at such a time we stamp the image of our one thought on everything.

Unlike her other books, which were conceived over months of consideration but then written down quickly and with little revision (her first book, *The Golden Arrow*, was reputedly put to paper in only three weeks' time), *Armour Wherein He Trusted* was written in slow fits and starts. Gladys Mary Coles says in *The Flower of Light* (1978) that Mary Webb (in her usual method) had worked out in her mind the entire plot and characterization of this novel before starting to write. Although she did not complete the book, from allusions in the fragment we know that Nesta (during the seven years when Sir Gilbert is away on Crusade) will be sought after by many men; that Sir Gilbert's arch-enemy Ranulph Jorwerth will woo Nesta; that Sir Gilbert (in spite of his hatred for the man) will do some good deed for Jorwerth's benefit; and that this act will lead to Sir Gilbert's harm. Nesta's early death is also intimated.

Sir Gilbert tells of his meeting Nesta, who is newly arrived from Wales to be lady-in-waiting to Lady Powys. The twenty-three-year-old Sir Gilbert is bewitched by Nesta's plaited golden hair and lissome body and falls in love:

> I knew it was my love, though I had never seen her afore, and I was bewildered, standing like an oaf looking upon her under the leaves. I mused on her long, struck, as the heron is when he sees his mate imaged in the water. She seemed not troubled at all, to have a great fellow standing there, and by this I was sure she was a faery, since they know not fear.

Nesta is also favored by the King's escheator (Sir Gilbert's hated rival), Ranulph Jorwerth. Under questioning by Jorwerth, Nesta associates herself with necromancy and Arthurian legend:

> "I come from the Cymru, sir," she made answer, "and my home is in the waste; and my lineage is elf-lineage."
> "Where, then, is this waste situate?" asked the Escheator, eager as men are when a thing touches their own special business. . . .
> "Why, lord, it is faery ground and you cannot measure it nor go round it, for though it is only a narrow piece, times, of the width of three horses head to tail, yet, times, it will widen to eternity and yet again it will shrink to a knife-edge."

. . . .
"And your lineage?"
"It is from Merlin, lord. . . . Our land is faery copyhold."

Sir Gilbert ignores numerous spiritual callings to help rescue the Holy Sepulcher from the Infidels, and instead courts Nesta. For her part, Nesta initially resists Gilbert's marriage proposal:

> "It would be best for me and thee," she said, in a strange bewitched voice, "best that I go back to Tochswilla. Nine old witch-women to tend the cooking-pot. Nine wizards to tend the fire. No commands to be given, no love to be given, nought to do or think or feel. With thee, so much heart's joy, but sorrow and pain and anxious cares. The bread to make and manchets to apportion. Spinning and weaving and the ordering of the house." . . .
> "It is thy love, Gilbert, it is lover's love I am afeard of. My clay likes it not. It is not altogether mortal clay, and nearness frights me."

Yet Sir Gilbert and Nesta do marry. He brings her as his wife to Castle Polrebec, where they live with Gilbert's parents and his Aunt Gundrun. At Castle Polrebec, Sir Gilbert and Nesta are ecstatically happy. Sir Gilbert reminisces:

> Yet in my garden methought I had security of joy. If God ever thought of any better Paradise than dawn and June and a mountain garden, He hath not showed it to me. . . . It clung like a nest, this my garden, to the grey wall of our castle, and it was grey itself with the quiet greyness of doves. The lavender was all spiked over like a castle guarded by halberd-men, and the maiden pink held up fresh buds, the grey-leaved rose bloomed white beneath the heavy dews. There were no citizens of the litel grey garden save Nesta and I, the grey-brown bees and the portly grey pigeons walking in the sun, like abbots. And for me, my joy was as the joy of holy recollected folk, still, with nought in it of the raving of lust. And meseems no joy is sweeter than this.

Sir Gilbert has a premonition that this gladness will not last. "And as I was with Nesta in the litel grey garden I knew well that the hours were glass, bright glass, to crackle inward when God pleased."

A strange hermit-like man, almost at death's door, calls on a stormy night at the castle. Sir Gilbert's wife and parents resist the man's message and protest Gilbert's separation from them:

> "Gilbert Polrebec," he said, in his strange tongue, mingled of Saxon and some country French, "I come from Peter Hermit. Thou must return with me now, swiftly, for because of his old kindness for thy mother he

wills that thou go with him in this first glorious Crusade, walking beside him as his own familiar friend." . . .

So, turning anywhere to save me from his eyes, that caught me and lured me into a spell of terror, I looked toward the Christus on the wall. And behold, a dreadful marvel! For even as I looked, the image shuddered and two tears rolled down the face, and He did bat His eyes at me. And when I saw the Lord God so shuddering and weeping upon our wall, and when, in the manner of some poor babe denied of some sweetmeat or some revel, He did so bat His eyes and droop His head, I knew that I must go, and my heart turned in my side and my soul uttered a cry, and I forgot myself falling on darkness.

And so in the grey dawn we departed, leaving the castle all blinded and folded in mist, and the litel grey garden blotted out, and those three beloved ones weeping and groaning at the door where I was to go in and out no more until many a year was fled. But in the wan light of morning I saw that the Christus on the rood wept no more, nor batted His eyes, but seemed more at ease, satisfied as a child at some promise long withheld but, at last given.

As the fragment ends, Sir Gilbert learns news of his family in the first of three letters that he will receive during his time away at the Crusades.

Armour Wherein He Trusted is written with restraint and coolness, and lacks the warmth and vigor of Mary Webb's other five novels. In presenting Sir Gilbert's struggle to renounce corporeal desire—especially to leave his Nesta, who symbolizes for Sir Gilbert all that is earthly love and loveliness, Webb is allegorizing her own struggles with physical and spiritual desire. Webb may be using this tale to work through her longing for earthly beauty, even as she feels her own imminent death. Sir Gilbert voices his own premonitions:

And He that was and is my friend has said:
"Look long on the apple-blow, for you will not see it agen. Listen well to the mavis, for come a year I shall have invited thee to my house. And leaning from heaven's wall you will see the white thorn shining deep down, like snow in summer, and you will hear the mavis sing so faint and far away that you must fill up the glats in the song from memory."

Webb struggled for more than two years with *Armour Wherein He Trusted* before abandoning it entirely. Arthur St. John Adcock (editor of the *Bookman*), relates in his memoir, *The Glory that was Grub Street* (1928), that Webb had telephoned him in early 1927:

. . . in evident distress, [Webb] began saying how unwell she had been, then interrupted herself to say abruptly, "I have destroyed all I had done of the new novel." There was no immediate reply to my surprised, "Good lord, whatever made you do that?" and I have seldom heard anything more piteous than the subdued, broken sound of her crying at the other end of the line. Presently, when she could speak again, she blamed herself miserably, said she had felt so dissatisfied, felt that she could not finish it, and would never write any more, so, on a sudden impulse, had torn it and put it on the fire.

Hilda Addison, in *Mary Webb: Her Life and Work* (1931), writes that Webb's husband Henry saved the manuscript of *Armour Wherein He Trusted* from the fire.

Armour Wherein He Trusted was published posthumously as a novel fragment by Jonathan Cape in 1929, as part of the seven-volume *Collected Works of Mary Webb*. The manuscript of *Armour Wherein He Trusted* is the only known surviving manuscript of Webb's six novels (cat. 148).

A Selection of Poems

Caradoc Evans, in a short essay he wrote for the *Colophon* (Winter 1938) said that Mary Webb told him: "You have no idea how hard I work over a poem. . . . But stories—well, they just come to me and I write them without thinking and often I'm surprised at what I've written, so strange it reads."

Mary Webb thought of herself, in large part, as a poet. Her verses reveal the natural working of her mind. Early biographer Hilda Addison observed: "Undoubtedly it is true to say that from early adolescence, even from childhood, she had an unusual perception of the indwelling of the eternal in the temporal, of spirit in matter." (*Mary Webb: A Short Study of her Life and Work,* 1931)

When Mary Webb expresses herself in verse, her sharp eye for detail and her delicate awareness of words and rhythms serve her well. To express her deeply felt, intuitive response to the natural world, Webb used conventional nineteenth-century forms and traditional poetic structures, which were second nature to her (as she had been trained in poetic form by her father from early childhood).

The minutiae of nature hold deep significance for her. She is conscious of "beauty unseen," able to be reflected in words, yet ineffably beyond them.

In a review entitled "The Wing of Psyche" for the July 1926 issue of the *Bookman,* Webb speaks of the creative mind, particularly of the mind of the poet:

> The poet lets not his right hand know what his left hand doeth. He has little choice, little will. He is simply a listener on the shelving shores of the subconscious, hearing the mighty roar of far seas . . . Hardly ever does he do any conscious thinking. He listens; then he writes. Often he is greatly astonished at what he writes.

Mary Webb's approach to poetry is reflected in these six selections from her work.

Treasures (for G. E. M.)

These are my treasures: just a word, a look,
A chiming sentence from his favourite book,
A large, blue, scented blossom that he found
And plucked for me in some enchanted ground,
A joy he planned for us, a verse he made
Upon a birthday, the increasing shade
Of trees he planted by the waterside,
The echo of a laugh, his tender pride
In those he loved, his hand upon my hair,
The dear voice lifted in his evening prayer.
How safe they must be kept! So dear, so few,
And all I have to last my whole life through.
A silver mesh of loving words entwining,
At every crossing thread a tear-drop shining,
Shall close them in. Yet since my tears may break
The slender thread of brittle words, I'll make
A safer, humbler hiding-place apart,
And lock them in the fastness of my heart.

Green Rain

Into the scented woods we'll go
And see the blackthorn swim in snow.
High above, in the budding leaves,
A brooding dove awakes and grieves;
The glades with mingled music stir,
And wildly laughs the woodpecker.
When blackthorn petals pearl the breeze,
There are the twisted hawthorn trees
Thick-set with buds, as clear and pale
As golden water or green hail —
As if a storm of rain had stood
Enchanted in the thorny wood,
And, hearing fairy voices call,
Hung poised, forgetting how to fall.

Freedom

When on the moss-green hill the wandering wind
Drowses, and lays his brazen trumpet down,
When snow-fed waters gurgle, cold and brown,
And wintered birds creep from the stacks to find
Solace, while each bright eye begins to see
A visionary nest in every tree —
Let us away, out of the murky day
Of sullen towns, into the silver noise
Of woods where every bud has found her way
Sunward, and every leaf has found a voice.

The Birds Will Sing

The birds will sing when I am gone
To stranger-folk with stranger-ways.
Without a break they'll whistle on
In close and flowery orchard deeps,
Where once I loved them, nights and days,
And never reck of one that weeps.

The bud that slept within the bark
When I was there, will break her bars —
A small green flame from out the dark —
And round into a world, and spread
Beneath the silver dews and stars,
Nor miss my bent, attentive head.

Good-bye to Morning

I will say good-bye to morning, with her eyes
Of gold, her shell-pale robe and crocus-crown.
Once her green veils enmeshed me, following down
The dewy hills of heaven: with young surprise
The daisies eyed me, and the pointed leaves
Came swiftly in green fire to meet the sun:
The elves from every hollow, one by one,
Laughed shrilly. But the wind of evening grieves
In the changing wood. Like people sad and old,
The white-lashed daisies sleep, and on my sight
Looms my new sombre comrade, ancient night.
His eyes dream dark on death; all stark and cold
His fingers, and on his wild forehead gleams
My morning wreath of withered and frozen dreams.

A Farewell

Beloved, once more I take the winter way
Through solitude's dark mountains, purple and cold
As frozen pansies, toward my house of clay
Where winds shall drink my tears, and shadows fold.

I dare not dwell so near to ecstasy
Lest I grow reckless, seeing the dear, the good,
And so, beseeching for it childishly,
Should spoil its beauty and my womanhood.

Yet will the breathless moments when you smiled,
Looking upon me, haunt me. It is not well
Remembering, when winter floods are wild,
Becalmed lilies and the summer's spell.

Farewell, beloved! Since you have grown too dear,
I must be gone. I take my pilgrimage
In haste — so much I love you, so much fear.
Wisdom may grow from tears, peace fall with age.

Selected Bibliography of Writings by and about Mary Webb
MARY E. CRAWFORD

Works listed chronologically in each section

NOVELS AND POETRY

The Golden Arrow. London: Constable & Company Ltd., 1916. Light tan cloth, pink dust jacket. Trial binding: blue cloth.

Gone to Earth. London: Constable and Company Ltd., 1917. Black-stamped red cloth, tan dust jacket.

Gone to Earth. New York: E. P. Dutton & Co., 1917. First American edition, red-stamped brown cloth.

The Spring of Joy: A Little Book of Healing. London and Toronto: J. M. Dent & Sons Ltd.; New York: E. P. Dutton & Co., 1917. Green cloth.

The House in Dormer Forest. London: Hutchinson & Co., 1920. Gold-stamped green cloth; 2nd binding state: black-stamped red cloth; 3rd binding state: blind-stamped green cloth; 4th binding state: blind-stamped ochre cloth.

The House in Dormer Forest. New York: George H. Doran Company, 1921. First American edition, black-stamped red cloth with tan dust jacket.

Seven for a Secret. London: Hutchinson & Co., 1922. Black-stamped olive cloth, illustrated dust jacket.

Seven for a Secret. New York: George H. Doran Company, 1923. First American edition, blue-stamped light blue cloth, illustrated dust jacket.

Precious Bane. London: Jonathan Cape Ltd., 1924. Gold-stamped green cloth, tan dust jacket.

Poems and The Spring of Joy. London: Jonathan Cape, 1928. Volume five of the seven-volume uniform *Collected Works of Mary Webb*. With an introduction by Walter de la Mare. Gold-stamped green cloth, tan dust jacket.

Poems and The Spring of Joy. New York: E. P. Dutton & Company, Inc., 1929. Volume five of the seven-volume uniform *Collected Works of Mary Webb*. With an introduction by Walter de la Mare. First American edition, quarter orange cloth over paper boards.

Armour Wherein He Trusted: A Novel and Some Stories. London: Jonathan Cape, 1929. Volume seven of the seven-volume uniform *Collected Works of Mary Webb*. With an introduction by Martin Armstrong. Gold-stamped green cloth, tan dust jacket.

Armour Wherein He Trusted: A Novel and Some Stories. New York: E. P. Dutton &

Company, Inc., 1929. Volume seven of the seven-volume uniform *Collected Works of Mary Webb*. With an introduction by Martin Armstrong. First American edition, gold-stamped orange cloth, illustrated dust jacket.

The Chinese Lion. London: Bertram Rota, 1937. Gold-stamped quarter red cloth over batik patterned boards, in green slipcase. Limited edition of 350 copies.

A Mary Webb Anthology. Henry Webb, ed. London: Jonathan Cape, 1939. Gold-stamped blue cloth, black floral dust jacket.

A Mary Webb Anthology. Henry Webb, ed. New York: E. P. Dutton & Co., Inc., 1940. First American edition, gold-stamped quarter red cloth over green cloth.

Fifty-One Poems: Hitherto Unpublished in Book Form. London: Jonathan Cape, 1946. Gold-stamped coarse turquoise cloth, tan dust jacket.

Fifty-One Poems: Hitherto Unpublished in Book Form. New York: E. P. Dutton & Co., Inc. [no date; 1946]. First American edition, gold-stamped fine turquoise cloth, tan dust jacket.

The Essential Mary Webb. Martin Armstrong, ed. London: Jonathan Cape, 1949. Gold-stamped brown cloth, turquoise dust jacket.

Mary Webb: Collected Prose and Poems. Gladys Mary Coles, ed. Shrewsbury: Wildings, 1977. Gold-stamped green cloth, gold dust jacket.

Selected Poems of Mary Webb: Collected Prose and Poems. Gladys Mary Coles, ed. Wirral: Headland, 1981. Pictorial wrappers.

CONTRIBUTIONS TO ANTHOLOGIES

1923. Walter De la Mare, ed. *Come Hither*. London: Constable & Co. Contains three poems: "Green Rain," "The Water Ousel," and "Market Day," p. 10, p. 106, and pp. 141–142.

1923. Ernest Rhys and C. A. Dawson-Scott, eds. *Thirty and One Stories by Thirty and One Authors*. London: Thornton Butterworth, Ltd. Contains the short story "Blessed are the Meek," pp. 444–453.

1923. Ernest Rhys and C. A. Dawson-Scott, eds. *31 Stories by Thirty and One Authors*. New York: D. Appleton and Company. Contains the short story "Blessed are the Meek," pp. 364–372.

1924. Edward O'Brien and John Cournos, eds. *Best Short Stories of 1923*. London: Jonathan Cape. Contains the short story "Blessed are the Meek," pp. 316–322.

1925. A. St. John Adcock, ed. *The Bookman Treasury of Living Poets*. London: Hodder & Stoughton, Ltd. Contains two poems: "Foxgloves," and "An Old Woman," pp. 458–460.

1926. Lady Cynthia Asquith, ed. *The Treasure Ship*. London: S. W. Partridge &

Co. [no date; 1926]. Contains the short story "A Marriage has been Arranged, A Fairy Tale," pp. 175–185.

1926. Lady Cynthia Asquith, ed. *The Treasure Ship.* New York: Charles Scribner's Sons. [no date; 1926]. First American edition. Contains the short story "A Marriage has been Arranged, A Fairy Tale," pp. 175–185.

1926. Lady Cynthia Asquith, ed. *The Ghost Book.* London: Hutchinson & Co. Contains the short story "Mr. Tallent's Ghost," pp. 290–306.

1927. Lady Cynthia Asquith, ed. *The Ghost Book.* New York: Charles Scribner's Sons. First American edition. Contains the short story "Mr. Tallent's Ghost," pp. 290–306.

1927. Lady Cynthia Asquith, ed. *Sails of Gold.* London: Jarrolds Publishers. Contains the poem "The Secret Joy," and the short story "The Cuckoo Clock," pp. 53–54 and 93–105.

1927. Lady Cynthia Asquith, ed. *Sails of Gold.* New York: Charles Scribner's Sons. First American edition. Contains the poem "The Secret Joy," and the short story "The Cuckoo Clock," pp. 53–54 and 93–105.

1928. Lady Cynthia Asquith, ed. *The Treasure Cave.* London: Jarrolds Publishers. [no date; 1928.] Contains two poems: "The Yellow Hammer," and "Fairy Led," pp. 62–65.

1928. Lady Cynthia Asquith, ed. *The Treasure Cave.* New York: Charles Scribner's Sons. First American edition. Contains two poems: "The Yellow Hammer," and "Fairy Led," pp. 62–65.

1934. [Dorothy M. Tomlinson, ed.] *A Century of Creepy Stories.* London: Hutchinson & Co. Contains "Mr. Tallent's Ghost."

1947. Ellery Sedgwick, ed. *Atlantic Harvest: Memoirs of the Atlantic.* Boston: Little, Brown and Company. Contains the short story "The Prize," pp. 375–381.

1993. Johnny Coppin, ed. *Between the Severn and the Wye: Poems of the Border Counties of England and Wales.* Gloucestershire: The Windrush Press. Contains two poems: "The Mountain Tree," and "Hill Pastures," pp. 18 and 34.

2003. Jack Adrian, ed. *The Ash-Tree Press Annual Macabre 2003: Ghosts at 'The Cornhill' 1931–1939.* Ashcroft, British Columbia: Ash-Tree Press. Contains the short story "The Sword," pp. 35–42 (previously published in the *Cornhill Magazine,* April 1934).

CONTRIBUTIONS TO NEWSPAPERS AND OTHER PERIODICALS

Signed "Mary Webb (Mrs. H. B. L. Webb)," "Mary Webb," or "Mrs. Mary Webb" unless otherwise noted.

1907

[Anonymous]. "Railway Accident Shrewsbury." *The Shrewsbury Chronicle*, October 18, 1907, p. 2. Poem.

1909

Lady Day [Gladys Mary Meredith]. "A Cedar Rose." *Country Life*, July 10, 1909, pp. 47–48. Short story.

1911

Gladys Mary Meredith. "The Difference." *The Sphere*, May 6, 1911. Poem.

1912

Gladys Mary Meredith. "Very Early. A Poem." *The Vineyard*, March 1912, p. 360. Poem.

1913

Mary-Meredith Webb. "The Wild Rose. A Poem." *The Vineyard*, June 1913, p. 527. Poem.

Mary-Meredith Webb. "My Father's Path. A Poem." *The Vineyard*, August 1913, p. 663. Poem.

1915

"The Vagrant." *The English Review*, January 1915, pp. 134–135. Poem.

"An Old Woman." *The English Review*, October 1915. Poem. [Cited by Gladys Mary Coles, *Mary Webb*, 1990, p. 66.]

1916

Unsigned book reviews for *The Liverpool Post*, 1916. [Cited by Caradoc Evans, *The Colophon*, Winter 1939.]

1920

"The Ancient Gods." *The Chapbook*, vol. 2, no. 7 (January 1920), pp. 19–20. Poem.

"The Core of Poetry." *The English Review*, vol. 30 (February 1920), pp. 142–144. Essay.

"The Lost Orchard." *The Sunday Pictorial*, April 25, 1920. Poem.

"When the Thorn Blows." *The English Review*, November 1920, p. 392. Poem.

1921

"Caer Cariad." *The Bookman* (New York), February 1921, pp. 487–491. Short story.

"Anne's Book." *The Nation,* July 9, 1921. Poem.

"The Water Ousel." *The Nation and the Athenaeum,* vol. 29 (July 30, 1921), p. 648. Poem.

"Anne's Book." *The Living Age,* October 1, 1921. Poem.

"Praise." *The Sunday Pictorial,* November 20, 1921. Poem.

"Fruits of the Earth." *The Nation,* November 26, 1921. Essay.

"The Watcher." *The Spectator,* November 1921. Poem.

"The Name Tree." *The English Review,* December 1921. Short story.

1922

"Blessed are the Meek." *The English Review,* September 1922, pp. 210–216. Short story.

"Roots." *The Spectator,* November 4, 1922. Book review.

"Birds, Beasts and Trees." *The Spectator,* December 2, 1922, pp. 812–814. Book review.

"The Watcher." *The Living Age,* December 4, 1922. Poem.

1923

"Our Birds, Their Haunts and Nests." *The Spectator,* January 27, 1923, p. 152. Book review.

"Green Rain." *The Spectator,* March 24, 1923. Poem.

"Birds, Beasts and Flowers." *The Spectator,* March 24, 1923, p. 488. Book review.

"A Dream of Uriconium: The Return of the Romans." *The Shrewsbury Chronicle,* March 30, 1923, p. 4. Prose story.

"Shrewsbury's Abbey Fair." *The Shrewsbury Chronicle,* April 6, 1923, p. 6. Prose story.

"Green Rain." *The Living Age,* May 26, 1923. Poem.

"Wild Life in Many Lands." *The Spectator,* August 11, 1923, pp. 194–195. Book review.

"Sense and Sensibility Out of Doors." *The Spectator,* October 6, 1923, p. 465. Book review.

"When the Pie Was Opened." *The Spectator,* December 1, 1923, p. 856. Book review.

"Three Pleasant Books." *The Bookman* (London), vol. 65, no. 387 (December 1923), p. 152. Book review of *Grey Wethers* by Vita Sackville West; *Old Days in Country Places* by two authors; and *Why They Married* by Mrs. Belloc Lowndes.

"Natural History." *The Spectator,* December 8, 1923, p. 910. Book review.

"Novels of Country Life." *The Spectator,* December 15, 1923. Book review.

"Quite Wild Animals." *The Spectator*, December 22, 1923, p. 1002. Book review.

"Novels of Country Life." *The Spectator*, December 29, 1923. Book review.

1924

"Viroconium." *The English Review*, January 1924. Poem. [Cited by Coles, *Mary Webb* (1990) p. 125.]

"Novels of Country Life." *The Spectator*, January 26, 1924. Book review.

"Novels of Country Life." *The Spectator*, February 2, 1924. Book review.

"The Honey Bee." *The Spectator*, February 8, 1924, pp. 207–208. Book review.

"The Prize." *The Atlantic Monthly*, April 1924, pp. 468–471. Short story.

"Glimpses of Old Shropshire." *Transactions of the Caradoc and Severn Valley Field Club*, vol. 7, no. 3 (June 1924), pp. 87–93. Prose story.

"Delicate Savagery." *The Bookman* (London), vol. 66, no. 395 (August 1924), pp. 278–279. Book review of *Ghosts in Daylight* by Oliver Onions; and *The Play Box* by Mrs. Henry Dudeney.

"Owd Blossom." *Hutchinson's Magazine*. Short story. [Cited in *Armour Wherein He Trusted: A Novel and Some Stories*, 1929, p. 9.]

"A Pedlar of Leaves." *The Daily News* (London), October 30, 1924. Prose story. [Cited in *A Mary Webb Anthology*, p. 251.]

"The Young Man Merciful." *The Bookman* (London), vol. 67, no. 399 (December 1924), pp. 185–186. Book review of *The Old Ladies* by Hugh Walpole.

"New Year Customs." *T. P. and Cassell's Weekly*, December 27, 1924, p. 387. Book review.

1925

"In Memory of Charles Dickens." *The Dickensian*, vol. 21, no. 1 (January 1925), p. 12. Poem.

"The Authoress in Fiction." *The Bookman* (London), vol. 67, no. 399 (January 1925), pp. 230–231. Book review of *Laura: A Cautionary Story* by Ethel Sidgwick; *The Colour of Youth* by V. H. Friedlaender; and *Justice Walk* by Constance Smedley.

"Dabbling in the Dew." *The Spectator*, March 21, 1925, pp. 471–472. Book review.

"Unpleasant Fiction." *The Bookman* (London), vol. 68, no. 403 (April 1925), pp. 6–15. Symposium: A range of authors are asked to give their views on current "sex novels;" Mary Webb's comments are on p. 12.

"Studies in Atmosphere." *The Bookman* (London), vol. 68, no. 403 (April 1925), pp. 32–33. Book review of *The Romantic Tradition* by Beatrice Kean Seymour; and *Soames Green* by M. R. Larminie.

"A Yellow Sanded Grove." *The Bookman* (London), vol. 68, no. 404 (May 1925), pp. 124–125. Book review of *The Goat and Compasses* by Martin Armstrong; and *The Twelve Saints* by Ruth Manning-Saunders.

"Morton Luce." *The Bookman* (London), vol. 68, no. 405 (June 1925), pp. 32–33. Bookman Gallery book review of *The Sonnets of Victorian Morton Luce.*

"The Wayfaring Tree." *The Spectator*, June 27, 1925, p. 1052. Book review.

"Hark How the Birds Do Sing." *T. P. and Cassell's Weekly*, June 27, 1925, p. 324. Book review.

"Over the Hills and Far Away." *The Road, A Quarterly Review*, vol. 4, no. 22 (July 1925), pp. 461–463. Short story.

"The Soul of Australia." *The Bookman* (London), vol. 69, no. 409 (October 1925), pp. 44–45. Book review of *Daimon* by E. L. Grant Watson.

"Helen Prothero Lewis." *The Bookman* (London), vol. 69, no. 410 (November 1925), pp. 111–112. Bookman Gallery book review of *The Hill Beyond* by Helen Prothero Lewis.

"A Will-o'-the-Wisp from the Steppes." *The Bookman* (London), vol. 69, no. 411 (December 1925), pp. 178–179. Book review of *The Dancer's Cat* by C. A. Nicholson.

1926

"Beyond the Sea." *The Bookman* (London), vol. 69, no. 412 (January 1926), pp. 226–227. Book review of *Doda* by Marcu Beza; *Barren Ground* by Ellen Glasgow; *Black Swans* by M. L. Skinner; *Mary Glenn* by Sarah G. Millin; and *Marsh Fires* by Mary Brearley.

"Glorious Apollo." *The Bookman* (London), vol. 69, no. 414 (March 1926), pp. 314–315. Book review of *Glorious Apollo* by E. Barrington.

"Contrast." *The Bookman* (London), vol. 70, no. 415 (April 1926), p. 52. Book review of *Hangman's House* by Donn Byrne; and *Whipped Cream* by Geoffrey Moss.

"John Halifax Gentleman." *T. P. and Cassell's Weekly*, April 3, 1926, p. 844. Book review.

"The Poetry of the Prayer Book." *T. P. and Cassell's Weekly*, April 17, 1926, p. 904. Essay.

"Plus Que De L'Esprit." *The Bookman* (London), vol. 70, no. 416 (May 1926), pp. 130–131. Book review of *Mape* by André Maurois.

"The Wing of Psyche." *The Bookman* (London), vol. 70, no. 418 (July 1926), p. 214. Book review of *The Art of Thought* by Graham Wallas.

"Pilgrims of Eternity." *The Bookman* (London), vol. 70, no. 419 (August 1926), pp. 265–266. Book review of *Desert: a Legend* by Martin Armstrong.

"A Posy of Sweet Flowers." *The Bookman* (London), vol. 70, no. 420

(September 1926), pp. 300–301. Book review of *A Bouquet from France* by Wilfred Thorley; and *A Hundreth Sundrie Flowres*, ed. Wilfred Thorley.

"Knowest Thou the Land?" *The Bookman* (London), vol. 71, no. 422 (November 1926), pp. 122–123. Book review of *Far End* by May Sinclair.

"One Coming from Calvary." *The Bookman* (London), vol. 71, no. 423 (December 1926), pp. 177–178. Book review of *Before the Bombardment* by Osbert Sitwell.

"Portrait of a Gentleman." *The Bookman* (London), vol. 71, no. 423 (December 1926), pp. 192–193. Book review of *Dust on the Wind* by C. A. Nicholson.

1927

"Our Immortal Jane." *The Bookman* (London), vol. 71, no. 425 (February 1927), pp. 256–258. Book review of the Clarendon Press edition of *The Novels of Jane Austen*, edited by R. W. Chapman and published by Oxford University Press.

"Little Miss Burney." *The Bookman* (London), vol. 72, no. 429 (June 1927), pp. 163–164. Book review of *The Story of Fanny Burney* by Muriel Masefield.

"Counsels of Perfection." *The Bookman* (London), vol. 72, no. 430 (July 1927), pp. 229–230. Book review of *From Place to Place* by Irvin Cobb; *The Golden Key* by Henry van Dyke; and *Lucky Numbers* by Montague Glass.

"Irony and Mrs. Wharton." *The Bookman* (London), vol. 72, no. 432 (September 1927), p. 303. Book review of *Twilight Sleep* by Edith Wharton.

1928

"Blessed are the Meek." *The Argosy*, vol. 4, no. 27 (August 1928), pp. 103–105. Short story. [Previously published in *The English Review*, September 1922.]

"In Affection and Esteem: A Hitherto Unpublished Story." *John o' London's Weekly*, vol. 20, no. 503 (December 8, 1928). Short story.

1929

"The Bread House." *The Argosy*, vol. 5, no. 33 (February 1929), pp. 73–76. Short story.

BIOGRAPHIES

1930. W. Reid Chappell. *The Shropshire of Mary Webb*. London: Cecil Palmer.

1931. Hilda Addison. *Mary Webb: A Short Study of Her Life and Work*. London: Cecil Palmer.

1932. Thomas Moult. *Mary Webb: Her Life and Work*. London: Jonathan Cape.

1948. W. Byford-Jones. *Shropshire Haunts of Mary Webb*. Shrewsbury (Shropshire): Wilding and Son, Ltd.

1964. Dorothy P. H. Wrenn. *Goodbye to Morning: A Biographical Study of Mary Webb*. Shrewsbury (Shropshire): Wilding and Son, Limited.

1970. Vincent Waite. *Shropshire Hill Country*. London: J. M. Dent and Sons Limited.

1977. Bernard Steff. *My Dearest Acquaintance: A Biographical Sketch of Mary and Henry Webb*. Ludlow (Shropshire): The Kings' Bookshop.

1978. Gladys Mary Coles. *The Flower of Light: A Biography of Mary Webb*. London: Duckworth; paperback reissue, Wirral (Wales): Headland Publications, 1998.

1981. Gordon Dickens. *Mary Webb: A Narrative Bibliography of her Life and Work*. Shrewsbury (Shropshire): Shropshire Libraries.

1986. Michèle Aina Barale. *Daughters and Lovers: The Life and Writing of Mary Webb*. Middletown (Connecticut): Wesleyan University Press.

1990. Gladys Mary Coles. *Mary Webb*. Bridgend (Wales): Seren Books, reprinted 1996.

1990. Linda Davies. *Mary Webb Country: An Introduction to her Life and Work*. Ludlow (Shropshire): Palmer's Press.

BOOKS WITH SECTIONS ABOUT WEBB

1928. G. K. Chesterton. "Introduction," *The Golden Arrow*. London: Jonathan Cape, pp. 7–10.

1928. John Buchan. "Introduction," *Gone to Earth*. London: Jonathan Cape, pp. 7–10.

1928. H. R. L. Sheppard. "Introduction," *The House in Dormer Forest*. London: Jonathan Cape, pp. 9–12.

1928. Robert Lynd. "Introduction," *Seven for a Secret*. London: Jonathan Cape, pp. 11–13.

1928. Stanley Baldwin. "Introduction," *Precious Bane*. London: Jonathan Cape, pp. 5–8.

1928. Walter De la Mare. "Introduction," *Poems and The Spring of Joy*. London: Jonathan Cape, pp. 13–19.

1928. A. St. John Adcock. *The Glory that was Grub Street: Impressions of Contemporary Authors*. London: Sampson, Lowe, Marston & Co., Ltd. [no date; 1928], pp. 321–330.

1929. Martin Armstrong. "Introduction," *Armour Wherein He Trusted: A Novel and Some Stories*. London: Jonathan Cape, pp. 11–16.

1933. A. Edward Newton. *End Papers: Literary Recreations*. Boston: Little, Brown & Company, pp. 36–46.

1934. Paul Jordan-Smith. *For the Love of Books: The Adventures of an Impecunious Collector.* New York: Oxford University Press, pp. 76–81.

1934. Frank Swinnerton. *The Georgian Literary Scene 1910–1935.* London: Hutchinson, pp. 246–248.

1934. Frank Swinnerton. *The Georgian Scene: A Literary Panorama.* New York: Farrar and Rinehart, pp. 313–315.

1935. A. R. Reade. *Main Currents in Modern Literature.* London: Ivor Nicholson and Watson Limited, pp. 197–213.

1935. Magdalene M. Weale. *Through the Highlands of Shropshire on Horseback.* London: Heath Cranton Limited, pp. 233–261.

1935. Ilse Knapp. *Die Landschaft im modernen englischen Frauen-roman.* Tübingen: University of Tübingen, pp. 81–94.

1936. Ernest A. Baker. *The History of the English Novel.* London: H. F. & G. Witherby, pp. 221–226 and p. 239.

1936. Margaret Lawrence. *The School of Femininity.* New York: Frederick A. Stokes, pp. 331–338.

1937. Susan Tweedsmuir. "Mary Webb," *Dictionary of National Biography, 1922–1930.* Oxford: Oxford University Press, pp. 901–902.

1937. Marcelle Magdinier. "Mary Webb: apôtre et poète de la pitié," *Études,* vol. 233 (December 20, 1937), pp. 752–764.

1938. James Carr. "The Novels of Mary Webb," *Papers of the Manchester Literary Club,* vol. 63 (1938), Manchester: Sherratt & Hughes, pp. 1–16.

1938. Oscar H. Shephard. "The Essays of Mary Webb," *Papers of the Manchester Literary Club,* vol. 63 (1938), Manchester: Sherratt & Hughes, pp. 17–22.

1946. Ellery Sedgwick. *The Happy Profession.* Boston: Little, Brown & Company, pp. 192–196.

1947. Ellery Sedgwick. *Atlantic Harvest: Memoirs of The Atlantic.* Boston: Little, Brown & Company, p. 375.

1949. Martin Armstrong. "Introduction," *The Essential Mary Webb.* London: Jonathan Cape, pp. 7–10.

1954. Susan Tweedsmuir. *A Winter Bouquet.* London: Gerald Duckworth & Co. Ltd., pp. 110–115.

1954. Lucien Leclaire. *Le Roman régionaliste dans les Iles Britanniques: 1800–1950.* Paris: Société d'Édition, pp. 168, 172–174, 177, 219, 245, 258n, and 274.

1954. Lucien Leclaire. *A General Analytical Bibliography of the Regional Novelists of the British Isles: 1800–1950.* Paris: Société d'Édition, pp. 288–290.

1956. Percy Muir. *Minding My Own Business: An Autobiography.* London: Chatto & Windus, pp. 198–201.

1960. Frank Shepherd. *Many Mansions.* Leigh-on-Sea: Citizen Publishing Co. Ltd., pp. 20–27.

1962. David A. Randall. *Dukedom Large Enough.* New York: Random House, pp. 170–174.

1966. Charles Sanders. "Mary Webb: An Introduction." *English Literature in Transition (1880–1920),* vol. 9, no. 3 (1966), pp. 115–118.

1966. Charles Sanders. "Mary Webb: An Annotated Bibliography of Writings about Her." *English Literature in Transition (1880–1920),* vol. 9, no. 3 (1966), pp. 119–136.

1967. Charles Sanders. "*The Golden Arrow:* Mary Webb's 'Apocalypse of Love.'" *English Literature in Transition (1880–1920),* vol. 10, no. 1 (1967), pp. 1–8.

1971. Michael S. Howard. *Jonathan Cape, Publisher.* London: Jonathan Cape, pp. 98–102.

1972. Claude Cockburn. *Bestseller: The Books Everyone Read 1900–1939.* London: Sidgwick & Jackson, pp. 173–181.

1972. Barbara Hannah. *Striving Towards Wholeness.* London: George Allen & Unwin Ltd., pp. 72–104.

1977. Glen Cavaliero. *The Rural Tradition in the English Novel 1900–1939.* London and Basingstoke: The Macmillan Press Ltd., pp. 133–146.

1984. Erika Duncan. *Unless Soul Clap its Hands: Portraits and Passages.* New York: Schocken Books, pp. 153–177.

1994. Gladys Mary Coles. *The Echoing Green.* Hexham (Northumberland): Flambard Press, pp. 51–70.

1998. Reggie Oliver. *Out of the Woodshed: The Life of Stella Gibbons.* London: Bloomsbury Publishing PLC, pp. 63–66 and 111–118.

REVIEWS AND BIOGRAPHICAL NOTICES OF WEBB

1916

"New Novels" (review of *The Golden Arrow*). *Times Literary Supplement,* September 7, 1916, p. 428.

1917

"New Novels" (review of *The Golden Arrow*). *The Nation,* March 29, 1917.

"The New Books" (review of *The Golden Arrow*). *The Outlook,* no. 115 (April 11, 1917), p. 668.

"The Golden Arrow." *The New York Times Book Review,* May 6, 1917, p. 183.

"Notes on New Fiction" (review of *The Golden Arrow*). *The Dial,* vol. 62 (May 7, 1917), pp. 443–444.

Helene Cross (review of *The Golden Arrow* and *Gone to Earth*). *The Bookman* (New York), vol. 45 (March–August 1917).

"Amid the Hills of Wales" (review of *The Golden Arrow*). *The Independent* (London), June 2, 1917, p. 438.

"Gone to Earth." *The New York Times Book Review,* August 26, 1917, p. 318.

Rebecca West. "Gone to Earth." *Times Literary Supplement,* August 30, 1917, p. 416.

"List of New Books" (review of *Gone to Earth*). *The Athenaeum,* no. 4621 (September 1917), p. 471.

D. P. Berenberg. "Gone to Earth." *New York Call,* September 9, 1917, p. 15.

"Notes on New Fiction" (review of *Gone to Earth*). *The Dial,* vol. 63 (September 13, 1917), p. 220.

"Among the 'Localists'" (review of *Gone to Earth*). *The Nation,* vol. 105 (September 20, 1917), p. 317.

"Readable Novels" (review of *Gone to Earth*). *The Spectator,* vol. 119 (September 22, 1917), p. 300.

1920

"New Novels" (review of *The House in Dormer Forest*). *Times Literary Supplement,* July 22, 1920, p. 471.

"Novels in Brief" (review of *The House in Dormer Forest*). *The Athenaeum,* no. 4710 (August 6, 1920), p. 179.

"The House in Dormer Forest." *The London Mercury,* no. 11 (September 1920), pp. 626–627.

1921

D. L. Mann. "The House in Dormer Forest." *Boston Evening Transcript,* vol. 26 (January 1921), p. 8.

"The House in Dormer Forest." *The New York Times,* January 30, 1921, p. 23.

Mary Alden Hopkins. "Family Fetishes" (review of *The House in Dormer Forest*). *Publisher's Weekly,* no. 99 (February 19, 1921), p. 574.

"New Novels" (review of *The House in Dormer Forest*). *The Outlook,* no. 128 (May 4, 1921), p. 28.

"Rebels" (review of *The House in Dormer Forest*). *The Nation,* no. 112 (May 25, 1921), p. 749 and pp. 791–792.

1922

"New Novels" (review of *Seven for a Secret*). *Times Literary Supplement,* November 9, 1922, p. 726.

"The Heart of the Country" (review of *Seven for a Secret*). *The Spectator*, no. 129 (November 11, 1922), p. 666.

Gerald Gould. "New Fiction" (review of *Seven for a Secret*). *Saturday Review*, vol. 134 (December 2, 1922), pp. 843–844.

Louis J. McQuilland. "Seven for a Secret." *John o' London's Weekly*, vol. 8, no. 191 (December 2, 1922), p. 324.

1923

Raymond Mortimer. "New Novels" (review of *Seven for a Secret*). *New Statesman*, no. 20 (January 27, 1923), p. 485.

Edwin Pugh. "Mary Webb" (review of *Precious Bane*). *The Bookman* (London), vol. 64 (April 1923), pp. 7–8.

"Seven for a Secret." *The New York Times*, May 20, 1923, p. 19.

E. W. Osborn. "His Love Points the Way of Life to Young Rideout" (review of *Seven for a Secret*). *The World* (New York), May 27, 1923, p. 6E.

H. W. Boynton. "Seven for a Secret." *The Independent*, no. 60 (June 23, 1923), p. 406.

J. K. Singleton. "New Novels" (review of *Seven for a Secret*). *The New Republic*, no. 30 (June 27, 1923), p. 129.

D. L. Mann. "Seven for a Secret." *Boston Evening Transcript*, July 3, 1923, p. 6.

Lillian Gilkes. "Rural Romance" (review of *Seven for a Secret*). *New York Tribune, Book News and Reviews*, July 22, 1923, p. 23.

"A Slender Welsh Story" (review of *Seven for a Secret*). *Springfield Republican* (Springfield, Massachusetts), July 22, 1923, p. 7A.

H. H. "Seven for a Secret." *Literary Digest International Book Review*, vol. 1 (September 1923), pp. 59–60.

"Books in Brief" (review of *Seven for a Secret*). *The Nation*, no. 67 (October 10, 1923), p. 410.

"Seven for a Secret." *The Evening Post* (New York), *Literary Review*, October 20, 1923, p. 165.

1924

"New Novels" (review of *Precious Bane*). *Times Literary Supplement*, July 17, 1924, p. 448.

L. P. Hartley. "Sacred and Profane Love" (review of *Precious Bane*). *The Spectator*, no. 138 (August 2, 1924), p. 168.

Austin Clarke. "Novels" (review of *Precious Bane*). *The Nation and the Athenaeum*, vol. 35 (August 2, 1924), pp. 560–570.

T. P. O'Connor. "The Hunger for the Land" (Book of the Week: review of *Precious Bane*). *T. P. & Cassell's Weekly*, August 24, 1924, pp. 487–488.

Gerald Gould. "New Fiction" (review of *Precious Bane*). *Saturday Review*, vol. 138 (August 30, 1924), p. 221.

John Franklin. "New Novels" (review of *Precious Bane*). *New Statesman*, no. 23 (August 30, 1924), p. 599.

Edwin Pugh. "Promise and Performance" (review of *Precious Bane*). *The Bookman* (London), vol. 66 (September 1924), p. 324.

"Mary Webb Writing Short Stories." *T. P.'s and Cassell's Weekly*, December 20, 1924. [Cited by Gladys Mary Coles in *The Flower of Light*, p. 273.]

1925

"Mary Webb returned from Shropshire and Radnorshire seeking inspiration for her new novel." *T. P.'s and Cassell's Weekly*, June 6, 1925, p. 200. [Cited by Gladys Mary Coles in *The Flower of Light*, p. 283.]

1926

"Telegrams in Brief" (notice of award of Prix Femina Vie Heureuse for 1924–1925 to Mary Webb for *Precious Bane*). *The Times* (London), February 12, 1926, p. 11.

L. M. Field. "Precious Bane." *Literary Review (New York Evening Post)*, May 29, 1926, p. 3.

S. L. Cook. "Precious Bane." *Boston Transcript*, June 5, 1926, p. 5.

J. W. C. "Precious Bane." *New York World*, June 6, 1926, p. 4.

Mary Kolars. "A Shropshire Tragedy" (review of *Precious Bane*). *New York Herald Tribune, Books*, June 6, 1926, p. 12.

"Precious Bane." *The New York Times*, June 20, 1926, p. 8.

"Anglo-French Literary Prizes Presented." *The Times* (London), July 7, 1926, p. 18.

"Precious Bane." *Saturday Review of Literature* (New York), vol. 2 (July 17, 1926), p. 939.

"The New Books" (review of *Precious Bane*). *The Outlook*, no. 143 (July 28, 1926), p. 449.

L. Moore. "Precious Bane." *Literary Digest International Book Review*, August 26, 1926, p. 548.

E. M. J. "Precious Bane." *Springfield Republican* (Springfield, Massachusetts), September 26, 1926, p. 7.

Marian Vaillant. "Precious Bane." *The Atlantic Monthly*, vol. 138, no. 22 (September 1926), p. 22 and p. 24.

"Precious Bane." *Booklist*, vol. 23 (November 1926), p. 85.

1927

Caradoc Evans, ed. (notice of Mary Webb's death). *T. P. and Cassell's Weekly*, December 31, 1927.

Arthur St. John Adcock, ed. "The Bookman's Diary" (notice of Mary Webb's death). *The Bookman* (London), vol. 72, no. 432 (December 1927).

"Notice of Mary Webb's Death on October 8, 1927." *The Dickensian*, vol. 24, no. 205 (Winter 1927–1928), p. 75.

1928

"Royal Literary Fund, 138th Anniversary Dinner: Mr. Baldwin's Speech." *The Times* (London), April 26, 1928, p. 18.

"Mrs. Mary Webb" (obituary). *The Times* (London), April 27, 1928, p. 21.

Arnold Bennett. "Books and Persons" (comments on Baldwin's speech and Mary Webb's novels). *The Evening Standard*, May 3, 1928.

"Books that Should Sell." *The New York Times*, May 9, 1928, p. 24.

J. C. Squire. "Mary Webb." *The London Mercury*, May 1928, pp. 6–8.

"The Case of Mary Webb." *Constable's Monthly List*, May 1928, pp. 5–6.

Ernest Marshall. "Baldwin Aids Sale of Obscure Books." *The New York Times*, May 13, 1928, section 3, p. 7.

"News and Views of Literary London." *The New York Times Book Review*, May 20, 1928, p. 10.

Daphne Clare. "The Life Story of Mary Webb." *The Evening Standard*, June 8, 1928, p. 18.

Mary Webb. "*The Golden Arrow.* Begin to enjoy it today" (the first installment of Webb's novel serialized daily through August 1928). *The Evening Standard*, June 9, 1928, p. 8.

"Who was Mary Webb?" *Literary Digest*, vol. 97 (June 9, 1928), p. 25.

Edwin Pugh. "Mary Webb." *The Bookman* (London), vol. 74, no. 442 (July 1928), pp. 193–196.

"New Fiction. Symbolism in Man and Nature" (review of *Collected Edition* of *Gone to Earth*). *Time and Tide*, August 31, 1928.

Kathleen Lee. "For Mary Webb," *The Bookman* (London), vol. 74 (September 1928), p. 299.

T. Earle Welby. "Reviews. Mr. Pound and Others" (review of *Poems and The Spring of Joy*). *Saturday Review*, vol. 146 (December 22, 1928), pp. 851–852.

"The Poems of Mary Webb" (review of *Poems and The Spring of Joy*). *Times Literary Supplement*, December 27, 1928, p. 102.

1929

"Mary Webb's Last Story" (review of *Armour Wherein He Trusted*). *The Times* (London), January 28, 1929, p. 17.

"New Novels" (review of *Armour Wherein He Trusted*). *Times Literary Supplement*, January 31, 1929, p. 8.

Wilfred Gibson. "The Poems of Mary Webb" (review of *Poems and The Spring of Joy*). *The Bookman* (London), vol. 75 (February 1929), pp. 269–270.

Almey St. John Adcock. "Armour Wherein He Trusted." *The Bookman* (London), vol. 75 (March 1929), p. 332.

Gertrude Diamant. "Armour Wherein He Trusted." *The World* (New York), vol. 28 (April 1929), p. 10.

H. P. Marshall. "Mary Webb" (review of Webb's *Collected Works*). *The Edinburgh Review*, vol. 249, no. 508 (April 1929), pp. 315–327.

L. M. Field. "Armour Wherein He Trusted." *The Evening Post* (New York), *Literary Review*, April 13, 1929, p. 10.

Walter R. Brooks. "Picked at Random" (review of *Armour Wherein He Trusted*). *The Outlook*, vol. 60 (April 17, 1929), p. 629 and p. 636.

Alice Beal Parsons. "Mary Webb's Last Book" (review of *Armour Wherein He Trusted*). *New York Herald Tribune, Books*, April 21, 1929, p. 4.

F. B. "Mary Webb's Poems" (review of *Poems and The Spring of Joy*). *Boston Transcript*, April 27, 1929, p. 5.

"Armour Wherein He Trusted." *The New York Times*, April 28, 1929, p. 6.

"Posthumous Fame." *The New Zealand Railways Magazine*, vol. 4, no. 1, (May 1, 1929), pp. 29-31.

Geraint Goodwin. "Mary Webb." *The Everyman*, May 2, 1929, pp. 14–15. [Cited in correspondence dated April 26, 1967 between Margaret Hardy and J. M. Dent & Sons Ltd.]

C. M. K. "Armour Wherein He Trusted." *Springfield Republican* (Springfield, Massachusetts), May 5, 1929, p. 7.

"Armour Wherein He Trusted." *The Bookman* (New York), vol. 69 (May 29, 1929), p. 23.

C. M. K. "Poems and The Spring of Joy." *Springfield Republican* (Springfield, Massachusetts), June 23, 1929, p. 7.

"Shropshire Moods" (review of the *Collected Works of Mary Webb*). *The Outlook and Independent*, vol. 152 (June 26, 1929), p. 348.

Charles Divine. "Sweet Music" (review of *Poems and The Spring of Joy*). *New York Herald Tribune*, July 14, 1929, p. 17.

J. Dana Tasker. "Potentialities" (review of *Poems and The Spring of Joy*). *The Nation*, vol. 129 (July 24, 1929), p. 96.

Alice Beal Parsons. "Mary Webb." *The Nation*, vol. 129 (August 7, 1929), pp. 145–146.

Louise Bogan. "Mary Webb" (review of *The House in Dormer Forest, Seven for a Secret*, and *Poems and The Spring of Joy*). *The New Republic*, vol. 59 (August 14, 1929), p. 348.

Ethel Wallace Hawkins. "The Books of Mary Webb" (review of *Poems and The Spring of Joy*). *The Atlantic Monthly*, vol. 144 (August 1929), p. 12 and p. 14.

"Poems and The Spring of Joy." *The Pratt Institute Quarterly Booklist*, Autumn 1929, p. 27.

1930s

Bernhard Fehr. *Die englische Literatur der Gegenwart und die Kulturfragen unserer Zeit*. Leipzig: Bernhard Tauchnitz, 1930, p. 80.

"Tours Through Literary England—X: The Mary Webb Country." *Saturday Review*, vol. 150 (August 30, 1930), pp. 251–252.

Mary Webb. "Owd Blossom." *The Argosy*, vol. 8, no. 55 (December 1930), pp. 104–106. Short story. (previously published in *Armour Wherein He Trusted: A Novel and Some Stories*. London: Jonathan Cape, 1929).

André Bellesort. "Littérature Étrangère" (review of French translation of *Precious Bane*). *Le Correspondant*, vol. 322, or new series, no. 286 (January 10, 1931), pp. 129–137.

Adrian Bury. "An Impression of Mary Webb." *Sufi Quarterly* (Geneva), vol. 7 (January 1931), pp. 7–10 and p. 330.

Grace Chapman. "Mary Webb" (review of Webb's *Collected Works*). *The London Mercury*, vol. 23, no. 136 (February 1931), pp. 364–371.

André Bellesort. "Littérature Étrangère": Un Roman de Mary Webb et quelques autres" (review of French translation of *The House in Dormer Forest*). *Le Correspondant*, vol. 328, or New Series, no. 242 (September 1932), pp. 777–783.

R. G. "Littératures Étrangères: Le poids des ombres" (review of French translation of *The House in Dormer Forest*). *Bravo: le magazine moderne*, no. 46 (November 1932), p. 25.

Hans Hecht. "Der Sündenesser," *Englische Studien*, vol. 47 (November 1932), pp. 238–246.

I. Shipton. "The Childhood of Mary Webb." *The Bookman* (London), December 1932, p. 195.

Gladys E. Peake. "The Religious Teachings of Mary Webb." *Congregational Quarterly*, vol. 11 (January 1933), pp. 41–51.

Lorna Collard. "Mary Webb" (review of Thomas Moult's biography of Mary Webb). *Contemporary Review*, vol. 143 (April 1933), pp. 455–464.

Mary Webb. "Over the Hills and Far Away." *The Argosy*, vol. 14, no. 86 (July 1933), pp. 100–102. Short story. (previously published in *Armour Wherein He Trusted: A Novel and Some Stories*. London: Jonathan Cape, 1929).

Mary Webb. "The Sword." *The Cornhill Magazine*, vol. 149, no. 892 (April 1934), pp. 401–409. Short story. (previously published in *Armour Wherein He Trusted: A Novel and Some Stories*. London: Jonathan Cape, 1929).

Bernhard Fehr. *Die englische Literatur der heutigen Stunde*. Leipzig: Bernhard Tauchnitz, 1934, p. 82–83.

Salvatore Rosati. "Letteratura inglese: George Moore—Katherine Mansfield—Mary Webb," *Nuova Antologia*, vol. 303 (October 1935), pp. 553–557.

Ernst Vowinckel. *Der englische Roman zwischen den Jahrzehnten 1927–1935*. Berlin: F. A. Herbig, 1936, pp. 101–102.

E. Thévenot. "Mary Webb," *Larousse mensuel*, Paris: Librairie Larousse, vol. 10 (1938), p. 658.

"Book Plebiscite by Czechs." *The Christian Science Monitor*, January 22, 1938. [In tenth annual symposium by Czech paper Lidové Noviny of Brno (Moravia), Mary Webb and Robert Graves voted the most popular English writers of 1937.]

"In Affection and Esteem." *Scholastic*, vol. 32 (May 21, 1938), p. 4.

Irene Marinoff. "Die Romane Mary Webbs," *Anglia*, vol. 60 (June 1938), pp. 434–448.

Edward Weeks. "Bookshelf" (review of *Gone to Earth*). *The Atlantic Monthly*, vol. 163 (July 1938).

Caradoc Evans. "Mary Webb." *The Colophon*, new series 3, no. 1 (Winter 1938), pp. 63–66.

"A Mary Webb Anthology." *Times Literary Supplement*, December 2, 1939, p. 697.

1940s

Ann Springer. "Woman's Genius Akin to Hardy's" (review of *A Mary Webb Anthology*). *Boston Transcript*, March 6, 1940, p. IE.

"A Mary Webb Anthology." *New York Herald Tribune, Books*, March 17, 1940, p. 26.

"Mary Webb's Writings" (review of *A Mary Webb Anthology*). *Springfield Republican* (Springfield, Massachusetts), April 3, 1940, p. 8.

"A Reader's List" (review of *A Mary Webb Anthology*). *The New Republic*, vol. 102 (April 15, 1940), p. 514.

"A Mary Webb Anthology." *Booklist*, vol. 36 (April 15, 1940), p. 322.

E. L. Tinker. "A Mary Webb Anthology." *The New York Times*, May 26, 1940, p. 23.

E. V. A. "A Mary Webb Anthology." *Forum*, vol. 103 (June 1940), p. 333.

Robert L. Pittfield. "The Shropshire Lass and her Goitre: Some Accounts of Mary Meredith Webb and her Works." *Annals of Medical History,* vol. 4 (July 13, 1942), pp. 284–293.

"Collection of Mary Webb," *Hobbies,* vol. 47 (September 1942), p. 97.

Caradoc Evans. "Mary Webb." *Welsh Review,* March 1, 1944.

J. Donald Adams. "Speaking of Books" (review of *The Spring of Joy*). *The New York Times,* December 31, 1944.

Hugo Manning. "Fifty-One Poems." *The Manchester Guardian,* December 31, 1946, p. 3.

Richard Church. "Fifty-One Poems." *The Spectator,* vol. 178 (January 3, 1947), p. 22.

P. J. H. H. "Fifty-One Poems." *The Christian Science Monitor,* February 8, 1947, p. 10.

"Fifty-One Poems." *Booklist,* vol. 44 (October 15, 1947), p. 65.

Weldon Kees. "Fifty-One Poems." *The New York Times,* November 9, 1947, p. 6.

"Fifty-One Poems." *Wisconsin Literary Bulletin,* vol. 43 (November 1947), p. 151.

Gerald MacDonald. "Fifty-One Poems." *Library Journal,* vol. 72 (December 1, 1947), p. 1688.

Wilfred Shepherd. "The Faith and Fiction of Mary Webb." *London Quarterly and Holborn Review,* October 1949, pp. 305–311.

1950s

Mary Webb. "Springtime." *The Argosy,* vol. 15, no. 5 (May 1954), p. 4. Excerpt from *Precious Bane.*

Mander, Constance A. "A Tramp Over the Country" (Mary Webb described in *Gone to Earth*). *Shropshire Magazine,* May 1956.

Fontinoy, Charles. "Thèmes de légendes dans *Gone to Earth.*" *Rivista di letterature moderne e comparate* (Florence), vol. 9 (Winter 1956), pp. 58–63.

Wright, A. J. "30th Anniversary of Mary Webb's Death." *Shropshire Magazine,* October 1957, pp. 11–13.

1960s

Sanders, Charles. "Webb's *Precious Bane,* Book III, Chapter 2." *The Explicator,* vol. 25, no. 2 (October 1966), p. 10.

Margaret Hardy. "Lost Poem is Found: Mary Webb's first published work comes to light after 60 years," March 17, 1967. Unpublished manuscript held at the Shropshire Archives, Castle Gates, Shrewsbury.

———. "Notes on the Meredith Family: from information given by Mr. Kenneth Meredith, eldest brother of Mary Webb," May 1967. Unpublished manuscript held at the Shropshire Archives, Castle Gates, Shrewsbury.

Margaret Hardy. "The Poems of Mary Webb." *Shropshire Magazine*, vol. 19, no. 5 (July 1967), p. 22.

Ralph Oldham. "The Bleak House on Wenlock Edge" ("Undern" in Mary Webb's *Gone to Earth*). *Shropshire Magazine*, vol. 19, no. 8 (October 1967), p. 30.

H. E. Gerber. "Mary Webb." *English Literature in Transition (1880–1920)*, vol. 11, no. 56 (1968), p. 56.

W. Eugene Davis. "The Poetry of Mary Webb: An Invitation." *English Literature in Transition (1880–1920)*, vol. 11, no. 2 (1968), pp. 95–101.

Michelle Dassie. "Mary Webb's Contribution to *The Bookman*." *Caliban*, no. 6 (1969), pp. 73–76.

1970s

Gladys Mary Coles. "Mary Webb as a Book Reviewer." *Shropshire Magazine*, September 1970, p. 17–18.

———. "Mary Webb's Roman Shropshire." *Country Quest*, August 1971, p. 8–10.

———. "Mary Webb's work . . . 'made a splendid fire which lasted a long time.'" *Shropshire Magazine*, vol. 24, no. 7 (September 1971), p. 18.

W. K. McNeil. "The Function of Legend, Belief and Custom in *Precious Bane*." *Folklore*, vol. 82 (1971), pp. 132–146.

Bernard Steff. "A Sketch of Mary Webb's Shropshire." *Country Life*, vol. 152 (October 12, 1972), pp. 888–890.

Julian Critchley. "Mary Webb's Love Letters to Nature." *The Illustrated London News*, January 1975, pp. 57–58.

Gladys Mary Coles. "Mary Webb: 50th Anniversary of her Death." *Shropshire Magazine*, December 1976, p. 23.

Flora McLeod. "Mary Webb as I Knew Her." [no date; 1970s?] Unpublished manuscript of a talk given to members of the Shropshire Women's Institute, held at the Shropshire Archives, Castle Gates, Shrewsbury

Paul Deane. "The Soul of the World: A Study of the Work of Mary Webb." *Modern British Literature*, vol. 2, no. 1 (Spring 1977), pp. 44–57.

Erika Duncan. "Portrait of the Artist as a Young Woman. A Study of the Life and Work of Mary Webb." 1977. [Carbon copy of typed draft catalogued by the University of Tulsa in the Rebecca West Special Collections holdings.]

Brian Watkins. "A Shropshire Lass: Mary Webb (1881–1927)." *Country Life*, October 20, 1977, pp. 1100–1101.

Gladys Mary Coles. "Mary Webb—Fifty Years On." *Shropshire Magazine*, October 1977, p. 21.

———. "Child of Spring." *Country Quest*, May 1978.

Erika Duncan. "Rediscovering Mary Webb." *Book Forum: An International Transdisciplinary Quarterly,* vol. 4 (1978), pp. 326–338.

Simon Appleyard. "The Shropshire World of Mary Webb." *This England,* Spring 1979, pp. 14–20.

1980s

Dorothy P. H. Wrenn. "*Seven for a Secret:* the Novel and Its Characters." [no date; 1980] Unpublished transcript of a lecture delivered at the Mary Webb Society's Summer School, held at the Shropshire Archives, Castle Gates, Shrewsbury.

Rosalind Coward. "This Novel Changes Lives: Are Women's Novels Feminist Novels? A Response to Rebecca O'Rourke's Article 'Summer Reading.'" *Feminist Review,* no. 5 (1980), pp. 53–64.

John H. Paterson and Evangeline Paterson. "Shropshire: Reality and Symbol in the Work of Mary Webb." *Humanistic Geography and Literature: Essays on the Experience of Place.* London: Croom Helm, 1981, pp. 209–220.

Marjorie Sykes. "Shropshire's Literary Landscape: A Centenary Tour of Mary Webb Country." *This England,* Spring 1981, pp. 50–53.

———. "The Anglo-Welsh Genius: Mary Webb." *Anglo-Welsh Review,* vol. 68 (1981), pp. 74–81.

Dorothy P. H. Wrenn. "Mary Webb's Husband," May 1981. Unpublished transcript of a lecture delivered at the Mary Webb Society's Summer School, Shropshire Archives, Castle Gates, Shrewsbury.

Gladys Mary Coles. "The Poetry of Mary Webb." *Poetry Wales,* vol. 17, no. 2 (Autumn 1981), pp. 83–93.

Gail Pool. "The Hunters and the Hunted" (review of *Gone to Earth*). *The Nation,* September 25, 1982, pp. 279–281.

Sarah Newell. "Two Country Classics" (review of *Gone to Earth* and *Precious Bane*). *The New York Times Book Review,* October 24, 1982, p. 30.

Patricia Craig. "Paperbacks in Brief" (review of *Seven for a Secret*). *Times Literary Supplement,* November 26, 1982, p. 1318.

Dorothy P. H. Wrenn. "Mary Webb and Thomas Hardy." [no date; 1980s?] Unpublished transcript of a lecture delivered at the Mary Webb Society's Summer School, held at the Shropshire Archives, Castle Gates, Shrewsbury.

1990s

Edmund Cusick. "Mary Webb's Borderland." *The New Welsh Review,* vol. 3 (Spring 1991), pp. 26–33.

Kenneth Milner. *Best Day of My Life: Mary Webb (Young Mary Meredith) at Much Wenlock.* Much Wenlock (Shropshire): Much Wenlock Dormer, 1999.

2000s

Hugo Jones. "The Webbs of Shropshire." *Shropshire Unfolded,* March 2001, pp. 21–25.

Eric Gardner. "A Nobler End: Mary Webb and the Victorian Platform." *Nineteenth Century Prose,* vol. 29, no. 1 (Spring 2002), pp. 103–116.

Ann Daniel. "Mary Gladys Webb: 1881–1927, Part One." *Shropshire Unfolded,* June 2002, pp. 14–15.

———. "Mary Gladys Webb: 1881–1927, Part Two." *Shropshire Unfolded,* July 2002, pp. 16–17.

———. "Mary Gladys Webb: 1881–1927, Part Three." *Shropshire Unfolded,* August 2002, pp. 18–19.

———. "Mary Gladys Webb: 1881–1927, Part Four." *Shropshire Unfolded,* September 2002, pp. 20–21.

Andrew Radford. "A Note on Hardy's Tess and Mary Webb's *Gone to Earth.*" *Thomas Hardy Journal,* February 2004, pp. 56–60.

———. "*Gone to Earth*: Hardy's Tess, Mary Webb and the Persephone Myth." *Thomas Hardy Yearbook,* no. 35 (February 2004), pp. 55–72.

Gladys Mary Coles. *The Magic of Shropshire with Mary Webb,* pamphlet. Shropshire: Shropshire Tourist (UK), Ltd., 2004.

Kenneth Milner. *Lullingford: Mary Webb's Much Wenlock.* Much Wenlock (Shropshire): K. Milner, 2004.

Andrew Radford. *The Lost Girls: Demeter-Persephone and the Literary Imagination, 1850–1930.* Amsterdam and New York: Rodopi, 2007.

Gladys Mary Coles. "Mary Webb: a Shropshire Naturalist." *Shropshire Wildlife.* Winter 2008, p. 7.

Millar, Eloise. "Mary Webb: brighter and better than Thomas Hardy." *The Guardian,* March 10, 2009. weblink: www.guardian.co.uk/books/booksblog/2009/mar/10/virago-mary-webb-thomas-hardy/print.

ACADEMIC THESES

1934. Zelina Florence Marcel. "A Dictionary of Characters in the Novels of Mary Webb." M.A. thesis, University of Kansas.

1934. Howard Parker Whitney. "Novels of Mary Webb." M.A. thesis, Boston University.

1934. Gertrud Schneider. "Die Verwendung und Bedeutung der Folklore in den Romanen von Mary Webb." Inaugural diss., University of Göttingen, Germany.

1936. Mary Mondy. "The Dialect in the Novels of Mary Webb, 1881–1927." M.A. thesis, Southern Methodist University.

1936. Marianne Tiemann. "Naturbetrachtung und Weltanschauung in den Werken von Mary Webb." Inaugural diss., University of Greifswald, Germany.

1956. Carolyn Emily Foster. "Folklore in Mary Webb's Novel, *Precious Bane.*" M.A. thesis, University of Maryland.

1956. M. P. G. Tolfree. "A Bibliography of Mary Webb." Submitted for Diploma in Librarianship, University of London.

1957. Ronald W. Butler. "The Relation of Art to Thought in the Novels of Mary Webb." M.A. thesis, University of Kentucky.

1959. Floyd Dale Fairweather. "Mary Webb: Her World." M.A. thesis, University of Idaho.

1960. W. J. de V. Prinsloo. "The Regional Novels of Arnold Bennett and Mary Webb: A Study in Contrasts." M.A. thesis, Potchefstroom University, South Africa.

1965. Mary Anne Mullally. "Mary Webb: Novelist of Shropshire Life." M.A. thesis, Université de Montréal.

1970. Virginia Griscom. "The Quest for Beauty; an Examination of the Life and Work of Mary Webb." M.A. thesis, Georgia State University.

1973. Donna Binnion Smith. "Character Interaction as an Expression of Theme in the Novels of Mary Webb." M.A. thesis, Tennessee Technological University.

1974. Beth Bowden. "Mysticism and Morbidity in the Work of Mary Webb." M.A. (Hons.) thesis, Victoria University of Wellington, Australia.

1977. Linda Morley. "Folklore in Mary Webb's Novel, *Precious Bane.*" Ph.D. diss., University of Pennsylvania.

1978. John Studley. "The Novels of Mary Webb: A Reading and Interpretation." Ph.D. diss., University of Toronto, Canada.

1982. Frances Josephine Dehn. "The Novels of Mary Webb as an Expression of a Mythology." Ph.D. diss., Kent State University.

1983. Helen Irish May. "Life as Lyric Drama in the Fiction of Mary Webb." Ph.D. diss., Florida State University, 1983.

1983. Michèle Aina Barale. "The Wish Unspoken: The Novels of Mary Webb." Ph.D. diss., University of Colorado, 1983.

1986. Barbara Duffin-Bates. "Mary Webb's Vision of the World: A Study in the Character Development, Patterning and Symbolism of her Novels." M.A. thesis, Acadia University (Ottawa).

1988. Becky Richards Edgerton. "Bright Glass: The Fictional World of Mary Webb." Ed.D. diss., University of Northern Colorado.

1991. Janice Miller Potter. "Both Fair and Good: The Novels of Mary Webb." Ph.D. diss., University of Connecticut.

1992. Christy Pesci. "The Poetry and Poetical Prose of Mary Webb." M.A. thesis, California State University, Dominguez Hills.

1992. Michelle R. Queen. "The Dragonfly's Shroud: Reading the Medieval Gothic Images in the Works of Mary Webb." M.A. thesis, North Carolina State University.

1996. Annemarie K. Gillin. "Monstrification: The Sign and the Condition in Three Fictional Heroines." M.A. thesis, University of Louisville.

2005. James Homer Thrall. "Mystic Moderns: Agency and Enchantment in Evelyn Underhill, May Sinclair and Mary Webb." Ph.D. diss., Duke University, 2005.

OTHER WORKS

1923. Michael Peele. *Shropshire in Poem and Legend.* Shrewsbury (Shropshire): Wilding and Son, Ltd.

1924. Joseph Collins. "Reading Matter for Invalids and the Novels of Mary Webb," *Taking the Literary Pulse: Psychological Studies of Life and Letters.* New York: George H. Doran, pp. 207–218.

1924. Gerald Gould. *The English Novel of Today.* London: John Castle, p. 218.

1925. Cornelius Weygandt. *A Century of the Novel.* New York: Century, p. 479.

1932. Robert M. Lovett, and Helen Sard Hughes. *The History of Novel in England.* Boston: Houghton-Mifflin, p. 440.

1933. Stanley J.Kunitz, ed. *Authors Today and Yesterday.* New York: H. W. Wilson, pp. 678–681.

1936. Elkin Mathews Ltd. *First and Last: A Catalogue of First Editions and Manuscripts. Bookseller's Catalogue Number 68.* Items 59–61, October 1936.

1937. E. Moore Darling. *Seeing Shropshire.* Shrewsbury (Shropshire): Adnitt & Naunton, Ltd.

1938. Elkin Mathews Ltd. *Books from the Libraries of Sir James Barrie and Mr. Aldous Huxley together with the Personal Library of Mary Webb consisting of only 30 Volumes. Bookseller's Catalogue Number 73.* Items 349–78, February 1938.

1939. S. P. B. Mais. *Highways and Byways in The Welsh Marches.* London: Macmillan and Co., Limited.

1941. Phyllis Bentley. *The English Regional Novel.* London: George Allen & Unwin, pp. 34–35.

1941. George Sampson. *The Concise Cambridge History of English Literature.* Cambridge: Cambridge University Press, pp. 975–976.

1941. Parke-Bernet Galleries, Inc. *The A. Edward Newton Collection of Books and Manuscripts, Part Three: N-Z, to be sold at Auction on October 29 and 30, 1941.* Items 503–509.

1942. Stanley J. Kunitz and Howard Haycraft, eds. *Twentieth Century Authors.* New York: H. W. Wilson, p. 1486.

1948. Samuel C. Chew. "The Nineteenth Century and After," *A Literary History of England*, Albert C. Baugh, ed. New York: Appleton-Century-Crofts, 1948, p. 1472, n. 23.

1950. Sherard Vines. *100 Years of English Literature.* London: Gerald Duckworth, p. 260.

1950. John Drinkwater, ed. "The Outline of Literature." London: George Newnes, p. 759.

1951. S. Diana Neill. *A Short History of the Novel.* London: Jarrolds, p. 282.

1952. G. M. Young. *Stanley Baldwin.* London: Rupert Hart-Davis, p. 109.

1952. Frederick Grice. *Folk Tales of the West Midlands.* London and Edinburgh: Thomas Nelson and Sons Ltd.

1954. Edward C. Wagenknecht. *Cavalcade of the English Novel.* New York: Henry Holt, pp. 574–575.

1956. Clarence L. Barnhart. *The New Century Handbook of English Literature.* New York: Appleton-Century-Crofts, pp. 1132–1133.

1956. William York Tindall. *Forces in Modern British Literature: 1885–1956.* New York: Vintage, pp. 303–304.

[no date; 1950s?] Lilian Hayward. *Twenty Shropshire Walks.* Shrewsbury (Shropshire): Shrewsbury Chronicle.

1960. Lionel Stevenson. *The English Novel: A Panorama.* Boston: Houghton-Mifflin, pp. 480 and 532–533.

1962. Parke-Bernet Galleries, Inc. *Modern First Editions & Fine Printing, Auction Catalogue Number 2106.* Items 250–267, from the Estate of the late Roland Bruce Barrett, April 24, 1962.

1963. Parke-Bernet Galleries, Inc. *First Editions and Manuscripts of American and British Authors, Auction Catalogue Number 220.* Items 230–243, from the Estate of the late George Matthew Adams, October 1, 1963.

1963. Maggs Brothers. *Bookseller's Catalogue Number 886.* Items 466–471.

1966. W. Eugene Davis. "New Light on a Neglected Novelist and Poet" *English Literature in Transition (1880–1920),* vol. 9, no. 3 (1966), p. 177. (Review of Dorothy H. P. Wrenn's *Goodbye to Morning: A Biographical Study of Mary Webb*).

[no date; 1970s?] Jean Hughes. *Shropshire Folklore Ghosts and Witchcraft.* Shrewsbury (Shropshire): Wilding and Son Limited.

1980. G. Dickins. *A Literary Guide to Shropshire*. Shrewsbury (Shropshire): Shropshire Libraries, p. 13.

1990. Sotheby's. *The Library of H. Bradley Martin: Highly Important English Literature*. New York: Sotheby's, 1990, Items 3307–3309.

1998. Peter Mastin. *The Mary Webb Society: The First Twenty-five Years 1972–1997*. Windhover (Leicestershire): Wigston Magna.

2001. Sotheby's. *The Library of Frederick B. Adams, Jr. Parts I and II*. London: Sotheby's, Items 71–81.

2002. Patricia A. Evans. *Poetic Landscapes: Watercolour Paintings, With Quotations from the Works of Mary Webb*. Pennerley (Shrewsbury): Tankerville Gallery, 2002.

MUSICAL SETTINGS

1933. Michael Head. *Foxgloves*. London: Boosey and Hawkes. Songs (high voice) with piano. Words by Gladys Mary Meredith Webb.

1933. Edmund Rubbra. *In Dark Weather: Song with Pianoforte*. London: Augener Ltd. Songs (high voice) with piano. Words by Gladys Mary Meredith Webb.

1936. Irvin Hinchliffe. *Green Rain*. London: Oxford University Press. Songs (low voice) with piano. Words by Gladys Mary Meredith Webb.

1937. Roland Leich. *Be Still, You Little Leaves*. Songs with piano. Words by Gladys Mary Meredith Webb. [A copy held in the Marian Anderson Papers, Rare Book & Manuscript Library, University of Pennsylvania, Collection of Music Manuscripts, Folder 1101.]

1938. Peggy Glanville-Hicks. *Be Still You Little Leaves*. Paris: Éditions de l'Oiseau lyre. Songs with piano. Words by Gladys Mary Meredith Webb.

1946. Vivienne Ada Maurice Lambelt. *Ah, Do Not Be So Sweet: Song (with Piano Accompaniment)*. London: J. & W. Chester Ltd.

1949. Bernard Naylor. *Rose-berries: Song*. Toronto: Western Music Co. Words by Gladys Mary Meredith Webb.

1962. Celius Dougherty. *Song for Autumn: For Voice and Piano*. New York: G. Schirmer. Songs (high voice) with piano. Words by Gladys Mary Meredith Webb.

2005. Richard Moult. *The Secret Joy*. Handricourt (France): Cynfeirdd. Compact disc of fifteen poems set to music sung by Kathy Taylor-Jones (mezzo-soprano), Kate Hopkins (soprano) and Nicholas Chalmers (piano). Words for thirteen of the fifteen songs by Mary Webb, including "Presences"; "A Hawthorn Berry"; "Dawn"; "A Summer Day"; "A Night Sky"; "Like a Poppy on a Tower"; "The Shell"; "The Snowdrop"; "The Secret Joy"; "Roseberries"; "A Rainy Day"; "Be Still, You Little Leaves"; and "The Sedge Warbler."

2007. Howard Skempton. *Five Poems of Mary Webb: For SSA Chorus.* Oxford: Oxford University Press.

DRAMATIC ADAPTATIONS

1930. Edward Lewis. *Precious Bane: A Play in a Prologue and Three Acts, Adapted from the Novel of Mary Webb.* London and New York: Samuel French, 1932. [Notice in *The Times* (London) for August 11, 1930: "On Monday, August 11, the Swanage Repertory Company will produce *Precious Bane,* a dramatization by Mr. Edward Lewis of the novel by Mary Webb." West End performance of *Precious Bane* at St. Martin's Theatre starring Robert Donat, Malcolm Keen, and Gwen Ferangcon-Davies opened during Easter week (March 27, 1932 was Easter Sunday) as cited in *The Times* (London) for February 25, 1932 and April 9, 1932.]

1930. T. G. Saville. *Gone to Earth,* a dramatization of the novel by Mary Webb. [Cited in *The Times* (London) for October 23, 1930: "Mary Webb's well-known novel *Gone to Earth* which has been adapted for the stage by Mr. T. G. Saville, a young actor who has been playing the leading parts at the Festival Theatre, Cambridge, is to be produced by the Swanage Repertory Company at the Players Theatre on Monday, November 3. A dramatization of another of Mary Webb's novels, *Precious Bane,* was recently performed at Swanage. *Gone to Earth* will open the first London season of the Swanage Repertory Theatre Company." Cited in *The Times* (London) November 3, 1930: "Another busy theatrical week opens tonight with the production by the Swanage Repertory Theatre Company of a dramatization of Mary Webb's novel *Gone to Earth.* This will be staged at the Players Theatre, with Miss Beatrix Lehmann as the heroine, Hazel Woodus, supported by Mr. Cecil Trouncer and Mr. Rupert Siddons. The dramatization consists of a series of eight episodes from the book. There will be three scenes, showing the cottage of Abel Woodus, the minister's house, and the squire's house."]

1939. Hugh Burden. *The House in Dormer Forest,* a dramatization of the novel by Mary Webb. [Cited in Sir Peter Ustinov's obituary in 2004. The play was produced in 1939 at the Barn Theatre in Surrey with eighteen-year-old Ustinov in the cast.]

1950. Michael Powell and Emeric Pressburger, director-writer-producers. *Gone to Earth.* U.K. release: November 6, 1950 by British Lion Films and Selznick International Pictures, 110 minutes. Starring Jennifer Jones as Hazel Woodus; David Farrar as Jack Reddin; and Cyril Cusack as Edward Marston.

1952. Michael Powell and Emeric Pressburger, director-writer-producers. *The Wild Heart.* American release: July 1952 by RKO Radio Pictures, Inc. 82 minutes. Additional scenes written and directed by Rouben Mamoulian (uncredited) and re-edited and produced by David. O. Selznick (uncredited). Starring Jennifer Jones as Hazel Woodus; David Farrar as Jack Reddin; and Cyril Cusack as Edward Marston.

1957. Constance Cox. *Precious Bane*. Six-part BBC Television dramatic series adapted from the novel by Mary Webb. Original air date: May 29, 1957 (season 1, episode 1). Starring Daphne Slater as Prue Sarn; Patrick Troughton as Gideon Sarn; and Paul Daneman as Kester Woodseaves.

1968. Claude Santelli, director. *Sarn*. Office de Radiodiffusion-Télévision Française (French television) play adapted from the novel by Mary Webb. Starring Dominique Labourier as Prue Sarn; Josep Maria Flotats as Gideon Sarn; and Pierre Vaneck as Kester Woodseaves.

1980. Carol Snape. *My Wife Did a Bit of Scribbling*. Unpublished script for radio play. [Script courtesy of Carol Snape-Barker. First performed at the Ludlow Arts Fesitival in 1982 as cited in *The Mary Webb Society: The First Twenty-Five Years (1972-1997)*, p. 46.]

1981. Micheline Wandor. *Precious Bane*. Three-part classic serial dramatisation of novel by Mary Webb. BBC Radio 4. 55 mins each. Starring Miriam Margolyes.

1989. Christopher Menaul, director *Precious Bane*. Film for television adapted from the novel by Mary Webb. BBC. Starring Janet McTeer as Prue Sarn; Clive Owen as Gideon Sarn; and John Bowe as Kester Woodseaves.

1996. Michelene Wandor. *Gone to Earth* by Mary Webb. Three-part classic serial. BBC Radio 4. 60 mins each.

2003. Bryony Lavery. *Precious Bane by Mary Webb; Dramatized by Bryony Lavery*. London: Oberon Books Ltd. A world premiere production by Pentabus Theatre in association with English Trust. First performed at Walcot Hall, Shropshire on July 11, 2003.

2004. Helen Edmundson. *Gone to Earth by Mary Webb; Dramatized by Helen Edmundson*. London: Nick Hern Books.

[no date.] *Seven for a Secret* / Mary Kellogg. Promptbook for the play *Seven for a Secret* adapted from the novel by Mary Webb. Includes cast list. [Belonged to and was annotated by the producer Herbert Prentice. Herbert M. Prentice Papers, *T-Mss 1964-005, Billy Rose Theatre Division, The New York Public Library for the Performing Arts, b. 34, f. 2.]

[no date.] *Precious Bane*. Typescript of a condensed version of the story *Precious Bane* considered by Cheryl Crawford (1920-1986) but not produced by her. [Cheryl Crawford Papers, *T-Mss 1973-004, Billy Rose Theatre Division, The New York Public Library for the Performing Arts, b. 81, f. 4.]

[no date.] Carol Snape. *Tangled Webb*. Unpublished script for biographical play. [Courtesy of Carol Snape-Barker and Jack Milner.]

Index

Numbers in *italics* refer to *page numbers*. Numbers in roman type refer to catalogue item numbers.

A

Adams, Frederick Baldwin, Jr., *51, 53, 54, 56*, 1, 3, 4, 10, 11, 18, 19, 21, 23, 24, 51, 53, 54, 56, 68, 69, 85, 100, 102, 103, 112, 119, 122, 125, 128, 129, 148, 152, 164, 166, 171, 180
Adams, George Matthew, *53, 54*, 112
Adcock, Almay St. John, *59*, 117
Adcock, Arthur St. John, *20, 55, 57*, 31, 43, 73, 99, 105, 109–111, 117, 121, 123, 130, 141, 148, *167*
Adcock, Marion St. John, 121
Addison, Hilda, *13, 18*, 12, 70, 164, 177, *168*
"Ah, Do Not Be So Sweet!," 28
"Alone," 22
"An Estray," 42
"Ancient Gods, The," 77, 78
"Antonio," 55
Arden, Deborah, *26, 28, 34, 35*, 52, 54, 58
Arden, John, *25, 28, 35*, 15, 54, 58
Arden, Patty, *28*, 54
Armour Wherein He Trusted, 7, 19, 20, 39, 52, 53, 56, 59, 56, 102, 119, 120, 148–151
Armstrong, Martin, *21, 60,* 9, 149, 163, 175
Arnold, Matthew, 84
Arthurian romance, 4
Atlantic Monthly, The, 97, 98
Auel, Jean, *47*
Auerbach, 55
Austen, Jane, *47*, 122, *152*

B

Baldwin, Stanley, Prime Minister, *7, 19–21, 45, 49, 50, 53, 55, 58,* 107, 127, 147, 149, 154, 161, 163, 176, 187, *163, 164*
Barn Theatre, 71
Barrett, Roland Bruce, *53*, 55
Barrie, Sir J. M., *20, 48*
Barrington, E. (pseud. Elizabeth Louisa Moresby), 116
Battle of the Somme, *17, 35*
Bayswater, 44, 84
Beast Walk, *38, 152, 153*
bees, *20, 26, 27,* 5, 109, *166*
Beguildy, Jancis, *27, 159–162*
Beguildy, Wizard, 132, *159–162*
Belgium, 59
Bennett, Arnold, *45, 57,* 159
Berg collection, 55
Bernard-Luc, Jean, 68
Bible, The, 39, 47, 13, 119, 148, *152, 159*
birds, *33, 36, 38, 41, 42, 44,* 19, 82, 117, 139, 142, 145, 175, *158, 170, 171*
"Birds, Beasts and Trees," *38*
"Birds will Sing, The," 145
Birmingham Post, The, 46, 180
Black Huntsman, *36,* 59, *149, 150*
Blake, William, *42,* 40
Board, Fred J., *51, 54,* 55, 116, 120
Bodley Head, *16,* 26
Book Forum, 61, 182
Bookman, The, 18, 20, 45, 57, 58, 24, 31, 43, 59, 73, 74, 88, 99, 105, 111–114, 116–118, 121–123, 130, 140, 141, 148, 154, *153, 167, 169*
Bookman Treasury of Living Poets, The, 99, 147
"Bookman's Diary, The," 105, 116
"Bookman's Gallery," 31, 112
Bristol, 29, 51, 115
British Broadcasting Corporation, *49*
BBC Radio 4, *46,* 180
British Film Institute National Archive, 67
British Library, *51*
Brontë, Emily, *44, 47*
Brontës, *7, 13, 47,* 122
Brothers, H. J., 167
Brown, Elvira, Miss, 120
Brown, Myrtle, 120
Browning, Elizabeth Barrett, *44*
Browning, Robert, *54,* 40
Buchan, John, *20, 21, 34, 48, 59,* 163, 176, *150*
Buck, Pearl, *47*
Burden, Hugh, 71
Burne, Charlotte Sophia, *27, 54,* 129
butterflies, *29,* 23
Byford-Jones, W., 171
Byron, George Gordon, Lord, 116
Byron, Lady Anne Isabella Noel, 116

C

"Caer Cariad: A Story of the Marches," 73, 74
Cambridge, *16, 26,* 53
Cambridge University Extension lectures, *16*
Campus Chat, 171
Canada, 41
Canadian Ambulance Unit, 41
Canavaggia, Maria, *61,* 151
Cannon, Beatrice, 4
Cape, Jonathan, *7, 21, 22, 49, 55, 60,* 134, 158–161, 163, 165, 166, 177, *164, 168*
Caradoc and Severn Valley Field Club, 101–104
Carnegie, Andrew, 11
"Carol for Peace, A," 114, 115
Castle Gates, 41
Celtic Literature, 84

201

Celtic mythology, 4
Celtic temperament, 4, 83, 84, 180
Challis, Christopher, 67
Chapbook, The, 78
Chapman, Grace, 163
Chapman, R. W., 122
Chappell, W. Reid, 162
Chaucer's Works, 54, 55
Chester, *10, 17, 35,* 42, 81
Chesterman, Hugh, 96
Chesterton, G. K., *21, 58,* 23, 163
Chinese Lion, The, 55, 124–126
Christianity, *61,* 12, 102, 148, *164, 167*
Christmas, *49,* 4, 81, 107, 115, 140, *163*
Church of St. Mary Magdalene, Bleddfa, Wales, 188
Clare, John, *44*
Clematisa, 2
Clematisa & Percival, 7, 10, 53, 56, 2
Coalbrookdale, 52
Coe, Jonathan, 67
Coles, Gladys Mary, as author or editor, 179, 180, 183–185, 187; cited, 7, *9, 10, 13, 14, 16–18, 21, 22, 33, 51,* 1, 3, 5, 10, 12, 13, 16, 18, 22, 25–28, 40–42, 51–53, 55, 59, 69, 70, 74, 88, 95, 99, 100, 103, 107, 125, 129, 142, 150, 155, 156, 164, 166, 176, 181, *152, 165*
Collected Works of Mary Webb, The, 7, 21, 34, 45, 49, 47, 99, 119, 120, 152, 157, 159, 163, 165, *164, 168*
"Colomen," 142, 143
Colophon, 30, *168*
Columbia University, *55*
Come Hither, 95
Composers' Guild of Great Britain, 178
Conrad, Joseph, 159
"Core of Poetry, The," *44,* 79
Cox, Harold, 161
Crane, Stephen, 159
Curtis Brown, 70, 74, 89

D

Dakers, Mr., 70, 74, 89
Dancer's Cat, The, 140
Dandelion Fairy, 2
Darke, Amber, *23, 38, 151–153*
Darke, Jasper, *38, 151–153*
Darke, Peter, *26, 151, 152*
Darke, Rachel (Mrs.), *26, 29, 151, 152*
Darke, Ruby, *38, 151, 152*
Darke, Solomon (Mr.), *29, 151*
Darke family, *26, 27, 29, 37, 38,* 69, *150–152*
Darling, E. Moore, 170
Das Kapital, 85
De la Mare, Walter, *15, 21, 43, 44, 48, 59,* 9, 95, 152, 153, 163
death-myths, *36, 37*
death-pack, *36, 37*
Dell paperback series, 63
Denton, *55,* 171
Devil's Chair, *35, 145–147*
Dickens, Charles, 107
Dickens Fellowship, *10,* 107
Dickensian, The, 107
Dictionary of National Biography, 7, 176
Dictionary of the English Language, A, 24
"Difference, The," 19, 20
Dinesen, Isak, *47*
Donat, Robert, 132
Dorchester, 128
Dormer Old House, *37,* 69, *150, 151*
Dorset, 85
Dorset County Museum, 85
Dorsetshire Folklore, 129
dove, 20, 142, *166, 170*
"Dream of Uricononium, A. The Return of the Romans," 103, 104
Dukedom Large Enough, 53, 127
Duncan, Erika, *61,* 182
Dutton, E. P., 11, 158, 174

E

Echoing Green, The, 22, 184
Edinburgh Review, The, 45, 58, 161

Edmundson, Helen, 186
"Elf, The," 7, 8
Eliot, George, 122
Elmer, Ralph, *31, 154–157*
Embassy Theatre, 132
End Papers, 49, 59, 11, 59, 167
English Review, The, 44, 12, 13, 79, 93, 103, 147
Essential Mary Webb, The, 60, 175
Evans, Caradoc, *48,* 1, 6, 30, *168*
Evans, Patricia A., 185
Evening Standard, The, 21, 45, 57, 140
Everlasting Quest, The, 32, 33
Everyman's Library, 54, 4

F

"Fallen Poplar, The," 25
Far End, 59, 88, 117, 118
"Farewell, A," 144
"Farewell to Beauty," 143, 144
Farrar, John, 74, 154
fascism, *38*
"Father's Path," *see* "My Father's Path."
Femina, 19
Fifty-One Poems, 55, 47, 99, 173, 174, 187
Financial Times, The, 46, 180
First Crusade, *19,* 102, 148, 150, *164*
First World War, *see* World War I
Fleming, Ian, *52*
"Flockmaster, The," 15, *146*
Flower of Light: A Biography of Mary Webb, The, (Coles), as main catalogue entry, 180; cited 7, *9, 13, 14, 18, 21, 34, 46,* 1, 12, 13, 16, 18, 25, 28, 40, 51, 53, 55, 59, 69, 70, 74, 88, 95, 100, 107, 129, 155, 156, 183, *165*
For the Love of Books, 60, 149
"Foxgloves," 99
Friends of "The Gustine Courson Weaver Mary Webb Shrine," The, 171
Fringal (the servant), *31, 155, 156*

202

G

G. P. Putnam and Sons, 86
"Garden in Winter, The," 47
"Gates of Gold and Green, The," 15
Gideon, *see* Sarn, Gideon
Gilgamesh, 32, 33
Girl Guide's Annual, 96
"Glimpses of Old Shropshire," 101–104
"Glorious Apollo," 55, 116
Glory That was Grub Street, The, 57, 130, 141, 148, *167*
God, *26, 58*, 12, 13, 15, 27, 39, 77–79, 93, 121, 144, 148, *146, 147, 152, 153, 163, 166, 167*
God's Little Mountain, 36, 184
Godfather, The, 86
Godson, Dr., 52
Goethe, Johann Wolfgang von, 59, 118
"Going for the Milk," 37
Golden Arrow, The, 17, 21, 25, 28, 34, 35, 50, 53, 54, 56, 58, 1, 10, 15, 16, 32, 44, 51–58, 87, 100, 127, 129, *145–147*
Golders Green, *21*
Goldwasser, Thomas, *9, 51*, 52
Gone to Earth, 17, 33, 35–37, 49, 55, 57, 58, 10, 32, 44, 59–63, 68, 88, 100, 118, 129, 167, 176, 184, 186, *148–150*
Gone to Earth, the film, 67
Gone with the Wind, 65
Goodbye to Morning, (Wrenn), as main catalogue entry, 177; cited, 70, 119, 123, 132, 137, 148
Gossip About Shropshire Folklore, A, 100
Grandmother Velindre, *see* Velindre, Hannah (Grandmother)
Graves' disease, *14, 16, 20, 40*, 10, 12, 14, 20, 26, 39, 52, 69, 123, 144, 145, *154*
Great War, *see* World War I
"Green Rain," 94, 95, *170*
Grolier Club, *9–11, 51*, 1, 11, 112
Grove Cottages, 46, 84, 119, 120, 124, 138
Guéritte, Madeleine T., 131
Guest, Lady Charlotte, *54*, 4

H

Hampstead, 46, 84, 115, 119, 120, 124, 138
"Hannah," 76; *see also*, "Neighbour's Children, The"
Happy Profession, The, 97
Hardy, Florence (Mrs. Thomas), *56*, 128
Hardy, Thomas, *13, 18, 31, 43, 56, 60*, 18, 85, 128, 129, *150, 151, 157*
Harrison, Austin, 13, 79, 93
Harvard University, *24*
Hassall, Joan, 174
Hawthorne, Nathaniel, *35*
"Heaven's Tower," 80
Hemingway, Ernest, 60
Hepple, Norman, 172, 175
Hickling, Dorothy, 1
Hilder, Roland, 165, 172, 175
"Hills of Heaven, The," 178
Hitz, Benjamin D., *51, 53, 54*, 173
Hollywood, 62, 159
Holmes, David, *55*
Holocaust, *38*
Horton, Betty M., *55*, 124
"House Beautiful, The," 6
House in Dormer Forest, The, 17, 18, 23, 26, 29, 37, 38, 44, 69–71, 73, 88, 89, *150–153*
House of Usher, *37*
Howard, Michael S., 60
Howell, John, 167
Huntbatch, Eli, *25–28*, 145
Huntbatch, Lily, *25, 26, 28, 34*, 52, *145, 146*

I

Idyllia, 112
"In Affection and Esteem," *55*, 120
"In April," 83, 84
In the Day of Battle, 55
Indiana University, 112
Ironbridge, 52

J

J. P. Pinker & Sons, Messrs., 159
Jackson, Georgina F., *54*, 18
James, Henry, 159
James, William, *24*, 21
Jancis, *see* Beguildy, Jancis
Jefferies, Richard, *13*
John Ardens Tochter, 58
John Howell Books, 167
Johnson, Samuel, *24*
Jonathan Cape, Publisher, 60
Jones, Jennifer, 62–64
Jonson, Ben, *47*
Jorwerth, Ranulph, 150, *165*
Joseph the Provider Books, *55*
Joyce, James, 159
Jung, Carl Gustav, *38, 48*

K

Karnac, H., (Books), *55*
Keats, John, 40
Keble College, 41
"Kennst du das Land," 59, 118
King, Maude Egerton, ed., 6, 9, 15
King Alfred School, *18*, 160, 164
King's School, *17*, 42
Kipling, Rudyard, *19*
"Knowest Thou the Land?", 59, 118
Kopelówny, Bolesławy, 133

L

La flèche d'or, 57
L'amour vient en jouant, 68
La renarde, 61
La renarde, pièce en 4 actes et 3 tableaux, 68
Lacretelle, Jacques de, 61, 131
"Lad Out There, The," 41
Lake District, *22*, 172
"Land Within, The," 138, 184
Lane, Allen, 60
Lawrence, D. H., *38*
Le Fleming, Christopher, 178
Le poids des ombres, 71

203

Leighton, 101
Leinster Square, 44, 84, 85, 87, 88, *158*
Lewis, Edward, 132
Lewis, Sinclair, 60
Library of Frederick Baldwin Adams, Jr., The, 85
Lilly Library, 55
Liverpool, 41
Liverpool Post, 6
Living Age, The, 95
Lloyd, Old John, 119
London, *17–19, 20, 48, 52, 59*, 1, 24, 59, 70, 72–74, 81, 82, 85, 107, 111, 112, 118–120, 124, 125, 127, 132, 137, 160, 164, 183, *154, 157, 158*
London, Jack, 159
London University, 160
Long Mynd, *35*
Longfellow, Henry Wadsworth, 3
Lory, Edith, Miss ("Minoni"), *13–15*, 3, 164
Lovekin, Gillian, *30, 31, 154–157*
Lovekin, Isaiah, *31, 155, 157*
"Lover of Roses, A," 22
Luce, Morton, 23, 31, 32, 44–46, 110–113, 115
Ludlow Festival, *10*, 181
Lynd, Robert, *21, 59, 163, 150, 157*
Lyric Theatre, Hammersmith, 186
Lyth Hill, *18, 20, 44, 39, 53*, 80, 86, 95, 103, 137, 184, 187

M

Mabinogion, The, 54, 4
"Maid in Shropshire," 186
Mamoulian, Rouben, 62
"Many Mansions," *60,* 119
Marble Faun, The, 35
Marigold (the servant), *26, 29, 151, 152*
"Market Day," 34, 35
Marshall, H. P., *45, 58,* 161
Marston, Edward, *36,* 149
Martin, H. Bradley, *51, 53–55,* 11, 118
Mary Webb (Coles), as main catalogue entry, 183; cited, *9, 16, 21, 34, 46,* 3, 5, 10, 26, 41, 42, 52, 142, 150, 164, 166, 181, 184, *152*
"Mary Webb" (Chapman), in the *London Mercury,* 163
"Mary Webb" (Marshall), in the *Edinburgh Review,* 161
"Mary Webb" (Pugh), in the *Bookman,* 154
Mary Webb: A Short Study of Her Life and Work (Addison), *18,* 12, 70, 164, 177, *168*
Mary Webb Anthology, A, 22, 172
"Mary Webb as I Knew Her" (McLeod), 13
Mary Webb: Collected Prose and Poems (Coles), as main catalogue entry, 179; cited, 99, 103, 125, 187
"Mary Webb Country," area known as, 162, 184, 187
Mary Webb: Her Life and Work (Moult), 166, 177
Mary Webb, photograph of, 1, 105, 107, 154, 183
"Mary Webb Pilgrims," travelers to Shropshire, 171
Mary Webb Society, The, *9, 46, 51*
"Mary Webb's Pathetic Little Library Sold, Shabby Volumes Now Rare Pieces," 148
Mathews, Elkin, *52–56, 59,* 4, 148
Matter, Form, and Style. A Manual of Practice in the Writing of English Composition, 10
McLeod, Flora, 13
Medici Society, 165
Meole Brace, 16
Meredith, Alice, *13, 14, 16, 18,* 19, 32, 42, 54, 81, 141, 156, 183
Meredith, Douglas, *17, 35,* 23, 41–43, 166, *148*
Meredith, George, *13–16, 28, 35, 43,* 3–5, 14–21, 23, 28, 31, 54, 129, 183

Meredith, Gladys Mary, *see* Webb, Mary
Meredith, Kenneth, *17, 35,* 5, 23, 41–43, 181, *148*
Meredith, Mervyn, *17, 35,* 23, 41–43, *148*
Meredith, Muriel, 183
Meredith, Olive, 42, 156
Meredith siblings, *13, 14,* 2, 3, 81, 155, 156, 183
Merry-Go-Round, The, 96
Meynell, Alice, *44*
Mew, Charlotte, *44*
Micheli, Odette, 71
Military Cross, 41
Milner, Jack, *10*
Miłość Prudencji Sarn, 133
Milton, John, *13, 40, 158*
Minding My Own Business, 52
Minkoff, G. R., *55*
Minoni, *see* Lory, Edith, Miss
Monro, Harold, 78
Moresby, Elizabeth Louisa, 116
"Morton Luce," in the *Bookman,* 112
Moult, Richard, 188
Moult, Thomas, 166, 177
Mrs. Walmsley's Finishing School, *14,* 3, 4
Muir, Percy H., *52, 54*
"My Father's Path," 14, 15
"My Own Town," 39
My People, 1
My Wife Did a Bit of Scribbling (Snape), *10,* 181
mysticism, *24, 25, 34, 38, 40, 50, 58, 60,* 12, 21, 80, 93, 100, 161, *146, 150–152, 161*

N

"Name-Tree, The," 93
Nation, The, 18, 146
Nation and the Athenaeum, The, 57
Naturbetrachtung und Weltanschauung in den Werken von Mary Webb, 169
"Nature's Call to City-dwellers," 36
nazism, *38*
"Neighbour's Children, The," 75, 76

Nesta, *20, 59,* 148, 150, *164–167*
New Forest, *21*
New Idyllia, 112
New Review, The, 31
New Statesman, The, 67, 146, 150
"New Year's Customs," 100
New York Public Library, *55*
New York Times, The, 152
New York University, 182
News Chronicle, The, 148
Newton, A. Edward, *49, 59,* 11, 59, 167
Nichols, Beverly, 60
Nicholson, C. A., 140, 141
"Night sky (1916), A," 43
"Nills, The," 42
North Texas State Teachers' College, Denton, Texas, 171
North Wales, 181
Novels of Jane Austen, The, 122

O

O'Grady, Hardress, 10
Old Market Hall, Shrewsbury, 136
"Old Woman, An," 99, 147
"On receiving a box of spring / flowers in London," 137
"Our Immortal Jane," 122
"Over the Hills and Far Away," *55,* 106
Owst, Gerald Robert, 148
Oxford, *13,* 3, 41, 84
Oxford Dictionary of National Biography, 7
Oxford University Press, 122, 176

P

pantheism, *24, 25, 61*
Paradise Lost, 13, 40, 158
Parke-Bernet, *54, 55*
Parry, Mary, 98, 126
Parry, Nicholas, 98, 126
Payne, Kerry, *55, 56,* 116, 120, 124
Penguin Books Ltd., 60
Percival, 2
Pernicious anemia, *19, 20,* 123, 144, 145

Peter the Hermit, 148, *164*
Philadelphia, *10*
Phillips, Henry, 11
Pierpont Morgan Library, 1, 11
Pinker, Eric, 159
Pinker, James Brand, 159
Pinker, James Ralph, 159
Poe, Edgar Allan, 37
Poems and The Spring of Joy, 15, 45, 54, 59, 7, 30, 47, 48, 99, 152, 153, 173, 187
Poetical Landscapes: Watercolour Paintings by Patricia A. Evans, 185
Poetical Works, (of Robert Browning), *54*
Poetical Works of Henry Wadsworth Longfellow, The, 3
"Poetry of the Prayer Book, The," *48,* 148
Polrebec, Sir Gilbert, *20, 59,* 148, 150, *164–167*
Pontesbury, *16,* 32, 34
poplars, 24, 25
Porthal, Centrine de, 68
Portofino, *22*
Potter, Beatrix, 178
Powell, Michael, 62, 63, 67
Poynton, Raymond, 181
Preaching in Medieval England, 148
Precious Bane, 7, 10, 13, 19, 20, 23, 25, 26, 30, 39–41, 47, 49, 53, 55–58, 60, 61, 46, 56, 85, 100, 102, 105, 108, 114, 127–135, 154, 156, 160, 163, 182, *158–164*
Precious Bane. A Play in a Prologue and Three Acts. Adapted from the Novel of Mary Webb, 132
Pressburger, Emeric, 62, 63, 67
Pride and Prejudice, 54
Priory School, *17*
Prix Femina Vie Heureuse Anglais, *19, 39,* 46, 114, *163*
"Prize, The," 97, 98
Prue, *see* Sarn, Prudence
Pugh, Edwin, *48, 57,* 105, 107, 130, 154
Puzo, Mario, 86

Q

Queen of Cornwall, The, 128
Quotation Calendar from Mary Webb, A, 165

R

Rainsford, Rebecca, *10*
Randall, David A., *53, 54,* 127
Rebecca, 65
Red Cross, *35*
Reddin, Squire Jack, *36,* 59, *149*
Rémon, Maurice, 91
"Return of the Romans: A Dream of Uriconium, A," 103, 104
"Reveille," *55*
Rideout, Robert, *30, 31,* *154–157*
RKO Radio Pictures Inc., 62, 64–66
Road, Quarterly Review, A, 106
Romantic poets, *13*
Rose Cottage, 32
Rossetti, Christina, *44,* 40
Rota, Bertram, *56,* 125
Royal Artillery, 41
Royal Literary Fund, *20, 49, 52,* 127, 147, 154, 161, *164*
Royal School of Church Music, 178
Rwth (the servant), *30, 155–157*

S

"Safe," 146
Salop, 50, 86
Salopians, 50, 52
San Francisco, *51,* 167
Sarn, 131, 133, 134
Sarn, Gideon, *26, 27, 39–41,* 132, *158–163*
Sarn, Prudence, *26, 27, 30, 39–41, 47, 60, 158–163*
Sarn Mere, *41, 159, 160, 162, 163*
Saturday Review, The, 146
Sayers, Dorothy L., *47*
Scafell Pike, *22,* 172, 184
Scarlet Letter, The, 54
"Science of Fiction, The," *31*

205

Scribner's, 52–54
Seasons and Castle of Indolence, The, 54
Second World War, see World War II
Secret Joy, The, 188
Sedgwick, Ellery, 97
Seeing Shropshire, 170
Selected Poems of Mary Webb (Coles), as main catalogue entry, 187; cited, 45, 22, 27, 99
Selznick, David O., 62–65, 67
Sense and Sensibility, 122
Sept pour un secret, 91
Seredy, Kate, 47
Seven For A Secret, 18, 30, 31, 41, 55, 56, 59, 59, 75, 85–92, 118, 128, 154–158
Shakespeare, William, 13, 14, 49, 31, 79, 85, 111
"Shell, The," 29, 30
Shelley, A. N. C., 24, 53
Shelley, Mary (née Webb), 24, 26, 53, 87
Sheppard, H. R. L., 21, 163
Shrewsbury, 16–19, 22, 7, 34, 39, 49, 50, 101, 104, 136, 170, 171, 177
Shrewsbury Chronicle, The, 101, 104
Shrewsbury Public Library, 13
"Shrewsbury's Abbey Fair," 104
Shropshire, 8, 9, 13, 16–21, 23, 25, 27, 33–36, 39, 40, 42–44, 48, 50, 51, 56, 58, 4, 7, 29, 39, 42, 44, 50–52, 54, 72, 82, 95, 100–104, 129, 137, 160, 162, 168, 170, 171, 181, 145, 148, 154, 158, 164
Shropshire Archives, 41
Shropshire dialect, 47, 18
Shropshire Folk-Lore: A Sheaf of Gleanings, 27, 54, 129
Shropshire Haunts of Mary Webb, The (Byford-Jones), 171
Shropshire of Mary Webb, The (Chappell), 162
Shropshire Women's Institute, 13
Shropshire Word-Book, A Glossary of Archaic and Provincial Words, etc., Used in the County, 54, 18
Siete para un secreto, 92
Silences of the Moon, The, 16, 24, 26
Sims, G. F., 55
Sin Eater, 27, 40, 159
Sinclair, May, 55, 59, 88, 117, 118
Six, Antoinette, 57
Smith College, 55
Smith, Paul Jordan, 60, 149
Snailbeach, 103
Snape, Carol, 10, 181
Somerset coast, 16
Sotheby's, 55, 56, 85, 128
Southernwood, Stephen, 26, 28, 52, 145–147
Southport, 14, 3
Spartacus, 71
Spectator, The, 18, 38, 46, 48, 95, 105, 114, 175
Sphere, The, 27
Spring Coppice, 44
Spring Cottage, 18, 20, 10, 39, 53, 86, 95, 123, 181, 184
Spring of Joy, The, 15, 42, 56, 9–11, 33, 175
St. Catherine's College, 16, 26
Stanford University Libraries, 9, 11, 51, 10
State Historical Museum, Teachers' College, Denton, Texas, 171
Stiperstones, 35, 103
subconscious, 29, 38, 45, 48, 79, 119, 153, 169
Sunday Pictorial, The, 145
Surrey, 71
"Swallows," 43, 139
Swanage Repertory Company, 132
Swinburne, Algernon Charles, 40

T

T. P. and Cassell's Weekly, 18, 48, 1, 100, 114, 148
Targ, William, 86
Tennyson, Alfred, 111, 112
"Their being is to be perceived," 143, 144
Thomas A. Goldwasser Rare Books, 55
Thomas, Edward, 44
Thomson, James, 54
Thoreau, Henry David, 39
Thorne, Mrs., 137
"Thornless Rose. A Carol for Peace. The," 115
Threnodies, 112
Through the Highlands of Shropshire on Horseback, 168
Thysia, 23, 31, 112
Tiemann, Marianne, 169
Times, The (London), 59, 132, 147, 154
Times Literary Supplement, 17, 57, 1, 59, 180, 186, 150, 153
"To a Blackbird Singing in London," 82
"To a little child begging," 72
"To Henry Webb," 22
Tolkien, J. R. R., 47
"To Mother Christmas 1920," 81
Topkapi, 71
Transactions of the Caradoc and Severn Valley Field Club, 101, 104
"Treasures (For G. E. M.)," 16, 169
Tweedsmuir, Lord, see Buchan, John
Tweedsmuir, Susan, 176

U

Udal, John Symonds, 129
University of Chicago, 54
University of Edinburgh, 24
University of London, 10
University of North Texas, 55
Unless Soul Clap Its Hands, 182
Uriconium, see Viroconium
Ustinov, Peter, 71

V

"Vagrant, The," 12, 13
Vander Poel, H. B., 51, 56, 2
Varieties of Religious Experience, The, 24, 21
Velindre, Catherine 151-153
Velindre, Hannah

(Grandmother), *26*, *29*, *30*, *151*,
Verbrugghe, Theobald, 92
"Very Early," 9
Vie Heureuse, 19
"Vigil," 47, 173
Vigilante amure, 151
Vineyard, The, 5, 6, 9, 14, 15, 36
"Viroconium," *43*, 101
Viroconium (the Roman city), 101, 103, 104
"Vis Medicatrix Naturae," 10

W

Walden, *39*
Wales, *33*, *48*, 181, 188
"Watcher, The," 48
Waterloo (the battle of), *47*, 102
Weale, Magdalene M., M.A., 168
Weaver, Gustine Courson, *53*, *54*, 171
Webb, Ethel, 26, 87
Webb, Henry Bertram Law, 10, 16–22, *34*, 2, 6, 10, 22, 24–29, 32, 33, 38, 42, 51, 53, 72, 86, 87, 111, 123, 128, 138, 148, 162, 183; his death a possible suicide, 22, 184; infatuation with Kathleen Wilson, *19*, *21*, 142, 160, *164*; nicknamed "Bertie," 16, 44, 45; widower, 21, *45*, *50*, *52*, *53*, 4, 18, 47, 99, 125, 127, 142, 148, 155–160, 164, 166, 171–173, 181, 184, 187, *163*, *164*

Webb, Mary, as Gladys Mary Meredith, 9; as Gladys Meredith, 19, 21, 23, 24; as Mary Gladys Meredith, *13*, 3, 52, 155; as Mary Meredith-Webb, 6, 15, 30, 36; advances from publishers, *17*, *18*, 70, 73, 74, 89, 108, *14*, *49*, 34, 70, 108, 110, 141; dressed as Madeleine from *Nicholas Nickleby*, 107; gives money to the poor, *17*, *18*, 70, 72, 108, 110; her didacticism, *39*, *48*, *153;* her manuscripts burned, 148; her methods of writing, 51, 85, 121, 137, 150; her siblings, *13*, *14*, 2, 3, 23, 41–43, 81, 155; Henry Webb negotiates for film rights to her novels, 156–160; knowledge of folklore, *13*, *23*, *25*, *36*, *48*, *56*, 100, 129, 148, *148*, *158*, *164;* longs for a child of her own, *29*, 75, 76; love of Shakespeare as a child, *14*; prevailing themes in her novels, *18*, *25*, *28*, *34*, *35–37*, *38*, *39*, *41*, *43*, *48*, 33, *146*, *160*, *164;* Prime Minister Baldwin comments on *Precious Bane*, 127, 154; sells at the Shrewsbury market, *17*, *19*, *52*, 32, 34, 35, 53; unconventional views, *30*, *34*, 26, 38, 52, 87; use of allegory, *33*, *35*, *39*, *48*, 48, 142, 148, *148*, *157*, *167;* views on poetry, *45*, *48*, 79, 112, *168*, *169*; yearning for Shropshire, *16*, *19*, *20*, *43*, 44, 51, 82, 95, 137

Webb, Mary (Henry's sister), *see* Shelly, Mary (*née* Webb)
Webb, Thomas, Dr., 19, 21
Webb, Thomas [Jr.], 87
Webb, Thomas, Mrs., 7, 16, 19, 21, 23–26, 29, 31, 45, 53, 87, 115
Wells, Edgar H., *54*
Wells, H. G., 159
Welsh Arts Council, 183
Welsh borderlands, *13*, *18*, *19*, *47*, 7, *164*
Wessex, 85
West, Rebecca, *17*, *48*, *57*, 59, *150*

Western Front, *17*, *35*, 42, 43, *148*
Weston-super-Mare, *16*, 29, 31, 44, 45, 51, 111, 115, *145*
"What has the sea swept up," *30;* see also, "Shell, The"
"White Moth, The," 55
"Why?," 27
Wicksteed, Ethel, Mrs., 164
Wicksteed, Joseph, 164
Wild Heart, The, 62, 64–66
"Wild Rose, The," 5, 6
Wilhelm Meister's Apprenticeship, 59, 118
"Will-O'-The-Wisp from the Steppes, The," 140
Wilson, Kathleen (later Mrs. Henry Webb), *19*, *21*, 22, *53*, 127, 142, 160, 164
"Wing of Psyche, The," *45*, *169*
Winter Bouquet, A, 176
"Winter Sunrise," 17
Wolfit, Donald, 132
"Wood, The," 44
Woodseaves, Kester, *26*, *30*, *40*, *160*, *161*, *163*
Woodus, Hazel, *35*, *36*, 59, 62–64, *148*–*150*
Woolmer, 55
Wordsworth, William, 112
World War I, *17*, *35*, *37*, *48*, 41, 43, 55, 59, 69, 101, 114, 117
World War II, *45*, *49*, 169
Worthington, Greville, *52*, *53*, *59*, 127
Wrenn, Dorothy P. H., 70, 119, 123, 132, 137, 148, 177
Wroxeter, 101

Y

"You are very brown," 38
Yutang, Lin, *47*

Z

Zaldívar, Eduardo, 92

207

Five hundred & twenty-five copies printed on Mohawk Options paper. Set in Baskerville and Bulmer types. Design & typography by Jerry Kelly.